Kanji Alchemy I
A Strategy for Reading
Japanese Characters

Harry Nap

CONTENTS

ACKNOWLEDGMENTS

Jim Breen's Kanjidic compilation of 6,355 kanji as specified in the JIS X0208 1990 standard has been used as the main source for Kanji Alchemy. This publication has included material from the JMdict (EDICT, etc.) dictionary files in accordance with the license provisions of the Electronic Dictionaries Research Group. See http://www.csse.monash.edu.au/~jwb/edict.html and http://www.edrdg.org/.

Kenneth Henshall's "A Guide to Remembering Japanese Characters" has been a major inspiration

INTRODUCTION

A different approach to kanji is required in order to facilitate reading proficiency:

- Start memorising kanji in groups or **clusters** rather than standalone characters.

- Study in a rational way by focusing on features within kanji that will aid kanji recognition such as **radicals** and an awareness of the etymology of the character.

- Study in a **systematic** way by imposing order and regularity on the multitude of characters. This means abandoning the conventional textbook format.

Japanese characters have a structure that allows for a modicum of understanding. There are recurring features that provide clues and it is clear that there is some kind of consistency in the proliferation of different forms. Characters have their own story to tell and that message can be reinforced when they are grouped together and treated as a set or a cluster. Within each cluster, it is possible to designate one character as a point of reference. 490 of these characters have been selected to act as a chunking device, representing anything from 2 to 14 similar characters in the set. This new allocation of kanji represents a radical departure from the way in which Japanese characters have been studied until now. To focus on approximately 23% of selected General Use characters means a considerable reduction in memorization and learning. The same set of 490 signature characters has also be used in the "Jinmei" series of the second volume and in the "Non General Use" (NGU) characters of the third volume of Kanji Alchemy. The entire range of kanji amounts to 6460 characters. Following is a synopsis of the method.

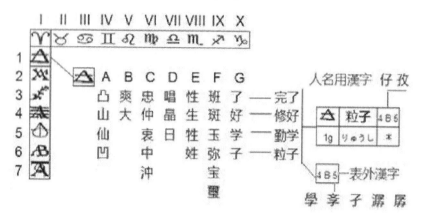

Note that there are ten chapters and that each chapter (named after a star sign) consists of seven weeks. Each week is represented by an alchemical symbol -the first week being AIR- containing seven days (A-G). The example of G shows that there are four characters in the General Use (Jouyou) Kanji range. The symbol in the left corner of the box features the glyph for AIR followed by the "Sight Word" and completed by information showing similar characters in Jinmei Kanji (A = 1, B = 2 etc.) and Non General Use Kanji (5). Learning to read 2136 characters and compounds is a formidable burden on the memory but it is a possible to considerably lessen this strain. Rather than exclusively focusing on memorization and retention, kanji recognition with an analytical focus should become one of the tools for coming to terms with Japanese characters. A case in point are the "semantic-phonetic" characters that represent 85% of all kanji. This category consists of two components: the phonetic component refers to the (long obsolete) pronunciation of the character (on-reading) while the semantic element indicates the meaning or context. An approach that highlights the salient features of kanji will significantly reduce reliance on memorization.

A clear understanding of radicals, in particular the ones that function as a semantic or phonetic indicator in the constituent character, will make the learning process much more efficient. Each kanji has one defining radical that is designated as a dictionary index. Although there are 214 radicals, the most frequent 18 account for 50% usage and the most frequent 48 radicals cover 75%.

Learning kanji means learning vocabulary in a convoluted way. Japanese vocabulary can broadly be classified into kango (words from Chinese origin or created from Chinese words), wago (native Japanese words) and garaigo (loanwords). Approximately 70% of dictionary entries are kanji compounds, the majority of these are kango. Kango consists of two (or more) kanji, each character having a reading that approximated the original Chinese at one stage (on-reading). Good knowledge of kango is indispensable for understanding texts. When learning how to read Japanese characters, strong emphasis should therefore be placed on kanji compounds. The key to more efficient study of kanji lies in the reordering of the 2136 general use characters. This is to be achieved through clustering and chunking. **Clustering** refers to the partitioning of a data set into subsets (clusters), so that the data in all subsets (ideally) share some common trait. **Chunking** is the practice of grouping units of information into smaller units or chunks in order to facilitate memorization. (signature characters) Just as a string of digits can be regrouped into a smaller number of meaningful units to form a date, Japanese characters can be re-arranged in order to emphasize shared elements that greatly facilitate recognition. Through careful selection 490 **signature characters** and their clusters represent over 1990 General Use Kanji. Each of these signature characters represents on average 3 to 4 other characters that share the same features; this means that over 90% of the General Use Kanji are related in a meaningful, learner-friendly way. Grouping together characters that share the same elements greatly facilitates the learning process and makes memorization less burdensome. In many cases radicals will make the distinction between characters that have common features. There are about 150 other characters in the 2136 General Use Kanji that are not related and are therefore not directly referenced to the signature characters. (7%) These characters feature of course in kanji compounds but seem to be otherwise singular, unique kanji such as some of the kanji denoting numerals (八 eight 百 hundred) as well as a number of pictographs (月 moon 毛 hair). This aspect changes when Jinmei and NGU kanji are considered: suddenly a great many of these characters become productive and in fact do have their own clusters of kanji with a similar structure.

A "productive" non-related character is indicated by an asterisk. The vertical bar or pipe character (|) in the key will sometimes show double or triple vertical bars if more than one of the approximately 150 non related characters have similar forms. Consider 礼 courtesy, salute:

礼	禮	屸	紤	軋
Non Related	Jinmei (Old Form)	Non General Use	Non General Use	Non General Use

The same set of 490 signature kanji is also used for "Jinmei Kanji" (862 kanji that are allocated for writing names) and Non General Use Kanji (more than 3460 kanji that belong neither to the General Use nor the Jinmei category). **Sight words and recall sentences** form an integral part of the learning process. The sight word is a kanji compound (粒子 particle) that refers to a range of similar characters that are grouped (clustered) together and that acts as a chunking device. Rather than learning one character at a time, a cluster of kanji should be memorized as a group and associated with the relevant signature character in a sight word. Sight words are sometimes used in English reading classes to teach young children high frequency words that are difficult to explain with phonics. (There are various, strongly disagreeing points of view on this subject.) It is part of the whole-word approach that emphasizes visual recognition of a word without analysis of the sub-parts after which the child is able to pronounce the whole word as a single unit. Given the large variety of kanji readings in the Japanese context, a visual approach makes sense because phonological clues are generally not so helpful. The relevant character that is used in the sight word is a bare or "stripped down" version of the similar kanji it represents, i.e. a character with the least complex radical of the kanji in the cluster or containing no radical at all. When the appropriate radicals are added to the character, the other related kanji in the group will become apparent. This applies not only to the 2136 general use characters but also, often to an even larger extent, to Jinmei and Non General Use characters as well.

A **recall sentence** is a verbal representation of all the characters in the cluster. In the 1G example this would be: **Completed a fine study in small parts**. (Completion 完了, friendship 修好, studying while working 勤学 and particle 粒子) The sentence functions as a mnemonic device incorporating all the compounds of the specific kanji. The recall sentence refers to the other General Use Kanji with a similar structure in the order in which they have been learned making retrieval of relevant information much easier. The learning process involves the expansion from one character to many: **signature character**; 子 **sight word**; 粒子 **sentence**; 完了/修好 /勤学 /粒子 **story**; "Notes from the House of Fashion", a short story for practicing kanji that covers a number of the characters featuring in that particular week. (See first week). It should be noted that, as kanji clusters cover the entire range of General Use Kanji, the conventional order of starting with only "Education Kanji" is no longer the case. Common elements in the structure of kanji can occur anywhere. This means that along with frequent characters － Education Kanji, the first 1006-- less frequent characters in the General Use Kanji range are introduced from the beginning of the series. The use of transliterated Japanese (romaji) should be discouraged. The convention of having katakana for on-reading and hiragana for kun-reading is to be followed. It is less effective to use romaji as it adds an extra step to the learning process. To use kana prepares for future use of Japanese-only materials and maps kanji to pronunciation in the most direct way. A more elaborate overview of kanji and Kanji Alchemy can be found on www.kanjialchemy.com.

Chapter 1 Aries

1A 山 AIR

△	仙術	4A7
1A 並	せんじゅつ	*

Convex, the Mountain Hermit, lives in a Concave

Pictograph of a mountain 山
Representation of convexity 凸

凸	トツ、でこ	convex, protrusion	凸
凸凹	でこぼこ；とつおう	unevenness; roughness	1A
山	サン、やま	mountain	山
山間	やまあい	ravine, gorge	1A
間	カン、ケン、あいだ、ま、あい	space, gap	1A
仙	セン	hermit, wizard	仙
仙術	せんじゅつ	wizardry; secret of immortality	1A
術	ジュツ	means, technique	1A
凹	オウ、ぼこ	hollow, concave, dent	凹
凹眼	おうがん	cavernous eyes	1A
眼	ガン、ゲン、まなこ	eye	1A

1B 大 AIR

△	大寒	2A1
1B	だいかん	*

It's Thrilling to be in the Big Chill

1

Pictograph of a standing person 大

爽	ソウ、さわ-やか	refreshing	爽
爽快	そうかい	thrilling	1B
快	カイ、こころよ-い	pleasant, cheerful	1B
大	ダイ、タイ、おお、おお-きい、おお-いに	big	大
大寒	だいかん	(time of) extreme cold	1B
寒	カン、さむ-い	cold, midwinter	1B

1C 中 AIR

△	中立	5 – 3
1C	ちゅうりつ	1‖2

The Loyal Go-between keeps his Innermost Neutrality in Okinawa

Arrow piercing centre of target 中

忠	チュウ	loyalty, devotion	忠
忠実	ちゅうじつな	loyal	1C
実*	ジツ、み、みの-る	(bear) fruit, truth, reality	1C
仲	チュウ、なか	relationship	仲
仲人	なこうど*	go-between	1C
人*	ジン、ニン、ひと	person	1C
衷	チュウ	inner feelings	衷
衷心	ちゅうしん	true feelings	1C
心	シン、こころ	heart, feelings	1C
中	チュウ、なか	middle, inside, China	中
中立	ちゅうりつ	neutrality	1C

2

立	リツ、リュウ、た-つ、た-てる	stand, rise, leave	1C
沖	チュウ、おき	open sea, soar	沖
沖縄	おきなわ	Okinawa	1C
縄	ジョウ、なわ	rope, cord	1C

1D 日 AIR

⏶		翌日	3B8
1D		よくじつ	*

All together now: it's a Sun Sun Sun-Shiny Day

Pictograph of the sun 日

唱	ショウ、とな-える	recite, preach	唱
唱和	しょうわ	group chant	1D
和	ワ、オ、やわ-らぐ、やわ-らげる、なご-む、なご-やか	Japan, peace, soft	1D
晶	ショウ	crystal, clear, bright	晶
液晶	えきしょう	liquid crystal	1D
液	エキ	liquid	1D
日	ニチ、ジツ、ひ、か	sun, day	日
翌日	よくじつ	next day	1D
翌	ヨク	next (of time)	1D

1E 生 AIR

⏶		性分	4A2
1E		しょうぶん	0‖5

The Nature of Survival has caused Victims with Surnames

3

Growing plant 生

性	セイ、ショウ	nature, sex	性
性分	しょうぶん	disposition	1E
分	ブン、フン、ブ、わ-ける、わ-かれる、わ-かる、わ-かつ	divide, minute, understand	1E
生	セイ、ショウ、い-きる、い-かす、い-ける、う-まれる、う-む	life, birth, grow	生
生存	せいぞん	existence, life, survival	1E
存*	ソン、ゾン	exist, know, think	1E
牲	セイ	sacrifice	牲
犠牲者	ぎせいしゃ	victim	1E
犠	ギ	sacrifice	1E
者	シャ、もの	person	1E
姓	セイ、ショウ	surname	姓
姓名	せいめい	surname	1E
名*	メイ、ミョウ、な	name, fame	1E

1F 玉 AIR

⛰	目玉	6D8
1F	めだま	*

The Relief Squad rescued a Spotty Eyeball and Increasingly Treasured it as an Imperial Seal

Originally string of beads, jade 玉

4

班	ハン	squad, group, allot	班
救護班	きゅうごはん	reliefs quad	1F
救	キュウ、すく-う	rescue, redeem	1F
護	ゴ	defend, protect	1F
斑	ハン、まだら	spot; blemish; speck; patches	斑
斑点	はんてん	speck; fleck	1F
点	テン	point, mark	1F
玉	ギョク、たま	ball, sphere, coin	玉
目玉	めだま	eyeball	1F
目	モク、ボク、め、ま	eye, ordinal, suffix	1F
弥	ミ、ビ、いや、や、あまねし、いよいよ	all the more; increasingly	弥
弥生	やよい	Yayoi period (ca.300BCE-300CE)	1F
生	セイ、ショウ、い-きる、い-かす、い-ける、う-まれる、う-む	life, birth, grow	1F
宝	ホウ、たから	treasure	宝
宝石	ほうせき	jewel	1F
石	セキ、シャク、コク、いし	stone, rock	1F
璽	ジ	imperial seal	璽
御璽	ぎょじ	imperial seal	1F
御	ギョ、ゴ、おん	handle, drive, honourable, your	1F

5

1G 子AIR

△	粒子	4B5
1G	りゅうし	*

Completed a Fine Study in Small Parts

Infant wrapped in clothes 子

了	リョウ	complete, finish, understand	了
完了	かんりょう	completion, conclusion	1G
完	カン	complete	1G
好	コウ、この-む、す-く	like, good, fine	好
修好	しゅうこう	amity, friendship	1G
修	シュウ、シュ、おさ-める、おさ-まる	practice, master	1G
学	ガク、まな-ぶ	study	学
勤学	きんがく	studying while working	1G
勤	キン、ゴン、つと-める、つと-まる	work, duties	1G
子	シ、ス、こ	child	子
粒子	りゅうし	particle	1G
粒	リュウ、つぶ	grain, particle	1G

Notes from the House of Fashion. Under excited twittering from the audience "Le Squelette", a model famous for her graceful emaciation, shuffled onto the catwalk. Her glittering 凹眼 scanned for the smallest 凸凹 lest she'd make a faux pas but her technique was impeccable. Even during 大寒 she had a 忠実 following but as far as her 衷心 were concerned she yearned for a warmer place like 沖縄. The audience broke out in 唱和 whilst celebrating her sunny 性分. She 生存 on minute helpings of organic sprouts but didn't consider herself a 犠牲者 of the industry. No need for a 救護班 she would say. The only motes I have are in my left 目玉 which I treasure like a 宝石. We should always follow the ways of 修好 and in 完了 I would like to proclaim to the world: if you must eat, eat sprouts!

2A 化 ALEMBIC

𝒲	化け物	3A6
2A	ばけもの	6‖12

Sundry Goods included Flower Beds and a Spook

Standing person, fallen person, change 化

貨	カ	goods, money	貨
雑貨	ざっか	sundry goods	2A
雑	ザツ、ゾウ	miscellany	2A
花	カ、はな	flower, blossom	花
花壇	かだん	flowerbed	2A
壇*	ダン、タン	stage, rostrum, podium	2A
化	カ、ケ、ば-ける、ば-かす	change, bewitch	化
化け物	ばけもの	spook	2A
物*	ブツ、モツ、もの	thing	2A

2B 丁 ALEMBIC

𝒲	丁寧	7D9
2B	ていねい	0|5

The Electric Town Light demands Striking Civil Reform from the Face-saving Authorities

Originally nail (now ngu character + metal) 丁

灯	トウ、ひ	light, lamp	灯
電灯	でんとう	electric light	2B
電	デン	electricity	2B
町	チョウ、まち	town	町
町外れ	まちはずれ	outskirts	2B
外	ガイ、ゲ、そと、ほか、はず-す、はず-れる	outside, other, undo	2B
打	ダ、う-つ	hit, strike	打
値打ち	ねうち	value; worth; price; dignity	2B
値	チ、ね、あたい	price, value	2B
丁	チョウ、テイ	block, exact	丁
丁寧	ていねい	civility, care	2B
寧*	ネイ	peace, preferably	2B
訂	テイ	correct, revise	訂
改訂	かいてい	revision	2B
改	カイ、あらた-める、あらた-まる	reform	2B
貯	チョ	store, save	貯
貯蔵	ちょぞう	storage; preservation	2B
蔵	ゾウ、くら	storehouse, harbor	2B
庁	チョウ	government, office, agency	庁
官庁	かんちょう	authorities	2B
官	カン	government, official	2B

8

2C 車 ALEMBIC

⋈	車庫	5D6
2C	しゃこ	*

The Depot Drives the Japanese Federation into Position

Two-wheeled chariot 車

庫	コ、ク	storehouse	庫
車庫	しゃこ	garage, depot	2C
車	シャ、くるま	vehicle, chariot	車
転	テン、ころ-がる、ころ-げる、ころ-がす、ころ-ぶ	rotate, roll, tumble	転
運転	うんてん	driving	2C
運	ウン、はこ-ぶ	transport, luck, move	2C
連	レン、つら-なる、つら-ねる、つ-れる	accompany, row	連
連邦	れんぽう	federation	2C
邦	ホウ	country, japan	2C
陣	ジン	position, camp	陣
堅陣	けんじん	stronghold	2C
堅	ケン、かた-い	firm, solid, hard	2C

2D 立 ALEMBIC

⋈	立場	5A4
2D	たちば	*

An Abducted Academic Degree Burst into Tears due to the Particle's Standpoint

Originally person standing on the ground 立

拉	ラツ、ラ、ロウ、らっ.する、ひし.ぐ、くだ.く	Latin; kidnap; crush	拉
拉致	らち	taking captive; carrying away; kidnapping	2D
致	チ、いた-す	do, send, cause	2D
位	イ、くらい	rank, extent	位
学位	がくい	academic degree	2D
学	ガク、まな-ぶ	study	2D
泣	キュウ、な-く	weep, cry	泣
泣き出す	なきだす	burst into tears	2D
出	シュツ、スイ、で-る、だ-す	emerge, put out	2D
粒	リュウ、つぶ	grain, particle	粒
粒子	りゅうし	particle	2D
子	シ、ス、こ	child	2D
立	リツ、リュウ、た-つ、た-てる	stand, rise, leave	立
立場	たちば	standpoint	2D
場	ジョウ、ば	place	2D

2E 石ALEMBIC

𝖬		嫉妬	4C4
2E		しっと	*

Rocky Ishikawa Reclaimed Rivers full of Jealous women

Cliff and (carved out) rock/boulder 石

岩	ガン、いわ		rock, crag	岩

岩手県	いわてけん	Iwate prefecture (Touhoku area)	2E
手	シュ、て、た	hand	2E
県	ケン	prefecture	2E
石	セキ、シャク、コク、いし	stone, rock	石
石川県	いしかわけん	Ishikawa prefecture (Hokuriku area)	2E
川	セン、かわ	river	2E
県	ケン	prefecture	2E
拓	タク	reclaim, clear, rub	拓
開拓	かいたく	reclamation (of wasteland); cultivation; (2) pioneering	2E
開	カイ、ひら-く、ひら-ける、あ-く、あ-ける	open	2E
妬	ト、ねたむ	be jealous	妬
嫉妬	しっと	jealousy	2E
嫉	シツ、そね.む、ねた.む、にく.む	jealous; envy	2E

2F 字 ALEMBIC

᙭		字幕	2 - 3
2F		じまく	*

Searching for a Sudden Outbreak of Subtitles

Originally house where children are raised, proliferation, numerous letters 字

勃	ボツ、にわ-かに	suddenness	勃
勃発	ぼっぱつ	outbreak	2F

発	ハツ、ホツ	discharge, start, leave	2F
字	ジ、あざ	letter, symbol	字
字幕	じまく	subtitle (movie)	2F
幕	マク、バク	curtain, tent, act	2F

2G 目 ALEMBIC

᙭		目撃者	4 - 5
2G		もくげきしゃ	*

Eye-witnesses issued Urgent reports on Overdue Home Nursing

Pictograph of an eye 目

目	モク、ボク、め、ま	eye, ordinal, suffix	目
目撃者	もくげきしゃ	eye-witness; witness	2G
撃	ゲキ、う-つ	strike, attack, fire	2G
者	シャ、もの	person	2G
眉	ビ、ミ、まゆ	eyebrow	眉
焦眉	しょうび	urgency	2G
焦	ショウ、こ-げる、こ-がす、こ-がれる、あせ-る	scorch, fret	2G
着	チャク、ジャク、き-る、き-せる、つ-く、つ-ける	arrive, wear	着
延着	えんちゃく	delayed arrival	2G
延	エン、の-びる、の-べる、の-ばす	extend, postpone	2G
看	カン	watch	看
家庭看護	かていかんご	home nursing	2G
家	カ、ケ、いえ、や	house, specialist	2G
庭	テイ、にわ	garden, courtyard	2G

護	ゴ		defend, protect	2G

The business that trafficketh in darkness. Portuguese might be the language of flowers but how do 化け物 communicate? Some say that in the 町外れ they use 電灯 but others maintain 丁寧 that this is disputed by the 官庁. And yet others state that they dwell in 車庫 -the so-called 堅陣 of mobile energy but that's a 立場 that would make me 泣き出す. (You don't need a 学位 to work that one out.) There might be some 嫉妬 involved but it can be argued that in 岩手県 they speak beautiful dialect. This would require 字幕 for the uninitiated although according to 目撃者 there is no need for 焦眉. I might settle with some strong spirits instead and leave it all to the good people in 家庭看護.

3A 先 ALUM

		指先		2A2
3A		ゆびさき		1|3

Tips for Finger Washing

Originally foot/stop + person, die, ancestors, precede, tip 先

先	セン、さき	previous, precede, tip	先
指先	ゆびさき	fingertip	3A
指	シ、ゆび、さ-す	finger, point	3A
洗	セン、あら-う	wash, investigate	洗
洗礼式	せんれいしき	baptism	3A
礼*	レイ、ライ	courtesy, salute, bow	3A
式	シキ	ceremony, form	3A

3B 左 ALUM

🌿	左側	3B7
3B	ひだりがわ	*

He lent Assistance to the Discriminating Left

Left hand + work upon, auxiliary, assist 左

佐	サ	assist, assistant	佐
補佐	ほさ	assistance	3B
補	ホ、おぎな-う	make good, stopgap	3B
差	サ、さ-す	difference, thrust	差
差別	さべつ	discrimination	3B
別	ベツ、わか-れる	split, differ, special	3B
左	サ、ひだり	left	左
左側	ひだりがわ	left side	3B
側	ソク、かわ	side	3B

3C 十 ALUM

🌿	十字路	4A4
3C	じゅうじろ	*

Measuring Ten Juicy Needles

Sewing needle used as a substitute for more a complex character 十

計	ケイ、はか-る、はか-らう	measure	計
愚計	ぐけい	foolish plan; one's plan	3C
愚	グ、おろ-か	foolish	3C
十	ジュウ、ジッ、とお、と	ten	十
十字路	じゅうじろ	crossroads	3C

字	ジ、あざ	letter, symbol	3C
路	ロ、じ	road, route	3C
汁	ジュウ、しる	juice, soup, liquid	汁
胆汁	たんじゅう	bile; gall	3C
胆	タン	liver, gall, courage	3C
針	シン、はり	needle	針
磁針	じしん	magnetic needle	3C
磁	ジ	magnet, porcelain	3C

3D 足 ALUM

	満足	4A1
3D	まんぞく	0|4

Stepping into Urgent and Captivating Satisfaction

Foot and kneecap, lower leg, able 足

踏	トウ、ふ-む、ふ-まえる	tread, step on	踏
踏み込む	ふみこむ	step into	3D
込	こ-む、こ-める	put in, be crowded	3D
促	ソク、うなが-す	urge, press	促
催促	さいそく	request; demand; claim	3D
催	サイ、もよお-す	organise, muster	3D
捉	ソク、とら-える	catch; capture	捉
捕捉	ほそく	capture; seizure	3D
捕	ホ、と-らえる、と-らわれる、と-る、つか-まえる、つか-まる	seize, capture	3D

15

足	ソク、あし、た-りる、た-る、た-す	leg foot, sufficient	足
満足	まんぞく	satisfaction	3D
満*	マン、み-ちる、み-たす	full, fill	3D

3E 青 ALUM

	青春	7C7
3E	せいしゅん	1‖10

A Refined, Bright, Youth can only be Requested with Calm, Friendly Cleanliness

Growth around a full well, fresh, green, immature 青

精	セイ、ショウ	spirit, vitality, refine, detail	精
精力	せいりょく	vitality	3E
力	リョク、リキ、ちから	strength, effort	3E
晴	セイ、は-れる、は-らす	clear, bright	晴
晴晴	はればれ	bright	3E
青	セイ、ショウ、あお、あお-い	blue, green, young	青
青春	せいしゅん	youth	3E
春*	シュン、はる	spring	3E
請	セイ、シン、こ-う、う-ける	request, undertake	請
請求	せいきゅう	request	3E
求	キュウ、もと-める	request, seek	3E
静	セイ、ジョウ、しず、しず-か、しず-まる、しず-める	quiet, calm	静
静粛	せいしゅく	silent, still, quiet	3E

粛*	シュク	solemn, quiet	3E
情	ジョウ、セイ、なさ-け	feeling, pity, fact	情
友情	ゆうじょう	friendship	3E
友	ユウ、とも	friend	3E
清	セイ、ショウ、きよ-い、きよ-まる、きよ-める	pure, clean	清
清潔	せいけつ	cleanliness	3E
潔	ケツ、いさぎよ-い	clean, pure	3E

3F 貝 ALUM

🦎	魚貝	2 – 6
3F	ぎょかい	3|2

Cockles and Mussels as in that long Japanese Song

Originally pictograph of a pointed bivalve 貝

貝	かい	shellfish	貝
魚貝	ぎょかい	marine products; seafood; fish and shellfish	3F
魚*	ギョ、うお、さかな	fish	3F
唄	バイ、うた	sing	唄
長唄	ながうた	long epic Japanese song	3F
長	チョウ、なが-い	long, senior	3F

3G 音 ALUM

🦎	発音	7 – 5
3G	はつおん	1|2

She Remembered her Dark Speculations on the Timid Sounds of a

Hundred Million Gloomy Thoughts

Originally form of speak with addition of tongue 音

闇	アン、くら-い、やみ	get dark; gloom; disorder	闇
夕闇	ゆうやみ	dusk; twilight	3G
夕	セキ、ゆう	evening	3G
憶	オク	think, remember	憶
憶測	おくそく	speculation	3G
測	ソク、はか-る	measure, fathom	3G
臆	オク、おしはか-る、むね	timidity; heart; mind; fear; cowardly	臆
臆病	おくびょう	cowardice; timidity	3G
病	ビョウ、ヘイ、や-む、やまい	illness	3G
音	オン、イン、おと、ね	sound	音
発音	はつおん	pronunciation	3G
発	ハツ、ホツ	discharge, start, leave	3G
億	オク	hundred million	億
億万長者	おくまんちょうじゃ	billionaire	3G
万*	マン、バン	ten thousand, myriad	3G
長	チョウ、なが-い	long, senior	3G
者	シャ、もの	person	3G
暗	アン、くら-い	dark, gloomy	暗
暗殺	あんさつ	assassination	3G
殺	サツ、サイ、セツ、ころ-す	kill	3G
意	イ	mind, thought, will	意
意見	いけん	opinion	3G
見	ケン、み-る、み-える、み-せる	look, see, show	3G

Finding your inner Viking at a smorgasbord. It is no use dipping 指先 into a bowl of carefully 洗礼式 organic sprouts on the right when you really want to dig into a plate of dripping deep fried on the 左側. So, what is the cunning 愚計 when we are at the 十字路: being plagued by 胆汁 or enjoying a 満足 braai? Suddenly there was a 催促 by green 晴晴 shapes in the corner. Resisting the eloquent 請求 of luscious 魚貝 is futile. 憶測 is rife and 意見 are divided but without going into character 暗殺 it could be said that the choice is clear. Fermented cod prepared by seven sturdy shield maidens should carry the day: simples!

4A 七 AMALGAM

志	七面倒	3 - 2
4A	しちめんどう	0|2

A Trump Card of Seven Troublesome Reprimands

Vaguely resembling a bent finger under a fist, old way to indicate seven 七

切	セツ、サイ、き-る、き-れる	cut	切
切り札	きりふだ	trump card	4A
札*	サツ、ふだ	paper money, note	4A
七	シチ、なな、なな-つ、なの	seven	七
七面倒	しちめんどう	great trouble; difficulty	4A
面	メン、おも、おもて、つら	face, aspect, mask	4A
倒	トウ、たお-れる、たお-す	fall, topple, invert	4A
叱	シツ、しかる	scold	叱
叱責	しっせき	reprimand	4A
責	セキ、せ-める	liability, blame	4A

4B 空 AMALGAM

本	寒空	2A4
4B	さむぞら	*

A Waiting Room is as inviting as a Wintry Sky

Hole (open space under roof) + work upon 空

控	コウ、ひか-える	refrain, write down, have near, wait	控
控え所	ひかえじょ	waiting room	4B
所	ショ、ところ	place, situation	4B
空	クウ、そら、あ-く、あ-ける、から	sky, empty	空
寒空	さむぞら	wintry sky, cold weather	4B
寒	カン、さむ-い	cold, midwinter	4B

4C 耳 AMALGAM

本	取出す	5H21
4C	とりだす	0|3

It is no Shame to take Out Health Care, in particular Otorhinology is Tempting

Pictograph of a pointed ear 耳

恥	チ、は-じる、はじ、は-じらう、は-ずかしい	shame, ashamed	恥
恥知らず	はじしらず	shameless (person)	4C
知	チ、しる	know	4C

取	シュ、と-る	take control	取
取出す	とりだす	take out	4C
出	シュツ、スイ、で-る、だ-す	emerge, put out	4C
摂	セツ	take, act as a proxy	摂
摂生	せっせい	health care	4C
生	セイ、ショウ、い-きる、い-かす、い-ける、う-まれる、う-む	life, birth, grow	4C
耳	ジ、みみ	ear	耳
耳鼻科	じびか	otorhinology	4C
鼻*	ビ、はな	nose	4C
科	カ	course, section	4C
餌	ジ、ニ、え、えば、えさ、もち	food; bait; prey	餌
好餌	こうじ	tempting offer	4C
好	コウ、この-む、す-く	like, good, fine	4C

4D 見 AMALGAM

太	見易い	4C4
4D	みやすい	*

Now Relax and Show the Look

Eye and (formerly) bent legs, kneeling to stare at something 見

現	ゲン、あらわ-れる、あらわ-す	appear, exist, now	現
現員	げんいん	present members	4D

21

員	イン	member, official	4D
寛	カン	magnanimous, relax	寛
寛厳	かんげん	leniency and severity	4D
厳	ゲン、ゴン、おごそ-か、きび-しい	severe, strict, solemn	4D
見	ケン、み-る、み-える、み-せる	look, see, show	見
見易い	みやすい	easy to see	4D
易	エキ、イ、やさ-しい	easy, change, divination	4D
視	シ	see, look, regard	視
可視	かし	visibility	4D
可	カ	approve, can, should	4D

4E 九 AMALGAM

本	九折	4B4
4E	きゅうせつ	*

Nine Round Soaking muses in a Rut

Bent elbow = nine when counting with one arm 九

九	キュウ、ク、ここの、ここの-つ	nine	九
九折	きゅうせつ	many turns (in a road)	4E
折	セツ、お-る、おり、お-れる	bend, break, occasion	4E
丸	ガン、まる、まる-い、まる-める	round, circle, ball, ship's mark	丸
丸太	まるた	log	4E

太	タイ、タ、ふと-い、ふと-る	fat, big	4E
染	セン、そ-める、そ-まる、し-みる、し-み	dye, soak, permeate	染
色染め	いろぞめ	dyeing	4E
色	ショク、シキ、いろ	colour, sensuality	4E
軌	キ	track, rut, way	軌
狭軌	きょうき	narrow gauge	4E
狭	キョウ、せま-い、せば-める、せば-まる	narrow, small	4E

4F 交 AMALGAM

交	外交	6 – 13
4F	がいこう	*

In Comparison, Effective Diplomacy Strangles Schools and Suburbs

Pictograph of person sitting with crossed legs, mix 交

較	カク	comparison	較
比較	ひかく	comparison	4F
比	ヒ、くら-べる	compare, ratio	4F
効	コウ、き-く	effect, efficacy	効
有効	ゆうこう な	valid	4F
有	ユウ、ウ、ある	have, exist	4F
交	コウ、まじ-わる、まじ-える、ま-じる、ま-ざる、ま-ぜる	mix, exchange	交
外交	がいこう	diplomacy	4F
外	ガイ、ゲ、そと、ほか、はず-す、はず-れる	outside, other, undo	4F

絞	コウ、しぼ-る、し-める、し-まる	strangle, wring	絞
絞め殺す	しめころす	strangle	4F
殺	サツ、サイ、セツ、ころ-す	kill	4F
校	コウ	school, (printing) proof	校
高校	こうこう	senior high school	4F
高	コウ、たか-い、たか、たか-まる、たか-める	tall, high, sum	4F
郊	コウ	suburbs	郊
郊外	こうがい	suburbs	4F
外	ガイ、ゲ、そと、ほか、はず-す、はず-れる	outside, other, undo	4F

4G 夕 AMALGAM

太		夕空	4A2
4G		ゆうぞら	*

Multilingual Transitional Greetings from an Evening Sky

Pictograph of a crescent moon 夕

多	タ、おお-い	many	多
多国籍言語	たこくせきげんご	multilingual; in many languages	4G
国	コク、くに	country, region	4G
籍	セキ	register	4G
言	ゲン、ゴン、い-う、こと	word, say, speak	4G
語	ゴ、かた-る、かた-らう	tell, speak, talk	4G

移	イ、うつ-る、うつ-す	transfer, move	移
遷移	せんい	transition	4G
遷	セン	move, change, shift	4G
挱	サツ	imminent	挱
挨拶	あいさつ	greetings	4G
挨	アイ	push open	4G
夕	セキ、ゆう	evening	夕
夕空	ゆうぞら	evening sky; twilight sky	4G
空	クウ、そら、あ-く、あ-ける、から	sky, empty	4G

Buyer's remorse and other grudges. Do not 叱責 the Magnificent 七 under a 寒空 when you just have visited a reputable practitioner of 耳鼻科. You should have refused that 好餌 made by that 恥知らず. And yet, what is 見易い now to 現員 appears to be 九 times more 色染め in the wool previously. Try 外交 and stop thinking about 絞め殺す that ruthless banker in his home in the 郊外. 多国籍言語 curses on his head and a thunderbolt from the 夕空: Argentarius delendus est!

5A 六 ANTIMONY

⊕	六角	2-7
5A	ろっかく	*

There are Six Sides to Happiness in the next world

Originally roof, then used as a substitute for clenched fist; six 六

六	ロク、む、む-つ、むっ-つ、むい	six	六
六角	ろっかく	hexagon	5A

角	カク、かど、つの	horn, angle	5A
冥	メイ、ミョウ	dark	冥
冥福	めいふく	happiness in the next world	5A
福	フク	good fortune	5A

5B 正 ANTIMONY

⊕	正直	8B8
5B	しょうじき な	0|1

There is Proof that the Failed Government's Agreement is Symptomatic of Honest Subjugation with Handcuffs

Originally variant of lower leg, straight, proper/correct 正

証	ショウ	proof	証
証明	しょうめい	proof	5B
明	メイ、ミョウ、あ-かり、あか-るい、あか-るむ	clear, open, bright	5B
綻	タン、ほころ.びる	be rent; ripped; unravel; run	綻
破綻	はたん	failure	5B
破	ハ、やぶ-る、やぶ-れる	break, tear	5B
政	セイ、ショウ、まつりごと	government	政
行政	ぎょうせい	administration	5B
行	コウ、ギョウ、アン、い-く、ゆ-く、おこな-う	go, conduct, column	5B
定	テイ、ジョウ、さだ-める、さだ-まる、さだ-か	fix, establish	定
協定	きょうてい	agreement	5B
協	キョウ	cooperate	5B

26

症	ショウ	symptom, illness	症
症状	しょうじょう	symptoms	5B
状	ジョウ	condition, letter	5B
正	セイ、ショウ、ただ-しい、ただ-す、まさ	correct	正
正直	しょうじき な	honest	5B
直	チョク、ジキ、ただ-ちに、なお-す、なお-る	direct, upright, fix	5B
征	セイ	subjugate, travel	征
征服	せいふく	subjugation	5B
服*	フク	clothes, yield, serve	5B
錠	ジョウ	lock, tablet	錠
手錠	てじょう	handcuffs	5B
手	シュ、て、た	hand	5B

5C 分 ANTIMONY

⊕		分子	6 - 9
5C		ぶんし	0‖3

Bonsai's Poverty caused a Dispute of Wheat Flower Molecules in the Atmosphere

Split, sword/cut 分

盆	ボン	tray, bon festival	盆
盆栽	ぼんさい	bonsai	5C
栽	サイ	planting	5C
貧	ヒン、ビン、まず-しい	poor, meagre	貧
貧困	ひんこん	poverty	5C

困*	コン、こま-る	quandary, annoyed	5C
紛	フン、まぎ-れる、まぎ-らす、まぎ-らわす、まぎ-らわしい	confusion, stray	紛
紛争	ふんそう	dispute	5C
争	ソウ、あらそ-う	conflict, vie	5C
粉	フン、こ、こな	powder	粉
麦粉	むぎこ	wheat flour	5C
麦*	バク、むぎ	wheat, barley	5C
分	ブン、フン、ブ、わ-ける、わ-かれる、わ-かる、わ-かつ	divide, minute, understand	分
分子	ぶんし	molecule	5C
子	シ、ス、こ	child	5C
雰	フン	atmosphere, air	雰
雰囲気	ふんいき	atmosphere	5C
囲	イ、かこ-む、かこ-う	surround	5C
気	キ、ケ	spirit	5C

5D 赤 ANTIMONY

| ⊕ | 赤面 | 3 – 3 |
| 5D | せきめん | * |

His Threatening Blush made us ask for Clemency

Originally big fire with ruddy glow 赤

嚇	カク	threaten, menace	嚇
威嚇的	いかくてき	threatening	5D
威	イ	authority, threaten	5D

28

的	テキ、まと	target, like, adjectival suffix	5D
赤	セキ、シャク、あか、あか-い、あか-らむ、あか-らめる	red	赤
赤面	せきめん	blush	5D
面	メン、おも、おもて、つら	face, aspect, mask	5D
赦	シャ	forgiveness	赦
赦免	しゃめん	clemency	5D
免	メン、まぬか-れる	escape, avoid	5D

5E 未 ANTIMONY

| ⊕ | | 姉妹 | 4 - 1 |
| 5E | | しまい | 3\|10 |

Future Sisters have Dark Meanings

Tree with additional branches at the top, still growing 未

未	ミ	immature, not yet	未
未来	みらい	future	5E
来*	ライ、く-る、きた-る、きた-す	come	5E
妹	マイ、いもうと	younger sister	妹
姉妹	しまい	sisters	5E
姉	シ、あね	elder sister	5E
昧	マイ、くら-い	dark; foolish	昧
曖昧	あいまい	vague; ambiguous; unclear	5E
曖	アイ、かげ-る	dark; not clear	5E
味	ミ、あじ、あじ-わう	taste, relish	味

意味	いみ	meaning	5E
意	イ	mind, thought, will	5E

5F 今 ANTIMONY

⊕	吟詠	7B9
5F	ぎんえい	1|3

On Second Thoughts, Indulging in Harp Play at this Year's Recital is Inclusive

Cover, put in a corner conceal 今

念	ネン	thought, concern	念
念力	ねんりき	will	5F
力*	リョク、リキ、ちから	strength, effort	5F
貪	タン、トン、むさぼ.る	covet; indulge in	貪
貪欲	どんよく	greed	5F
欲	ヨク、ほっ-する、ほ-しい	greed, desire	5F
琴	キン、こと	koto	琴
琴線	きんせん	heartstrings	5F
線	セン	line	5F
捻	ネン、ね-じる、ひね-る	twirl; twist; play wit	捻
捻挫	ねんざ	sprain	5F
座	ザ、すわ-る	seat, sit, gather	5F
今	コン、キン、いま	now	今
今年	ことし*	this year	5F
年	ネン、とし	year	5F
吟	ギン	recite	吟
吟詠	ぎんえい	recital	5F
詠	エイ、よ-む	poem, recite, compose	5F

30

含	ガン、ふく-む、ふく-める	include, contain	含
含めて	ふくめて	including	5F

5G 虫 ANTIMONY

⚗		蛍雪	6 - 9
5G		けいせつ	0|4

Mosquito's and Studious Fireflies fight Anglo-Saxon Worms and Cocooned Insects

Insect 虫

蚊	カ	mosquito	蚊
蚊帳	かや*	mosquito net	5G
帳	チョウ	register, drape	5G
蛍	ケイ、ほたる	firefly	蛍
蛍雪	けいせつ	studying	5G
雪*	セツ、ゆき	snow	5G
独	ドク、ひと-り	alone, Germany	独
独英	どくえい	Anglo-Saxon	5G
英	エイ	superior, England	5G
蚕	サン、かいこ	silkworm	蚕
養蚕	ようさん	sericulture	5G
養	ヨウ、やしな-う	rear, support	5G
繭	ケン、まゆ	cocoon	繭
繭糸	けんし	silk thread	5G
糸	シ、いと	thread	5G
虫	チュウ、むし	insect, worm	虫
毒虫	どくむし	poisonous insect	5G
毒	ドク	poison	5G

31

Geometry in the humming of strings. Squares are bland but 六角 are exciting and the 証明 for that requires just an 正直 look at the 症状 of any indisposed geometrist. Keep your 手錠 at home when you want to 紛争 this and don't give me that 貧困 of data reply. (Excuse me while I kiss the 雰囲気). There will be no 赦免 for 威嚇的 Cartesian mountebanks and other 曖昧 twisted 姉妹. This 今年 Pythagoras 吟詠 will pull your 琴線 so that the 貪欲 for fabulous formula, buzzing like a 毒虫, will be contained within a 蚊帳: wild 繭糸 from a crazy silkworm's ass!

6A 土 ARMENIAN BOLE

𝓐𝓑	土煙	3D3
6A	つちけむり	0|4

Doing the Dirt on that Company

Pictograph of a clod of earth on the ground 土

吐	ト、は.く、つ.く	disgorge, vomit	吐
音吐	おんと	voice	6A
音	オン、イン、おと、ね	sound	6A
土	ド、ト、つち	earth	土
土煙	つちけむり	cloud of dust	6A
煙*	エン、けむ-る、けむり、けむ-い	smoke	6A
社	シャ、やしろ	company, Shinto shrine	社
御社	おんしゃ	(hon) (pol) your company	6A
御	ギョ、ゴ、おん	handle, drive, honourable, your	6A

6B 王 ARMENIAN BOLE

AB		王位	4D16
6B		おうい	*

An Emperor is a Vigorous King with a Crazy crown

Originally blade of a large battle axe 王

皇	コウ、オウ	emperor	皇
皇居	こうきょ	Imperial Palace	6B
居	キョ、い-る	be, reside	6B
旺	オウ	flourishing; successful; beautiful; vigorous	旺
旺盛	おうせい	full of vim and vigour	6B
盛	セイ、ジョウ、も-る、さか-る、さか-ん	prosper, heap, serve	6B
王	オウ	king	王
王位	おうい	the thrown, the crown	6B
位	イ、くらい	rank, extent	6B
狂	キョウ、くる-う、くる-おしい	lunatic, mad	狂
熱狂	ねっきょう	wild enthusiasm; being crazy about	6B
熱	ネツ、あつ-い	heat	6B

6C 園 ARMENIAN BOLE

AB		公園	3B7
6C		こうえん	1|4

The Round Monkey made a Detour in the Park

Chinese only long robe, phonetic long 園

猿	エン、さる	monkey, ape	猿
猿丸	さるまる	Sarumaru (name, round monkey)	6C
丸	ガン、まる、まる-い、まる-める	round, circle, ball, ship's mark	6C
遠	エン、オン、とお-い	distant	遠
遠回り	とおまわり	detour	6C
回*	カイ、エ、まわ-る、まわ-す	turn, rotate	6C
園	エン、その	garden, park	園
公園	こうえん	park	6C
公	コウ、おおやけ	public, fair, lord	6C

6D 白 ARMENIAN BOLE

𝐀𝐁	告白	6C5
6D	こくはく	*

The Shipping(magnate) Threatened to Beat the White Count for Ten Nights

Literally thumbnail, white 白

舶	ハク	ship, shipping	舶
船舶	せんぱく	shipping	6D
船	セン、ふね、ふな	boat, ship	6D
迫	ハク、せま-る	press, draw near	迫
脅迫	きょうはく	threat	6D
脅	キョウ、おびや-かす、おど-す、おど-かす	threaten, coerce	6D
拍	ハク-ヒョウ	beat, tap, clap	拍
拍手	はくしゅ	hand clapping	6D

手	シュ、て、た	hand	6D
白	ハク、ビャク、しろ、しら、しろ-い	white	白
告白	こくはく	confession; acknowledgment	6D
告	コク、つ-げる	proclaim, inform	6D
伯	ハク	count, senior figure	伯
伯父	おじ*	uncle	6D
父	フ、ちち	father	6D
泊	ハク、と-まる、と-める	stay, lodge	泊
十泊	じゅうはく	ten night's stay	6D
十	ジュウ、ジッ、とお、と	ten	6D

6E 色 ARMENIAN BOLE

| ÆB | 好色 | | 4E7 |
| 6E | こうしょく | | * |

The Never-Ending Grasping at Enriching Sensuality

Person bending over another person 色

絶	ゼツ、た-える、た-やす、た-つ	cease, sever, end	絶
絶望	ぜつぼう	despair	6E
望	ボウ、モウ、のぞ-む	wish, hope, gaze	6E
把	ハ	grasp, comprehend	把
把持	はじ	grasp; hold; grip	6E
持	ジ、も-つ	like, good, fine	6E
肥	ヒ、こ-える、こえ、こ-やす、こ-やし	fatten, enrich	肥

肥育	ひいく	fattening	6E
育	イク、そだ-つ、そだ-てる	raise, educate	6E
色	ショク、シキ、いろ	colour, sensuality	色
好色	こうしょく	amorous	6E
好	コウ、この-む、す-く	like, good, fine	6E

6F 同 ARMENIAN BOLE

AB	銅像	5A2
6F	どうぞう	*

The Copper's Cylindrical Body Cavity was the Same

Possible variant of boat, convey + mouth/say (the same thing?) 同

銅	ドウ	copper	銅
銅像	どうぞう	bronze statue	6F
像	ゾウ	image	6F
筒	トウ、つつ	tube, cylinder	筒
筒形	つつがた	cylindrical	6F
形	ケイ、ギョウ、かた、かたち	shape, pattern	6F
胴	ドウ	body, trunk, torso	胴
胴体	どうたい	body, trunk	6F
体	タイ、テイ、からだ	body	6F
洞	ドウ、ほら	cave, penetrate	洞
空洞	くうどう	cavern, cavity	6F
空	クウ、そら、あ-く、あ-ける、から	sky, empty	6F
同	ドウ、おな-じ	same	同
同時	どうじ	same time	6F
時	ジ、とき	time	6F

6G 系 ARMENIAN BOLE

AB	系統	7A3
6G	けいとう	0|7

The Modest Matron in Charge Searches with an Elementary System of Descending Woollen Yarns

Pictogram of skein of yarn, originally doubled 系

遜	ソン、へりくだ-る	humble	遜
謙遜	けんそん	humble; humility; modesty	6G
謙	ケン	humble, modest	6G
係	ケイ、かか-る、かかり	involvement	係
係員	かかりいん	clerk in charge	6G
員	イン	member, official	6G
索	サク	rope, search	索
思索	しさく	speculation; thinking; meditation	6G
思	シ、おも-う	think	6G
素	ソ、ス	element, base, bare	素
簡素	かんそ な	simplicity; plain	6G
簡	カン	simple, brief	6G
系	ケイ	lineage, connection	系
系統	けいとう	system, line	6G
統	トウ、す-べる	supervise, lineage	6G
孫	ソン、まご	descendants, grandchildren	孫
子孫	しそん	descendants	6G
子	シ、ス、こ	child	6G
糸	シ、いと	thread	糸

37

毛糸	けいと	woollen yarn	6G
毛*	モウ、け	hair	6G

A kingdom for a primate. The 音吐 of 熱狂 King George sounded in the 公園 whilst he called his favourite 猿丸: come hither my sexy scientist. He then 拍手 to summon his nutty 伯父 and ordered him to 把持 the animal after he 絶望 to get hold of the 好色 one. At the 同時 as a life-size 銅像 of Cornelius toppled over the monarch raised his 筒形 sceptre and spoke the 簡素 and 謙遜 words: Zira, no more drinking and stop dissecting my 子孫!

7A 田 ATHANOR

𝔸	田打ち	4B12
7A	たうち	*

Hata's Ritzy Dental Floss

Pictograph of a rice field 田

畑	はた、はたけ	field	畑
営業畑	えいぎょうばたけ	sales field	7A
営	エイ、いとな-む	conduct, barracks	7A
業	ギョウ、ゴウ、わざ	profession, deed, karma	7A
畝	せ、うね	ridge, square, measure	畝
畝織	うねおり	ridged fabric; corduroy	7A
織	ショク、シキ、お-る	weave	7A
田	デン、た	rice field	田
田打ち	たうち	tilling a paddy field	7A

打	ダ、う-つ	hit, strike	7A
細	サイ、ほそ-い、ほそ-る、こま-か、こま-かい	slender, fine	細
詳細	しょうさい	detail particulars	7A
詳	ショウ、くわ-しい	detailed	7A

7B 工 ATHANOR

𝔄	大工	8A8
7B	だいく	*

The Successful Carpenter and a Colourful Aggressor made a Crimson Contribution to the Inlet with a Clause

Carpenter's adze-cum-square 工

功	コウ、ク	merit, service	功
成功	せいこう	success	7B
成	セイ、ジョウ、な-る、な-す	become, make, consist	7B
工	コウ、ク	work	工
大工	だいく	carpenter	7B
大	ダイ、タイ、おお、おお-きい、おお-いに	big	7B
虹	コウ、にじ	rainbow	虹
虹色	にじいろ	rainbow-coloured	7B
色	ショク、シキ、いろ	colour, sensuality	7B
攻	コウ、せ-める	attack	攻
攻撃者	こうげきしゃ	aggressor	7B
撃	ゲキ、う-つ	strike, attack, fire	7B
者	シャ、もの	person	7B

紅	コウ、ク、べに、くれない	red, crimson, rouge	紅
真紅	しんく	crimson	7B
真	シン、ま	true, quintessence	7B
貢	コウ、ク、みつぐ	tribute	貢
貢献	こうけん	contribution	7B
献	ケン、コン	dedicate, present	7B
江	コウ、え	inlet, river	江
入り江	いりえ	creek, inlet	7B
入	ニュウ、い-る、い-れる、はい-る	to get in, to go in, to come in	7B
項	コウ	clause, item, nape	項
項目	こうもく	clause, item	7B
目	モク、ボク、め、ま	eye, ordinal suffix	7B

7C 明 ATHANOR

𝔄		克明		2B
7C		こくめい		0|2

Diligence of the Federation

Sun and moon symbolising light, very bright 明

明	メイ、ミョウ、あ-かり、あか-るい、あか-るむ	clear, open, bright	明
克明	こくめい	diligence	7C
克*	コク	conquer, overcome	7C
盟	メイ	alliance, pledge	盟
連盟	れんめい	federation	7C

連	レン、つら-なる、つら-ねる、つ-れる	accompany, row	7C

7D 寸 ATHANOR

	一寸		10A8
7D	いっすん		1|9

Danton Hunts, Attacks and Interrogates Armed Tiny Groups of Drunk Rural American Conservatives

Originally pulse being one sun (width of finger) from base palm 寸

狩	シュ、か-る、か-り	hunt	狩
狩猟	しゅりょう	hunting	7D
猟*	リョウ	game-hunting	7D
討	トウ、う-つ	attack	討
追討	ついとう	tracking down and killing	7D
追	ツイ、お-う	chase, pursue	7D
尋	ジン、たず-ねる	ask, inquire, a fathom	尋
尋問	じんもん	questioning, interrogation	7D
問	モン、と-う、と-い、とん	ask	7D
肘	チュウ、ひじ	elbow; arm	肘
肩肘	かたひじ	shoulder and elbow	7D
肩	ケン、かた	shoulder	7D
寸	スン	measure, inch	寸
一寸	いっすん	tiny bit, one inch	7D
一	イチ、イツ、ひと、ひと-つ	one	7D

41

団	ダン、トン	group, body, mass, ball, round	団
団体	だんたい	group	7D
体	タイ、テイ、からだ	body	7D
酎	チュウ	sake	酎
焼酎	しょうちゅう	distilled spirits shouchuu	7D
焼	ショウ、や-く、や-ける	burn, roast	7D
村	ソン、むら	village	村
農山漁村	のうさんぎょそん	agricultural, mountain and fishing villages; rural districts	7D
農	ノウ	farming	7D
山	サン、やま	mountain	7D
漁	ギョ、リョウ	fishing	7D
対	タイ、ツイ	against, vis-a-vis, versus, anti-	対
対米	たいべい	toward/with America	7D
米	ベイ、マイ、こめ	rice, America	7D
守	シュ、ス、まも-る、もり	protect, keep	守
保守	ほしゅ	conservatism	7D
保	ホ、たも-つ	preserve, maintain	7D

7E 己 ATHANOR

𝕬		自己	7B3
7E		じこ	*

In the new Era of Accountability an Odious Princess Reformed Herself by Distributing twisting threads

Twisted thread, first person pronoun 己

紀	キ	chronicle, start	紀
紀元	きげん	epoch, era	7E
元	ゲン、ガン、もと	originally, source	7E
記	キ、しる-す	account, chronicle	記
下記	かき	the following	7E
下	カ、ゲ、した、しも、もと、さ-げる、さ-がる、くだ-る、くだ-す	base, under, lower	7E
忌	キ、い-む、い-まわしい	mourn, abhor, odious	忌
忌中	きちゅう	mourning	7E
中	チュウ、なか	middle, inside, China	7E
妃	ヒ	queen, princess	妃
王妃	おうひ	queen, princess	7E
王	オウ	king	7E
改	カイ、あらた-める、あらた-まる	reform	改
改革	かいかく	reform	7E
革	カク、かわ	leather, reform	7E
己	コ、キ、おのれ	I, me, you, self	己
自己	じこ	self	7E
自	ジ、シ、みずか-ら	self	7E
配	ハイ、くば-る	distribute	配
配達	はいたつ	delivery	7E
達	タツ	attain	7E

7F 合 ATHANOR

A	合唱	6B14
7F	がっしょう	*

A Harmonious Solution Boarded on tight Control of the Supply of Tombstones

Lid, cover, mouth say, cap off remark, reply fittingly 合

合	ゴウ、ガッ、カッ、あ-う、あ-わす、あ-わせる	meet, join, fit	合
合唱	がっしょう	chorus	7F
唱	ショウ、とな-える	recite, preach	7F
答	トウ、こた-える、こた-え	answer	答
解答	かいとう	solution	7F
解	カイ、ゲ、と-く、と-かす、と-ける	unravel, explain, solve	7F
搭	トウ	load, board	搭
搭乗	とうじょう	boarding	7F
乗	ジョウ、の-る、の-せる	ride, mount, load	7F
拾	シュウ、ジュウ、ひろ-う	pickup, gather, ten	拾
収拾	しゅうしゅう	control	7F
収	シュウ、おさ-める、おさ-まる	obtain, store, supply	7F
給	キュウ	supply, bestow	給
供給	きょうきゅう	supply	7F
供	キョウ、ク、そな-える、とも	offer, attendant	7F
塔	トウ	tower, monument	塔
石塔	せきとう	tombstone	7F

石	セキ、シャク、コク、いし	stone, rock	7F

7G 北 ATHANOR

𝕬	敗北	2A5
7G	はいぼく	*

Carry on your Back the cold Defeat

Originally two persons sitting back to back, coldest direction 北

背	ハイ、せ、せい、そむ-く、そむ-ける	back, stature, defy	背
背負	せおう	carry on one's back, shoulder	7G
負	フ、ま-ける、ま-かす、お-う	defeat, bear	7G
北	ホク、きた	north, flee	北
敗北	はいぼく	defeat	7G
敗	ハイ、やぶ-れる	defeat	7G

Tea for the tillerman. Wearing 畝織 long johns whilst 田打ち is superb but I don't want to go into 詳細. The 成功 貢献 of the 真紅 大工 speak for themselves. Work hard and 克明 is all I need to say and this applies as well to ambient 団体 of 狩猟 hillbillies armed with large flasks of 焼酎 in the 農山漁村. It is the 紀元 of 改革 and no Appalachian 王妃 can stop it. The 配達 of 供給, however, will provide a 解答 to the urgent needs of the Caraway 合唱 in the uppermost northern part. Make no mistake: nothing can 敗北 their awesome yodelling aunties!

Chapter 2 Taurus

8A 内 BALM

𓃰	獄内	2 – 6
8A	ごくない	0|1

Paying Tax in Prison, no strings attached

Originally enter + dwelling = inside 内

納	ノウ、ナッ、ナ、ナン、トウ、おさ-める、おさ-まる	obtain, store, supply	納
納税	のうぜい	tax payment	8A
税	ゼイ	tax, tithe	8A
内	ナイ、ダイ、うち	inside	内
獄内	ごくない	in prison	8A
獄*	ゴク	prison, litigation	8A

8B 広 BALM

𓃰	広告	3B9
8B	こうこく	*

Advertising Mineral Magnification

Originally spacious building illuminated by flaming arrow 広

広	コウ、ひろ-い、ひろ-まる、ひろ-める、ひろ-がる、ひろ-げる	wide, spacious	広

広告	こうこく	advertisement	8B
告	コク、つ-げる	proclaim, inform	8B
鉱	コウ	mineral, ore	鉱
鉱物	こうぶつ	mineral	8B
物	ブツ、モツ、もの	thing	8B
拡	カク	spread	拡
拡大	かくだい	magnification	8B
大	ダイ、タイ、おお、おお-きい、おお-いに	big	8B

8C 馬 BALM

	馬乗り	6A10
8C	うまのり	*

Riding Park's Cheap Goods is Completely Sick and will end in Noisy Abuse

Pictograph of a horse 馬

馬	バ、うま、ま	horse	馬
馬乗り	うまのり	riding	8C
乗	ジョウ、の-る、の-せる	ride, mount, load	8C
駐	チュウ	stop, stay	駐
駐車	ちゅうしゃ	parking	8C
車	シャ、くるま	vehicle, chariot	8C
駄	ダ	pack-horse, poor quality	駄
駄物	だもの	cheap goods	8C
物	ブツ、モツ、もの	thing	8C
篤	トク	sincere, serious	篤

47

危篤	きとく	seriously ill	8C
危	キ、あぶ-ない、あや-うい、あや-ぶむ	dangerous	8C
騒	ソウ、さわ-ぐ	noise, disturbance	騒
大騒ぎ	おうさわぎ	uproar, chaos	8C
大	ダイ、タイ、おお、おお-きい、おお-いに	big	8C
罵	バ、ののし.る	abuse; insult	罵
罵声	ばせい	jeers	8C
声	セイ、ショウ、こえ、こわ	voice	8C

8D 陽 BALM

| 𢼊 | | 太陽 | 8C11 |
| 8D | | たいよう | 0|4 |

Secretive Males caused Casualties in the Fishing Grounds: Fried Intestines in Hot Water produce Ulcers

Chinese only bright and open out, sun rising high and shining down 陽

陰	イン、かげ、かげ-る	shadow, secret, negative (yin)	陰
陰口	かげぐち	back biting	8D
口*	コウ、ク、くち	mouth, opening	8D
陽	ヨウ	sunny, male, positive (yang)	陽
太陽	たいよう	sun	8D
太	タイ、タ、ふと-い、ふと-る	fat, big	8D
傷	ショウ、きず、いた-む、いた-める	wound, injury	傷

48

死傷者	ししょうしゃ	casualties	8D
死	シ、し-ぬ	death	8D
者	シャ、もの	person	8D
場	ジョウ、ば	place	場
漁場	ぎょじょう、りょうば	fishing grounds/banks	8D
漁	ギョ、リョウ	fishing	8D
揚	ヨウ、あ-げる、あ-がる	raise, fry	揚
揚げ物	あげもの	fried food	8D
物	ブツ、モツ、もの	thing	8D
腸	チョウ	intestine(s)	腸
腸炎	ちょうえん	enteritis	8D
炎	エン、ほのお	inflammation, flame, blaze	8D
瘍	ヨウ、かさ	boil; carbuncle	瘍
潰瘍	かいよう	ulcer	8D
潰	カイ、エ、つぶ.す、つぶ.れる、つい.える	crush; smash; break; dissipate	8D
湯	トウ、ゆ	hot water	湯
銭湯	せんとう	public bath	8D
銭	セン、ぜに	sen, coin, money	8D

8E 首 BALM

ꙭ	首肯	4A2
8E	しゅこう	*

It Appears that Mountain Pass Guidance is coming to a Head

Originally eye with exaggerated eyebrow, eye area of face 首

貌	ボウ、かお、かたち	appearance	貌
変貌	へんぼう	transformation	8E
変	ヘン、か-わる、か-える	change, strange	8E
道	ドウ、トウ、みち	way, road	道
峠道	とうげみち	road through a mountain pass	8E
峠	とうげ	mountain pass	8E
導	ドウ、みちび-く	guide, lead	導
指導	しどう	guidance	8E
指	シ、ゆび、さ-す	finger, point	8E
首	シュ、くび	head, neck, chief	首
首肯	しゅこう	assent; consent	8E
肯	コウ	consent, agree, vital	8E

8F 売 BALM

売 (image)		売り物	4A9
8F		うりもの	*

Sell the Reader a new Purchasing Procedure

Formerly to buy, put out for buying; sell 売

売	バイ、う-る、う-れる	sell	売
売り物	うりもの	item for sale	8F
物	ブツ、モツ、もの	thing	8F
読	ドク、トク、トウ、よ-む	read	読
読者	どくしゃ	reader	8F
者	シャ、もの	person	8F
買	バイ、か-う	buy	買
故買	こばい	buying stolen goods	8F

故	コ、ゆえ	past, reason	8F
続	ゾク、つづ-く、つづ-ける	continue, series	続
手続き	てつづき	procedure	8F
手	シュ、て、た	hand	8F

8G 池 BALM

ꙮ		用水池	3C3
8G		ようすいち	0|1

The Underground is a Reservoir of Strangers

Twisting creature, snake undulating ground 池

地	チ、ジ	ground, land	地
地下	ちか	underground	8G
下	カ、ゲ、した、しも、もと、さ-げる、さ-がる、くだ-る、くだ-す	base, under, lower	8G
池	チ、いけ	pond, lake	池
用水池	ようすいち	reservoir	8G
用	ヨウ、もち-いる	use	8G
水*	スイ、みず	water	8G
他	タ	other	他
他人	たにん	stranger	8G
人	ジン、ニン、ひと	person	8G

The Tax Man cometh. It is tax time again so many innocent citizens were targeted to make 納税 by unscrupulous conmen 獄内 sending false 広告 and leaving threatening messages. Pay now or there will be 大騒ぎ as the police will lead you away under taunts and 罵声 from a hostile crowd and no hero will be 馬乗り to the rescue. A black 太陽 will be shining and you shall be afflicted by

51

腸炎 and horrible 潰瘍 if you don't ring the number. Did I mention an untimely accident on 峠道 if you withhold your 首肯? We have 手続き for turning your family into 売り物 my dear 読者. So, come and meet me 地下 near the 用水池 where a 他人 will relieve you of your precious possessions.

9A 楼 BATH OF VAPOURS

🅱	鐘楼	3A22
9A	しょうろう	*

Count Cherries from the Tower

Shamaness chanting whilst holding counting stick 楼

数	スウ、ス、かず、かぞ-える	number, count	数
数学	すうがく	mathematics	9A
学	ガク、まな-ぶ	study	9A
桜	オウ、さくら	cherry	桜
徒桜	あだざくら	ephemeral (easily scattered) cherry blossom; fickle woman	9A
徒	ト、あだ	follower, futility	9A
楼	ロウ	tower	楼
鐘楼	しょうろう	bell tower	9A
鐘	ショウ、かね	bell	9A

9B 里 BATH OF VAPOURS

🅱	古里	5E13
9B	ふるさと	2|3

It is Unreasonable to suggest that Back in my Hometown Burial is a Trifling affair

Ground with fields and dividing paths, settlement 里

理	リ	reason, rational	理
無理	むり	unreasonable	9B
無*	ム、ブ、な-い	not, non, cease to be	9B
裏	リ、うら	reverse, side, rear, inside, lining	裏
裏面	りめん	inside, back	9B
面	メン、おも、おもて、つら	face, aspect, mask	9B
里	リ、さと	village, league	里
古里	ふるさと	hometown	9B
古	コ、ふる-い、ふる-す	old	9B
埋	マイ、う-める、う-まる、う-もれる	bury	埋
埋葬	まいそう	burial	9B
葬	ソウ、ほうむ-る	bury	9B
厘	リン	rin, tiny amount	厘
厘毛	りんもう	a trifle	9B
毛	モウ、け	hair	9B

9C 黄 BATH OF VAPOURS

𝕍𝔹	黄色	3C
9C	きいろ	*

Present the Yellow Profile

Original meaning flaming arrow, yellow 黄

演	エン	performance, play, presentation	演

演歌	えんか	enka; traditional-style Japanese popular ballad	9C
歌	カ、うた、うた-う	song	9C
黄	コウ、オウ、き、こ	yellow	黄
黄色	きいろ	yellow	9C
色	ショク、シキ、いろ	colour, sensuality	9C
横	オウ、よこ	side, cross ways	横
横顔	よこがお	profile	9C
顔	ガン、かお	face	9C

9D 家 BATH OF VAPOURS

ℬ		作家	3A7
9D		さっか	*

The lazy Writer's Bride must forgo a Dual Income

Pictograph of a pig 家

家	カ、ケ、いえ、や	house, specialist	家
作家	さっか	writer	9D
作	サク、サ、つく-る	make	9D
嫁	カ、よめ、とつ-ぐ	marry, bride	嫁
花嫁	はなよめ	bride	9D
花	カ、はな	flower, blossom	9D
稼	カ、かせ-ぐ	work, earn money	稼
共稼ぎ	ともかせぎ	dual income	9D
共	キョウ、とも	together	9D

9E 原 BATH OF VAPOURS

𝕍𝔹	原子	4 - 1
9E	げんし	*

Atomic Prayer needs Cracked Resources

Cliff + variant of spring 原

原	ゲン、はら	plain, origin	原
原子	げんし	atom	9E
子	シ、ス、こ	child	9E
願	ガン、ねが-う	request, wish	願
願い事	ねがいごと	prayer	9E
事	ジ、ズ、こと	thing, matter, act	9E
隙	ゲキ、すき	crevice; fissure; discord; opportunity; leisure	隙
隙間	すきま	crevice; crack; gap; opening	9E
間	カン、ケン、あいだ、ま	space, gap	9E
源	ゲン、みなもと	source, origin	源
資源	しげん	resources	9E
資	シ	capital, resources	9E

9F 斗 BATH OF VAPOURS

𝕍𝔹	北斗星	3 - 6
9F	ほくとせい	*

Big Dipper Fertiliser is a School Subject

Pictograph of a ladle 斗

斗	ト		dipper, measure	斗

北斗星	ほくとせい	Big Dipper	9F
星	セイ、ショウ、ほし	star	9F
北	ホク、きた	north	9F
料	リョウ	materials, measure, charge	料
肥料	ひりょう	fertiliser	9F
肥	ヒ、こ-える、こえ、こ-やす、こ-やし	fatten, enrich	9F
科	カ	course, section	科
学科	がっか	school subjects	9F
学	ガク、まな-ぶ	study	9F

9G 戸 BATH OF VAPOURS

₿		戸籍	5B5
9G		こせき	*

Equally Ranked (Registered) Families had a Blast and Brightened Up the House of Ill Repute

Pictograph of "half" a door 戸

肩	ケン、かた	shoulder	肩
比肩	ひけん	rank equal with; compare favourably with	9G
比	ヒ、くら-べる	compare, ratio	9G
戸	コ、と	door	戸
戸籍	こせき	family register	9G
籍	セキ	register	9G
炉	ロ	furnace	炉
高炉	こうろ	blast furnace	9G

高	コウ、たか-い、たか、たか-まる、たか-める	tall, high, sum	9G
啓	ケイ	enlighten, state	啓
啓発	けいはつ	enlightenment; development; edification	9G
発	ハツ、ホツ	discharge, start, leave	9G
所	ショ、ところ	place, situation	所
悪所	あくしょ	dangerous place; house of ill repute; bad place	9G
悪	アク、オ、わる-い	bad, hate	9G

Bleak lodgings & humble abodes. Bats live in 鐘楼 whilst devotees of 数学 live in suitcases. There is nothing 無理 about dwelling 裏面 a sturdy trunk as long as it is not 黄色 and 演歌 proof. It also provides an elegant solution for young 花嫁 and aspiring 作家 who perhaps might be light on financial 資源 but have plenty of 願い事 for better times ahead. Indeed, an appropriate topic for 学科 and 啓発. Only a batty barrister in full court dress would complain about the lack of a 高炉 but he changed his tune after being exposed in 悪所.

10A 申 BISMUTH

B	申し込む	6E16
10A	もうしこむ	*

A Gentleman Applies his Mesmerizing Spirits & First Person Pronouns to great Extends

Originally forked lightning, 'voice of the gods?' 申

紳	シン	gentleman, belt	紳
紳士	しんし	gentleman	10A

士	シ	warrior, scholar, man	10A
申	シン、もう-す	say, expound	申
申し込む	もうしこむ	apply	10A
込	こ-む、こ-める	put in, be crowded	10A
電	デン	electricity	電
荷電	かでん	electric charge	10A
荷	カ、に	load, burden	10A
神	シン、ジン、かみ、かん、こう	god, spirit	神
精神	せいしん	spirit	10A
精	セイ、ショウ	spirit, vitality, refine, detail	10A
俺	エン、おれ	I	俺
伸	シン、の-びる、の-ばす	stretch, extend	伸
伸縮	しんしゅく	elasticity	10A
縮	シュク、ちぢ-む、ちぢ-まる、ちぢ-める	shrink, reduce	10A

10B 作 BISMUTH

ℬ	製作		5A9
10B	せいさく		*

The Production of Yesterday's Lies Pickles contemporary Exploits

Non General Use character adze on wood, make/construct 作

| 作 | サク、サ、つく-る | make | 作 |

58

製作	せいさく	production	10B
製	セイ	manufacture	10B
昨	サク	yesterday, past	昨
昨日	さくじつ	yesterday	10B
日	ニチ、ジツ、ひ、か	sun, day	10B
詐	サ	lie, deceive	詐
詐欺	さぎ	fraud	10B
欺	ギ、あざむ-く	cheat, deceive	10B
酢	サク、す	vinegar, sour	酢
酢の物	すのもの	pickles	10B
物	ブツ、モツ、もの	thing	10B
搾	サク、しぼ-る	wring, press	搾
搾取	さくしゅ	exploitation	10B
取	シュ、と-る	take control	10B

10C 弱 BISMUTH

	文弱	2B6
10C	ぶんじゃく	*

A Weakness for Learning is not Blind Love

Doubling of bow, bending and delicate hairs, easily bent 弱

弱	ジャク、よわ-い、よわ-る、よわ-まる、よわ-める	weak	弱
文弱	ぶんじゃく	(enervating) attraction to learning	10C
文	ブン、モン、ふみ	writing, text	10C
溺	デキ、おぼれる	drown	溺
溺愛	できあい	blind love	10C

59

愛	アイ	love	10C

10D 曜 BISMUTH

B	曜日	3D3
10D	ようび	*

Leap into Washing any Day of the Week

Bird and wings, passing 曜

躍	ヤク、おど-る	leap, dance, rush	躍
飛躍	ひやく	leap, activity, rapid progress	10D
飛	ヒ、と-ぶ、と-ばす	fly	10D
濯	タク	wash, rinse	濯
洗濯	せんたく	washing	10D
洗	セン、あら-う	wash, investigate	10D
曜	ヨウ	day of the week	曜
曜日	ようび	day of the week	10D
日	ニチ、ジツ、ひ、か	sun, day	10D

10E 寺 BISMUTH

B	侍女	8A5
10E	じじょ	1|5

At the Time in a Well-Maintained Buddhist Temple a First-Class Lady-In-Waiting Ambushed the Poetic priest in Patently samurai fashion

Growing plant, hand, regular use of hands, clerical work 寺

時	ジ、とき	time	時
時代	じだい	era	10E

代	ダイ、タイ、か-わる、か-える、よ、しろ	replace, world, generation, fee	！	10E
持	ジ、も-つ	hold, have, maintain		持
長持ち	ながもち	durability		10E
長	チョウ、なが-い	long, senior		10E
寺	ジ、てら	temple		寺
寺院	じいん	Buddhist temple		10E
院	イン	institute		10E
等	トウ、ひと-しい	class, equal, et cetera		等
一等	いっとう	first class		10E
一	イチ、イツ、ひと、ひと-つ	one		10E
侍	ジ、さむらい	attend (upon)		侍
侍女	じじょ	lady-in-waiting		10E
女*	ジョ、ニョ、ニョウ、おんな、め	woman		10E
待	タイ、ま-つ	wait		待
待ち伏せ	まちぶせ	ambush		10E
伏	フク、ふ-せる、ふ-す	prostrated, bend down		10E
詩	シ	poetry		詩
詩抄	ししょう	selected poems		10E
抄	ショウ	excerpt, extract		10E
特	トク	special		特
特許	とっきょ	patent		10E
許	キョ、ゆる-す	permit, allow, place, home		10E

61

10F 語 BISMUTH

B	語調	3C7
10F	ごちょう	*

Telling Enlightenment makes Sense

Words + ngu character I/me (originally two identical reels) 語

語	ゴ、かた-る、かた-らう	tell, speak, talk	語
語調	ごちょう	tone	10F
調	チョウ、しら-べる、ととの-う、ととの-える	adjust, investigate, tone, tune	10F
悟	ゴ、さと-る	perceive, discern	悟
悟り	さとり	enlightenment	10F
五	ゴ、いつ、いつ-つ	five	五
五感	ごかん	the five senses	10F
感	カン	feeling	10F

10G 方 BISMUTH

B	見方	12A20
10G	みかた	02|03

The Devoted Wife's Fragrance and Way of Looking Liberated the Constrained Priest as the Fat husband was Looking on but she Defended his Visit by Spinning a Model Yarn

Possibly tethered boats in the current, square 方

房	ボウ、ふさ	room, wife, tuft	房
世話女房	せわにょうぼう	devoted wife	10G
世*	セイ、セ、よ	world, society, age, generation	10G

話	ワ、はな-す、はなし	tale, talk	10G
女	ジョ、ニョ、ニョウ、おんな、め	woman	10G
芳	ホウ、かんば-しい	fragrant, good, your	芳
芳香	ほうこう	fragrance	10G
香	コウ、キョウ、か、かお-り、かお-る	fragrance, incense	10G
方	ホウ、かた	side, way, square, direction, person	方
見方	みかた	way of looking	10G
見	ケン、み-る、み-える、み-せる	look, see, show	10G
放	ホウ、はな-す、はな-つ、はな-れる	release, emit	放
解放	かいほう	liberation	10G
解	カイ、ゲ、と-く、と-かす、と-ける	unravel, explain, solve	10G
妨	ボウ、さまた-げる	hamper, obstruct	妨
妨害	ぼうがい	obstruction	10G
害	ガイ	harm, damage	10G
坊	ボウ、ボッ	priest, boy, town	坊
坊主	ぼうず*	priest	10G
主	シュ、ス、ぬし、おも	master, owner, main	10G
肪	ボウ	fat	肪
脂肪	しぼう	fat	10G
脂	シ、あぶら	fat, grease, resin	10G
傍	ボウ、かたわ-ら	side, beside(s)	傍

63

傍観	ぼうかん		looking on	10G
観	カン		watch, observe	10G
防	ボウ、ふせ-ぐ		prevent, defend	防
防衛	ぼうえい		defence	10G
衛	エイ		guard, protect	10G
訪	ホウ、おとず-れる、たず-ねる		visit, inquire	訪
訪問	ほうもん		visit	10G
問	モン、と-う、と-い、とん		ask	10G
紡	ボウ、つむ-ぐ		spin, (yarn)	紡
紡機	ぼうき		spinning machine	10G
機	キ、はた		loom, device, occasion	10G
倣	ホウ、なら-う		imitate, follow	倣
模倣	もほう		imitation	10G
模	モ、ボ		copy, model, mould	10G

The rain in Albion stays mainly in the plain. Dan Dare and 紳士 Jim, spiffy chaps 俺'd say, found themselves in a spot of 荷電 bother and in a bit of a 酢の物 one day. Or was it 昨日? They were, you see, investigating a case of 詐欺 where a 文弱 boffin was 溺愛 with a 洗濯 wench. On a certain 曜日 when said boffin used to read 詩抄 in a 寺院 she 待ち伏せ him and persuaded him to hand over his 特許. Resistance was futile as he listened to the 語調 of her seductive voice whilst her fragrance overpowered his 五感. Her delightful 見方 and top notch 芳香 were enough to make him drop his 防衛 after which he exclaimed: By George, I think you've got it!

11A 仏 BLACK BRIMSTONE

♔	仏教	6C13
11A	ぶっきょう	*

In the Pine Grove of Buddhism Private Plaintiffs Refund Fairness

Nose, self 仏

松	ショウ、まつ	pine	松
松原	まつばら	pine grove	11A
原	ゲン、はら	plain, origin	11A
仏	ブツ、ほとけ	Buddha, France	仏
仏教	ぶっきょう	Buddhism	11A
教	キョウ、おし-える、おそ-わる	teach	11A
私	シ、わたくし	I, private, personal	私
私立	しりつ	private	11A
立	リツ、リュウ、た-つ、た-てる	stand, rise, leave	11A
訟	ショウ	accuse, sue	訟
訴訟人	そしょうにん	plaintiff	11A
訴	ソ、うった-える	sue, appeal	11A
人	ジン、ニン、ひと	person	11A
払	フツ、はら-う	pay, sweep away, rid	払
払い戻し	はらいもどす	refund	11A
戻	レイ、もど-す、もど-る	return, bring back, rebel, bend, vomit	11A
公	コウ、おおやけ	public, fair, lord	公
公平	こうへい	fairness	11A
平	ヘイ、ビョウ、たい-ら、ひら	flat, even, calm	11A

11B才 BLACK BRIMSTONE

♨	天才	4 - 2
11B	てんさい	6‖8

The Financial Lumber Genius Closed Shop

Originally dam across a stream 才

財	ザイ、サイ	wealth, assets	財
財政的	ざいさいてき	financial	11B
政	セイ、ショウ、まつりごと	government	11B
的	テキ、まと	target, like, adjectival suffix	11B
材	ザイ	timber, resource	材
材木	ざいもく	wood, lumber	11B
木*	ボク、モク、き、こ	tree, wood	11B
才	サイ	talent, year of age	才
天才	てんさい	genius	11B
天*	テン、あめ、あま	heaven, sky	11B
閉	ヘイ、と-じる、と-ざす、し-める、し-まる	close, shut	閉
閉店	へいてん	closing store	11B
店	テン、みせ	store, premises	11B

11C 至 BLACK BRIMSTONE

♨	至らない	9B17
11C	いたらない	2‖‖10

Bankrupted, squeezed out of financial Means and with an Imperfect Understanding they Arrived Occupying the Living

Room where they Choked on Fine Alcohol from the Liquor Shop

Pictograph of an arrow falling to the ground 至

倒	トウ、たお-れる、たお-す	fall, topple, invert	倒
倒産	とうさん	bankruptcy	11C
産*	サン、う-む、う-まれる、うぶ	birth, produce	11C
致	チ、いた-す	do, send, cause	致
致し方	いたしかた	means	11C
方	ホウ、かた	side, way, square, direction, person	11C
至	シ、いた-る	go, reach, peak	至
至らない	いたらない	imperfect	11C
握	アク、にぎ-る	grasp, grip	握
把握	はあく	grasp	11C
把	ハ	grasp, comprehend	11C
到	トウ	go, reach, arrive	到
到達	とうたつ	arrival	11C
達*	タツ	attain	11C
室	シツ、むろ	room, house	室
居室	きょしつ	living room	11C
居	キョ、い-る	be, reside	11C
窒	チツ	block up, plug	窒
窒死	ちっし	asphyxia	11C
死	シ、し-ぬ	death	11C
緻	チ、こまか.い	fine (i.e. not coarse)	緻
緻密	ちみつ	minute; fine; delicate; accurate; elaborate	11C
密	ミツ	dense, secret	11C

屋	オク、や	store, building	屋
酒屋	さかや	liquor store	11C
酒*	シュ、さけ、さか	alcohol, sake	11C

11D 止 BLACK BRIMSTONE

| ♨ | 中止 | 3B13 |
| 11D | ちゅうし | * |

The Dentist Grudgingly Suspended a Tooth

Foot, stop, planting the foot 止

歯	シ、は	tooth	歯
歯医者	はいしゃ	dentist	11D
医	イ	doctor	11D
者	シャ、もの	person	11D
渋	ジュウ、しぶ、しぶ-い、しぶ-る	hesitate, astringent	渋
渋々	しぶしぶ	grudgingly	11D
止	シ、と-まる、と-める	stop	止
中止	ちゅうし	suspension	11D
中	チュウ、なか	middle, inside, China	11D

11E 心 BLACK BRIMSTONE

| ♨ | 愛国心 | 3C7 |
| 11E | あいこくしん | * |

The Reply: Patriotism can be Wicked

Pictograph of a heart 心

応	オウ	respond, react	応
応答	おうとう	reply; answer; response	11E
答	トウ、こた-える、こた-え	answer	11E
心	シン、こころ	heart, feelings	心
愛国心	あいこくしん	patriotic feelings; patriotism	11E
愛	アイ	love	11E
国	コク、くに	country, region	11E
芯	シン	inner part	芯
灯芯	とうしん	wick	11E
灯	トウ、ひ	light, lamp	11E

11F 行 BLACK BRIMSTONE

♨		運行	2 - 9
11F		うんこう	*

Operations Differ Greatly

Pictograph of crossroads 行

行	コウ、ギョウ、アン、い-く、ゆ-く、おこな-う	go, conduct, column	行
運行	うんこう	service (bus, train); operation; (2) motion	11F
運	ウン、はこ-ぶ	transport, luck, move	11F
桁	コウ、けた	beam; girder; spar; unit or column (accounting)	桁
桁違い	けたちがい	differing greatly	11F
違	イ、ちが-う、ちが-える	differ	11F

11G 羽 BLACK BRIMSTONE

⛾	羽毛	5A12
11G	うもう	*

A Fan hit an Old Man the Next Day during Plumage Practice

Pictograph of bird's wings 羽

扇	セン、おうぎ	fan	扇
扇子	せんす	(folding) fan	11G
子	シ、ス、こ	child	11G
翁	オウ	old man, venerable	翁
翌	ヨク	next (of time)	翌
翌日	よくじつ	next day	11G
日	ニチ、ジツ、ひ、か	sun, day	11G
羽	ウ、は、はね	wing, feather, bird counter	羽
羽毛	うもう	plumage	11G
毛	モウ、け	hair	11G
習	シュウ、なら-う	learn, train	習
練習	れんしゅう	practice	11G
練	レン、ね-る	refine, knead, train	11G

Reasons to be cheerful. Questionable 払い戻し always have a high degree of 公平 if the right 私立 individuals are concerned such as 財政的 demi-gods and 天才 of the stock market. Of course, 倒産 are regrettable but anyone with a firm 把握 of the situation should avoid running to the 酒屋. No maudlin drunkenness in the 居室 please! Just bear it 渋々 like sweating it out at the 歯医者. The appropriate 応答 is to light the 灯芯 of introspection and to stare deeply into your navel. Public 運行 are still available so the 翌日, each day as a matter of fact, you could go to the park and loiter with intent or watch 翁 geezers 練習

gentle exercises.

12A 外 BLOOD STONE

⊂	占い者	11F14
12A	うらないしゃ	1|1

An Outsider Called a Sticky yet Chaste Diviner who "Post Eviction" Detected and Appended Unsophisticated Obituaries

Crescent moon and divination (crack in turtle shell) 外

外	ガイ、ゲ、そと、ほか、はず-す、はず-れる	outside, other, undo	外
外側	そとがわ	exterior	12A
側	ソク、かわ	side	12A
点	テン	point, mark	点
点呼	てんこ	roll call	12A
呼*	コ、よ-ぶ	call, breathe	12A
粘	ネン、ねば-る	sticky, glutinous	粘
粘着	ねんちゃく	adhesion	12A
着	チャク、ジャク、き-る、き-せる、つ-く、つ-ける	arrive, wear	12A
貞	テイ	chastity, virtue	貞
貞操	ていそう	chastity	12A
操	ソウ、みさお、あやつ-る	handle, chastity	12A
占	セン、し-める、うらな-う	divine, occupy	占
占い者	うらないしゃ	diviner	12A
者	シャ、もの	person	12A
赴	フ、おもむ-く	proceed, go	赴
赴任地	ふにんち	post, posting	12A
任	ニン、まか-せる、まか-す	duty, entrust	12A

地	チ、ジ	ground, land	12A
店	テン、みせ	store, premises	店
店立て	たなだて	eviction	12A
立	リツ、リュウ、た-つ、た-てる	stand, rise, leave	12A
偵	テイ	spy, investigate	偵
探偵	たんてい	detection	12A
探	タン、さぐ-る、さが-す	search, probe	12A
貼	チョウ、テン、は-る	stick; paste; apply	貼
貼付	ちょうふ	pasting; paste; appending	12A
付	フ、つ-ける、つ-く	attach, apply	12A
朴	ボク	simple, magnolia	朴
純朴	じゅんぼく	simplicity, naïve, unsophisticated	12A
純	ジュン	pure	12A
訃	フ、しらせ	obituary	訃
訃報	ふほう	news of a death	12A
報	ホウ、むく-いる	report, reward	12A

12B 楽 BLOOD STONE

⊆		楽観的		2B7
12B		らっかんてき		*

Music is the Drug

Originally a type of oak whose leaves were eaten by silk worms 楽

楽	ガク、ラク、たの-しい、たの-しむ	pleasure, music	楽
楽観的	らっかんてき	optimistic	12B

観	カン		watch, observe	12B
的	テキ、まと		target, like, adjectival suffix	12B
薬	ヤク、くすり		medicine, drug	薬
丸薬	がんやく		pill	12B
丸	ガン、まる、まる-い、まる-める		round, circle, ball, ship's mark	12B

12C 舌 BLOOD STONE

⊆		二枚舌		6A9
12C		にまいじた		*

Bind that Duplicitous Talkative Tongue, bringing to Life Riotous Words

Originally mouth + dry/forked thrusting weapon, phonetic emerge 舌

括	カツ	bind, wrap, fasten	括
括弧	かっこ	parentheses	12C
弧	コ	arc, arch, bow	12C
話	ワ、はな-す、はなし	tale, talk	話
哀話	あいわ	sad story	12C
哀	アイ、あわ-れ、あわ-れむ	sorrow, pity	12C
舌	ゼツ、した	tongue	舌
二枚舌	にまいじた	duplicity	12C
二	ニ、ふた、ふた-つ	two	12C
枚	マイ	sheet, counter	12C
活	カツ	activity, life	活
生活	せいかつ	life	12C

生	セイ、ショウ、い-きる、い-かす、い-ける、う-まれる、う-む	life, birth, grow	12C
乱	ラン、みだ-れる、みだ-す	disorder, riot	乱
反乱	はんらん	rebellion	12C
反	ハン、ホン、タン、そ-る、そ-らす	oppose, anti, reverse	12C
辞	ジ、や-める	word, decline, leave	辞
辞職	じしょく	resignation	12C
職	ショク	employment, job	12C

12D 周 BLOOD STONE

| ⊑ | | 六百周 | 4A7 |
| 12D | | ろっぴゃくしゅう | 0\|9 |

Six Hundred Weekly Laps were enough to Tone the Investigator

Originally field completely full of crops, complete, cycle 周

周	シュウ、まわ-り	circumference, around	周
六百周	ろっぴゃくしゅう	800 laps	12D
六	ロク、む、む-つ、むっ-つ、むい	six	12D
百*	ヒャク	hundred	12D
週	シュウ	week	週
週間	しゅうかん	week	12D
間	カン、ケン、あいだ、ま	space, gap	12D
彫	チョウ、ほ-る	carve, sculpture	彫
彫刻	ちょうこく	sculpture	12D

刻	コク、きざ-む	chop, mince, engrave	12D
調	チョウ、しら-べる、ととの-う、ととの-える	adjust, investigate, tone, tune	調
調査	ちょうさ	investigation	12D
査	サ	investigate	12D

12E 毎 BLOOD STONE

| ⊂ | | 毎日 | 9I8 |
| 12E | | まいにち | * |

Regrettably, Each and Every day Mummy's Buman was Scorned to the Quick in a Poisonous Sea of Rich and Plummy Insults

Plant and mother, fertility, richly growing plant 毎

悔	カイ、く-いる、く-やむ、くや-しい	regret, repent, vexed	悔
悔恨	かいこん	regret	12E
恨	コン、うら-む、うら-めしい	resent, regret	12E
毎	マイ	each, every	毎
毎日	まいにち	every day	12E
日	ニチ、ジツ、ひ、か	sun, day	12E
母	ボ、はは	mother	母
母艦	ぼかん	mother ship	12E
艦	カン	warship	12E
侮	ブ、あなど-る	scorn, despise	侮
侮慢	ぶまん	contempt; insult; offense; offence	12E
慢	マン	lazy, rude, boastful	12E
敏	ビン	agile, quick, alert	敏

75

過敏	かびん	nervousness; over sensitivity	12E
過	カ、す-ぎる、す- ごす、あやま-つ、あやま-ち	pass, exceed, error	12E
毒	ドク	poison	毒
中毒	ちゅうどく	poisoning; addiction	12E
中	チュウ、なか	middle, inside, China	12E
海	カイ、うみ	sea	海
公海	こうかい	high seas; international waters	12E
公	コウ、おおやけ	public, fair, lord	12E
繁	ハン	profuse, rich, complex	繁
繁雑	はんざつ	complex; intricate	12E
雑	ザツ、ゾウ	miscellany	12E
梅	バイ、うめ	plum (fertility)	梅
梅花	ばいか	plum blossom	12E

12F 筆 BLOOD STONE

| ⊂ | | 筆者 | 4 – 5 |
| 12F | | ひっしゃ | 3\|6 |

The Writer had a brush with the Law after Crossing out his Postcards

Hand holding brush 筆

筆	ヒツ、ふで	writing brush	筆
筆者	ひっしゃ	writer	12F
者	シャ、もの	person	12F
律	リツ、リチ	law, control	律

法律	ほうりつ	law	12F
法	ホウ、ハッ、ホッ	law	12F
津	シン、つ	harbour, crossing	津
津波	つなみ	tsunami	12F
波	ハ、なみ	wave	12F
書	ショ、か-く	write	書
葉書	はがき	postcard	12F
葉*	ヨウ、は	leaf	12F

12G 須 BLOOD STONE

⊏	必須	3F7
12G	ひっす	*

Impudence of a Necessary Subclass

Head and attractive forehead, face 須

顔	ガン、かお	face	顔
厚顔	こうがん	impudence; audacity	12G
厚	コウ、あつ-い	thick, kind	12G
須	ス、あごひげ、すべか-らく …べ-し	ought; by all means; necessarily	須
必須	ひっす	necessary	12G
必	ヒツ、かなら-ず	necessarily	12G
類	ルイ	resemble, variety, sort	類
下位分類	かいぶんるい	subclass; subdivision	12G

下	カ、ゲ、した、しも、もと、さ-げる、さ-がる、くだ-る、くだ-す	base, under, lower	12G
位	イ、くらい	rank, extent	12G
分	ブン、フン、ブ、わ-ける、わ-かれる、わ-かる、わ-かつ	divide, minute, understand	12G

Baking buns in the oven of the universe. On the New Age Fair, there was a 点呼 of hirsute practitioners of such arts as the 探偵 of lives past and 占い者 specialising in lives of the future. The latter were generally more 楽観的 than the former who occasionally had 哀話 of 生活 ruined by 二枚舌 and 反乱. For an entire 週間 the public was invited to be receptive to an 調査 of every spiritual nook & cranny. 毎日 offered opportunities to wash away 悔恨 and 侮慢 of previous reincarnations and to prepare oneself for the vexing 過敏 of things to come. As one of the 筆者 in the field expressed it: there are plenty of alien 葉書 out there! And as the cosmic 法律 of 必須 and gratuitous 厚顔 states: never mind the bollocks!

13A 孝 BORAX

| ☥ | 孝行 | 3 - 1 |
| 13A | こうこう | * |

It is Taught that Filial Piety Ferments like Yeast

Old man + child 孝

教	キョウ、おし-える、おそ-わる	teach	教
教化	きょうか	culture; education; civilisation	13A
化	カ、ケ、ば-ける、ば-かす	change, bewitch	13A

孝	コウ	filial piety	孝
孝行	こうこう	filial piety	13A
行	コウ、ギョウ、アン、い-く、ゆ-く、おこな-う	go, conduct, column	13A
酵	コウ	ferment, yeast	酵
発酵	はっこう	fermentation	13A
発	ハツ、ホツ	discharge, start, leave	13A

13B 氏 BORAX

	氏名	7C14
13B	しめい	2|6

From the Depths of a Full Name through the Decline of Resistance the Residence of Paper Marriage can be reached

Originally ladle, now hill, prominent hilltop living 氏

底	テイ、そこ	bottom, base	底
奥底	おくそこ	depths	13B
奥*	オウ、おく	heart, interior	13B
氏	シ、うじ	clan, family, Mr	氏
氏名	しめい	full name	13B
名	メイ、ミョウ、な	name, fame	13B
低	テイ、ひく-い、ひく-める、ひく-まる	low	低
低落	ていらく	decline	13B
落	ラク、お-ちる、お-とす	fall, drop	13B
抵	テイ	resist, match	抵
抵抗	ていこう	resistance	13B
抗	コウ	resist, oppose	13B

邸	テイ	mansion, residence	邸
邸宅	ていたく	mansion	13B
宅	タク	house, home	13B
紙	シ、かみ	paper	紙
鼻紙	はながみ	tissue paper, handkerchief paper	13B
鼻	ビ、はな	nose	13B
婚	コン	marriage	婚
結婚	けっこん	marriage	13B
結	ケツ、むす-ぶ、ゆ-う、ゆ-わえる	bind, join, end	13B

13C 刀 BORAX

⚒	竹刀	4C17
13C	しない*	*

At the Riverside he was struck by a Bamboo Sword and Bladed Love

Curved sword, cut 刀

辺	ヘン、あた-り、べ	vicinity, boundary	辺
川辺	かわべ	riverside	13C
川	セン、かわ	river	13C
刀	トウ、かたな	sword	刀
竹刀	しない*	bamboo sword (kendo)	13C
竹	チク、たけ	bamboo	13C
刃	ジン、は	blade sword	刃
刃物	はもの	bladed object	13C

物	ブツ、モツ、もの	thing	13C
初	ショ、はじ-め、はじ-めて、はつ、うい、そ-める	beginning, first	初
初恋	はつこい	first love	13C
恋	レン、こ-う、こい、こい-しい	love, beloved	13C

13D 黒 BORAX

𝄞		黒人	3D
13D		こくじん	*

Black Men were Silently studying Ink Drawings

Originally flame with window and marks of soot, black 黒

黒	コク、くろ、くろ-い	black	黒
黒人	こくじん	negro	13D
人	ジン、ニン、ひと	person	13D
黙	モク、だま-る	be silent	黙
沈黙	ちんもく	silence	13D
沈	チン、しず-む、しず-める	sink	13D
墨	ボク、すみ	ink, ink stick	墨
墨絵	すみえ	ink drawing	13D
絵	カイ、エ	picture	13D

13E 通 BORAX

𝄞		通勤	4B7
13E		つうきん	*

Re-employed Dancing Girls in Labour Pains don't like Commuting

Chinese only raised, originally sun rising above a brushwood fence
通

用	ヨウ、もち-いる	use	用
再雇用	さいこよう	re-employment	13E
再	サイ、サ、ふたた-び	again, twice, re-	13E
雇	コ、やと-う	employ, hire	13E
踊	ヨウ、おど-る、おど-り	dance, leap, double	踊
踊り子	おどりこ	dancing girl	13E
子	シ、ス、こ	child	13E
痛	ツウ、いた-い、いた-む、いた-める	pain, painful	痛
陣痛	じんつう	labour pains	13E
陣	ジン	position, camp	13E
通	ツウ、ツ、とお-る、とお-す、かよ-う	pass, way, commute	通
通勤	つうきん	commuting	13E
勤	キン、ゴン、つと-める、つと-まる	work, duties	13E

13F 沿 BORAX

	鉛筆	3
13F	えんぴつ	*

The Captain traces the Coast line with his Pencil

Hollowed out boat 沿

船	セン、ふね、ふな	boat, ship	船
船長	せんちょう	captain	13F
長	チョウ、なが-い	long, senior	13F

沿	エン、そ-う	go, alongside	沿
沿岸	えんがん	coast	13F
岸	ガン、きし	bank, shore	13F
鉛	エン、なまり	lead	鉛
鉛筆	えんぴつ	pencil	13F
筆	ヒツ、ふで	writing brush	13F

13G 夜 BORAX

⚸	夜明け	2 - 4
13G	よあけ	*

A Dawn as beautiful as a Blood Type

Clear moon 夜

夜	ヤ、よ、よる	night	夜
夜明け	よあけ	dawn	13G
明	メイ、ミョウ、あ-かり、あか-るい、あか-るむ	clear, open, bright	13G
液	エキ	liquid	液
血液型	けつえきがた	blood type	13G
血	ケツ、ち	blood	13G
型	ケイ、かた	type, model, mould	13G

Plus c'est la meme chose. The long standing 発酵 of popular music 教化 has reached such breathtaking 奥底 of terminal 低落 that we are just dancing in the ashes. Let's sit back at a nice spot near the 川辺 and let the dreary repetition of 初恋, second love and fiftieth love float along in 沈黙 like endless carbon copies of a once original 墨絵. Send in the 踊り子 to help forget the clumsy 通勤 of hoary old tunes from the past. 船長 Courageous -Disko comes to mind- from the contemporary music business are dipping their 鉛筆 in ancient 血液型. May the 夜明け of a new era petrify them like mountain trolls!

14A 辛 BRICK

IIIII	辛苦	5A11
14A	しんく	0|6

After having Known much Hardship the Parents requested an Interview with the Prime Minister

Tattooist's needle, piercing, slaves, hardship, bitterness 辛

弁	ベン	speech, know, valve	弁
勘弁	かんべん	pardon; forgiveness; forbearance	14A
勘	カン	endure, consider, investigate, sense	14A
辛	シン、から-い	sharp, bitter	辛
辛苦	しんく	hardship	14A
苦	ク、くる-しい、くる-しむ、くる-しめる、にが-い	painful, bitter	14A
親	シン、おや、した-しい、した-しむ	intimate, parent	親
両親	りょうしん	parents	14A
両*	リョウ	both, pair, coin	14A
接	セツ、つ-ぐ	contact, join	接
面接	めんせつ	interview	14A

面	メン、おも、おもて、つら	face, aspect, mask	14A
宰	サイ	administer	宰
宰相	さいしょう	prime minister	14A
相	ソウ、ショウ、あい	mutual, minister, aspect	14A

14B 前 BRICK

ⅢⅢ		朝飯前	2A5
14B		あさめしまえ	*

Rice Crackers are no Piece of Cake

Originally putting on one's clogs (hollowed out wood) and go 前

煎	セン、いる	parched	煎
煎餅	せんべい	rice crackers	14B
餅	ヘイ、もち	mochi rice cake	14B
前	ゼン、まえ	before, front	前
朝飯前	あさめしまえ	trivial matter; easy as pie; it's a piece of cake	14B
朝	チョウ、あさ	court, morning	14B
飯	ハン、めし	cooked rice, food	14B

14C 台 BRICK

ⅢⅢ		台風	6B9
14C		たいふう	*

The Lazy and "Methallargic" Typhoon Started to Rule over the Foetus

Originally mound of earth on the top of which one is stationed 台

怠	タイ、おこた-る、なま-ける	be lazy, neglect	怠
怠り勝ち	おこたりがち	neglectful	14C
勝	ショウ、か-つ、まさ-る	win, surpass	14C
冶	ヤ、と-ける	melting; smelting	冶
冶金	やきん	metallurgy	14C
金	キン、コン、かね、かな	gold, money, metal	14C
台	ダイ、タイ	platform, stand	台
台風	たいふう	typhoon	14C
風	フウ、フ、かぜ、かざ	wind, style	14C
始	シ、はじ-める、はじ-まる	begin, first	始
始終	しじゅう	throughout	14C
終	シュウ、お-わる、お-える	end, finish	14C
治	ジ、チ、おさ-める、おさ-まる、なお-る、なお-す	govern, rule, cure	治
政治	せいじ	politics	14C
政	セイ、ショウ、まつりごと	government	14C
胎	タイ	womb	胎
胎児	たいじ	foetus	14C
児	ジ、ニ	child	14C

14D 弟 BRICK

Ⅲ		弟子	4C4
14D 並		でし	*

Young Iota Programs Love Affairs

86

Previously showing two and large, double large, supersize; fat 太
Set order in binding a stake (used as a weapon), sequence 弟

弟	テイ、ダイ、デ、おとうと	younger brother	弟
弟子	でし	pupil; disciple; adherent; follower; apprentice	14D
子	シ、ス、こ	child	14D
太	タイ、タ、ふと-い、ふと-る	fat, big	太
与太	よた	idle gossip; nonsense; good-for-nothing fellow	14D
与	ヨ、あた-える	give, convey, impart, involvement	14D
第	ダイ	grade, order	第
次第	しだい	1) dependent upon; (2) as soon as; immediately (upon); (3) circumstances; (4) order; precedence; program	14D
次	ジ、シ、つ-ぐ、つぎ	next, follow	14D
汰	タ	luxury; select	汰
色恋沙汰	いろこいざた	love affair	14D
色	ショク、シキ、いろ	colour, sensuality	14D
恋	レン、こ-う、こい、こい-しい	love, beloved	14D
沙	サ、すな	sand	14D

14E 妻 BRICK

IIIII	夫妻	8E14
14E	ふさい	*

A Conjugal Vacuum Cleaner was Returned with the Widow's Bedding to Soak Up a Ghastly Violation

Hand holding broom, house wife 妻

妻	サイ、つま	wife	妻
夫妻	ふさい	husband and wife	14E
夫	フ、フウ、おっと	husband, man	14E
掃	ソウ、は-く	sweep	掃
掃除機	そうじき	vacuum cleaner	14E
除	ジョ、ジ、のぞ-く	exclude, remove	14E
機	キ、はた	loom, device, occasion	14E
帰	キ、かえ-る、かえ-す	return	帰
帰り道	かえりみち	way back	14E
道	ドウ、トウ、みち	way, road	14E
婦	フ	woman, wife	婦
寡婦	かふ	widow	14E
寡	カ	few, minimum, widow	14E
寝	シン、ね-る、ね-かす	sleep, lie down	寝
寝具	しんぐ	bedding	14E
具	グ	equip, means	14E
浸	シン、ひた-す、ひた-る	soak, immerse	浸
浸水	しんすい	inundation	14E
水	スイ、みず	water	14E

凄	サイ、セイ、すさま-じい	uncanny; weird; threatening; horrible	凄
凄惨	せいさん	ghostliness; gruesomeness	14E
惨	サン、ザン、みじ-め	cruel, miserable	14E
侵	シン、おか-す	invade, violate	侵
侵害	しんがい	violation	14E
害	ガイ	harm, damage	14E

14F 西 BRICK

▐▊▊▊▌		泰西	2E4
14F		たいせい	*

The Occident, The Horror

Originally basket, wine press 西

西	セイ、サイ、にし	west	西
泰西	たいせい	the Occident; the West	14F
泰	タイ	calm, serene, big, Thai	14F
慄	リツ、ふる.える、おそ.れる、おのの.く	fear	慄
慄然	りつぜん	in horror	14F
然	ゼン、ネン	duly, thus, so, but	14F

14G 少 BRICK

▐▊▊▊▌	即妙	8B8

14G	そくみょう		*

A Few Seconds in the Ministry of Silly Construction & Neglect to Quote the Witty Sandy Tsunahama

Original meaning is "smaller than small", tiny size 少

少	ショウ、すく-ない、すこ-し	a little, few	少
軽少	けいしょう	trifling; slight	14G
軽	ケイ、かる-い、かろ-やか	light, flippant	14G
秒	ビョウ	second (of time)	秒
寸秒	すんびょう	a moment	14G
寸	スン	measure, inch	14G
省	セイ、ショウ、かえり-みる、はぶ-く	ministry, omit, examine	省
建設省	けんせつしょう	Ministry of Construction	14G
建	ケン、コン、た-てる、た-つ	build, erect	14G
設	セツ、もう-ける	establish, build	14G
劣	レツ、おと-る	be inferior	劣
愚劣	ぐれつ	foolishness; stupidity; silliness	14G
愚	グ、おろ-か	foolish	14G
沙	サ、すな	sand	沙
ご無沙汰	ごぶさた	neglect to write/contact	14G
無	ム、ブ、な-い	not, non, cease to be	14G
汰	タ	luxury; select	14G
抄	ショウ	excerpt, extract	抄
抄録	しょうろく	quotation; abstract; selection; summary	14G

録	ロク	record, inscribe	14G
妙	ミョウ	exquisite, strange, mystery	妙
即妙	そくみょう	ready wit	14G
即	ソク	immediate, namely, accession	14G
砂	サ、シャ、すな	sand, gravel, grain	砂
砂浜	すなはま	sandy beach	14G
浜	ヒン、はま	beach, shore	14G

And Atlas kind of shrugged. Speaking about 辛苦 in a recent 面接 the 宰相 remarked that there should be an end to 勘弁 and feelings of entitlement. Life is not 朝飯前 and his 政治 were a clarion call to all 怠り勝ち and other 与太 to no longer 次第 on government programs. We are all 弟子 of market forces now and there is no 帰り道 to a situation where people could stretch out on comfortable 寝具 provided by the common weal. There might be an 浸水 of such cases but I say: let the 泰西 recoil in 慄然 from such 愚劣 and not for 寸秒 consider an idle and joyful existence on a 砂浜. There are foreign bondholders to be paid you know!

Chapter 3 Gemini

15a 古 CALCINATION

ⓇR	考古学	9D17
15A	こうこがく	*

In the Past an Old and Bitter Individual was Imprisoned in the "County" of Seven Dead Leaves in the Lake

Skull-like mask, ancestors, old 古

故	コ、ゆえ	past, reason	故
事故	じこ	accident	15A
事	ジ、ズ、こと	thing, matter, act	15A
古	コ、ふる-い、ふる-す	old	古
考古学	こうこがく	archaeology	15A
考	コウ、かんが-える	consider	15A
学	ガク、まな-ぶ	study	15A
苦	ク、くる-しい、くる-しむ、くる-しめる、にが-い	painful, bitter	苦
苦味	にがみ	bitterness; bitter taste	15A
味	ミ、あじ、あじ-わう	taste, relish	15A
個	コ	individual, counter	個
個人	こじん	individual	15A
人	ジン、ニン、ひと	person	15A
錮	コ、ふさ.ぐ	to tie	錮
禁錮	きんこ	imprisonment; confinement	15A

禁	キン	ban, forbid	15A
箇	カ、コ	item (counter)	箇
七箇	ななこ	seven items	15A
七	シチ、なな、なな-つ、なの	seven	15A
固	コ、かた-める、かた-まる、かた-い	hard, firm, solid	固
固執	こしつ	persist in, hold fast to	15A
執	シツ、シュウ、と-る	take, grasp, execute	15A
枯	コ、か-れる、か-らす	wither, decay	枯
枯葉	かれは	dead leaf	15A
葉	ヨウ、は	leaf	15A
湖	コ、みずうみ	lake	湖
湖水	こすい	lake	15A
水	スイ、みず	water	15A

15B 番 CALCINATION

ℝ		順番	4E12
15B		じゅんばん	*

It's your Turn to Referee the Flapping Feudal Lord

Rice plant + field, planting follows set order, roster, turn 番

番	バン	turn, number, guard	番
順番	じゅんばん	turn	15B
順	ジュン	sequence, compliance	15B
審	シン	judge, investigate	審
審判	しんぱん	judging, refereeing	15B

判	ハン、バン	seal; stamp; judgment	15B
翻	ホン、ひるがえ-る、ひるがえ-す	flap, change	翻
翻って	ひるがえって	on second thoughts	15B
藩	ハン	fief, clan, fence	藩
藩主	はんしゅ	feudal lord	15B
主	シュ、ス、ぬし、おも	master, owner, main	15B

15C 斤 CALCINATION

℞	斤目	11C25
15C	きんめ	1‖4

A Short Time after the New Year the Quality of Cutting-Edge Wood chopping in the Near East Gradually caused the Master to Pray and to engage in Weighty Analysis

Axe with shaped handle 斤

暫	ザン		a while, briefly	暫
暫時	ざんじ		short time	15C
時	ジ、とき		time	15C
新	シン、あたら-しい、あら-た、にい		new	新
新年	しんねん		new year	15C
年	ネン、とし		year	15C
質	シツ、シチ、チ		quality, pawn	質
品質	ひんしつ		quality	15C
品*	ヒン、しな		goods, quality, kind	15C
斬	ザン、サン、セン、ゼン、き.る		beheading; kill; murder	斬

94

斬新	ざんしん	novel, i.e. cutting-edge	15C
新	シン、あたら-しい、あら-た、にい	new	15C
薪	シン、たきぎ	firewood, kindling	薪
薪割り	まきわり	wood chopping	15C
割	カツ、わ-る、わり、わ-れる、さ-く	divide, rate	15C
近	キン、ちか-い	near	近
近東	きんとう	the near east	15C
東	トウ、ひがし	east	15C
漸	ゼン	gradual advance	漸
漸次	ぜんじ	gradually	15C
次	ジ、シ、つ-ぐ、つぎ	next, follow	15C
匠	ショウ	craftsman, plan	匠
師匠	ししょう	master	15C
師*	シ	teacher, model, army	15C
祈	キ、いの-る	pray, hope	祈
祈念	きねん	prayer	15C
念	ネン	thought, concern	15C
斤	キン	axe, weight	斤
斤目	きんめ	weight	15C
目	モク、ボク、め、ま	eye, ordinal, suffix	15C
析	セキ	divide, analyse	析

95

分析	ぶんせき	analysis	15C
分	ブン、フン、ブ、わ-ける、わ-かれる、わ-かる、わ-かつ	divide, minute, understand	15C

15D 市 CALCINATION

⊕	市場	4 - 7
15D	しじょう	*

Elder Sister Lunges at the Market for Shingles

Originally stop + confines + water weed, levelling out of sell/buy
市

姉	シ、あね	elder sister	姉
姉貴	あねき	elder sister	15D
貴	キ、たっと-い、とうと-い、たっと-ぶ、とうと-ぶ	precious, revered	15D
肺	ハイ	lung(s)	肺
肺臓	はいぞう	lungs	15D
臓	ゾウ	entrails, viscera	15D
市	シ、いち	city, market	市
市場	しじょう	market	15D
場	ジョウ、ば	place	15D
柿	シ、かき	persimmon; shingle	柿
柿色	かきいろ	reddish-brown; yellowish-brown	15D
色	ショク、シキ、いろ	colour, sensuality	15D

15E 形 CALCINATION

CR	人形	4 – 4
15E	にんぎょう	*

Conventional Dolls need Refined Punishment

Lattice window + hairs/pattern 形

型	ケイ、かた	type, model, mould	型
紋切れ型	もんきれがた	conventional	15E
紋	モン	(family) crest, pattern	15E
切	セツ、サイ、き-る、き-れる	cut	15E
形	ケイ、ギョウ、かた、かたち	shape, pattern	形
人形	にんぎょう	doll	15E
人	ジン、ニン、ひと	person	15E
研	ケン、と-ぐ	hone, refine	研
研ぎ澄ます	とぎすます	to sharpen; to grind; to whet; to hone; to make keen	15E
澄	チョウ、す-む、す-ます	clear, settle	15E
刑	ケイ	punish	刑
処刑	しょけい	punishment	15E
処	ショ	deal with, place	15E

15F 事 CALCINATION

CR	一事	4 – 2
15F	いちじ	*

According to Official History Servants do Matter

Formerly hand and flag on a pole, identifying guild? Work, worker/servant 事

吏	リ	official	吏
公吏	こうり	public official	15F
公	コウ、おおやけ	public, fair, lord	15F
史	シ	history, chronicler	史
現代史	げんだいし	contemporary history	15F
現	ゲン、あらわ-れる、あらわ-す	appear, exist, now	15F
代	ダイ、タイ、か-わる、か-える、よ、しろ	replace, world, generation, fee	15F
使	シ、つか-う	use, servant, messenger	使
酷使	こくし	exploitation, abuse	15F
酷	コク	severe, intense, cruel, harsh	15F
事	ジ、ズ、こと	thing, matter, act	事
一事	いちじ	one thing	15F
一	イチ、イツ、ひと、ひと-つ	one	15F

15G 谷 CLACINATION

ℝ		幽谷	7A10
15G		ゆうこく	*

Bathing in the Deep Ravine Dissolves Rich Slang and Tolerable Desire

Deeply, widely split opening, valley 谷

浴	ヨク、あ-びる、あ-びせる	bathe	浴

水浴び	みずあび	bathing	15G
水	スイ、みず	water	15G
谷	コク、たに	valley, gorge	谷
幽谷	ゆうこく	deep ravine	15G
幽	ユウ	dark, obscure, faint, lonely	15G
溶	ヨウ、と-ける、と-かす、と-く	melt, dissolve	溶
溶解	ようかい	melt, dissolve	15G
解	カイ、ゲ、と-く、と-かす、と-ける	unravel, explain, solve	15G
裕	ユウ	rich, plentiful	裕
裕福	ゆうふく	opulence	15G
福	フク	good fortune	15G
俗	ゾク	worldly, vulgar, custom	俗
俗語	ぞくご	slang	15G
語	ゴ、かた-る、かた-らう	tell, speak, talk	15G
容	ヨウ	contain, looks	容
寛容	かんよう	tolerance	15G
寛	カン	magnanimous, relax	15G
欲	ヨク、ほっ-する、ほ-しい	greed, desire	欲
欲望	よくぼう	desire	15G
望	ボウ、モウ、のぞ-む	wish, hope, gaze	15G

Reflections of the Lakeshore Strangler. 枯葉 floating on the 湖水 of 苦味 memories: the 考古学 of unfortunate 順番 and mistaken 審判. An 分析 of sloppy financial 薪割り whilst muddling through on a wing and a 祈念. 漸次 the 市場 for 柿色 murderous horror 人形 dried up resulting in strict 処刑 for 公吏 and considerable 酷使 hardly seen before in 現代史. Investors took a

水浴び and that quickly 溶解 any hopeful 欲望 for 裕福. Chucky didn't get lucky.

16A 長 CAMPHOR

XO	長持ち	3B3
16A	ながもち	*

The Long Stretch to the register Draped Off

Originally showing an old man with flowing long hair 長

長	チョウ、なが-い	long, senior	長
長持ち	ながもち	long-lasting	16A
持	ジ、も-つ	hold, have, maintain	16A
張	チョウ、は-る	stretch	張
伸張	しんちょう	expansion; extension; elongation	16A
伸	シン、の-びる、の-ばす	stretch, extend	16A
帳	チョウ	register, drape	帳
帳消し	ちょうけし	cancellation; writing off	16A
消	ショウ、き-える、け-す	extinguish, vanish, consume	16A

16B 京 CAMPHOR

XO	東京	8G8
16B	とうきょう	0|2

With some Influence in Tokyo I Found Employment where I Yearned for the Kick of applying Whale Oil to Scenic Benches

House on a hill, noble 京

影	エイ、かげ	shadow, light, image	影
影響	えいきょう	influence	16B
響	キョウ、ひび-く	resound, echo, effect	16B
京	キョウ、ケイ	capital	京
東京	とうきょう	Tokyo	16B
東*	トウ、ひがし	east	16B
就	シュウ、ジュ、つ-く、つ-ける	take up, be involved	就
就職	しゅうしょく	finding employment	16B
職	ショク	employment, job	16B
憬	ケイ、あこが.れる	yearn for; aspire to; admire	憬
憧憬	しょうけい; どうけい	longing; aspiration	16B
憧	ショウ、ドウ、あこが-れる	yearn after; long for; aspire to; admire; adore	16B
蹴	シュウ、け-る	kick	蹴
一蹴	いっしゅう	kick; rejection	16B
一	イチ、イツ、ひと、ひと-つ	one	16B
鯨	ゲイ、くじら	whale	鯨
鯨油	げいゆ	whale oil	16B
油	ユ、あぶら	oil	16B
景	ケイ	scene, view, bright	景
景色	けしき	scenery	16B
色	ショク、シキ、いろ	colour, sensuality	16B
涼	リョウ、すず-しい、すず-む	cool	涼
涼み台	すずみだい	bench	16B
台	ダイ、タイ	platform, stand	16B

16C 高 CAMPHOR

𝕏𝕆	高最	2E8
16C	こうさい	*

Tall Manuscripts

Pictograph of a tall watchtower 高

高	コウ、たか-い、たか、たか-まる、たか-める	tall, high, sum	高
高最	こうさい	highest	16C
最	サイ、もっと-も	most, -est	16C
稿	コウ	manuscript, straw	稿
原稿	げんこう	manuscript	16C
原	ゲン、はら	plain, origin	16C

16D 朝 CAMPHOR

𝕏𝕆	朝廷	4C3
16D	ちょうてい	*

Emperor "Self-Depreciator" Manages to hold Court as the Tide comes in

Originally sun rising through plants, rise + river 朝

朝	チョウ、あさ	court, morning	朝
朝廷	ちょうてい	imperial court	16D
廷	テイ	court, government office	16D
嘲	チョウ、トウ、あざけ.る	ridicule; insult	嘲

自嘲	じちょう	self-derision	16D
自	ジ、シ、みずか-ら	self	16D
幹	カン、みき	trunk, main	幹
幹事	かんじ	manager	16D
事	ジ、ズ、こと	thing, matter, act	16D
潮	チョウ、しお	tide, seawater	潮
潮流	ちょうりゅう	tide, current	16D
流	リュウ、ル、なが-れる、なが-す	flow, stream	16D

16E 可 CAMPHOR

XO	可決	12C20
16E	かけつ	1|3

"Say Tammy", How should one Send a Burdensome Cavalry of Harshly Singing Hippopotamus to the Odd Cape Palanquin

Mouth + twisting water weed/ seek an exit 可

埼	キ、さき、さい、みさき	cape; spit; promontory	埼
埼玉県	さいたまけん	Saitama Prefecture	16E
玉	ギョク、たま	ball, sphere, coin	16E
県	ケン	prefecture	16E
何	カ、なに、なん	what, how many	何
如何	いかが*	how	16E
如*	ジョ、ニョ	similar, equal	16E
可	カ	approve, can, should	可

可決	かけつ	approval	16E
決	ケツ、き-める、き-まる	decide, settle, collapse	16E
寄	キ、よ-る、よ-せる	draw near, send, visit	寄
立ち寄る	たちよる	visit, call	16E
立	リツ、リュウ、た-つ、た-てる	stand, rise, leave	16E
荷	カ、に	load, burden	荷
荷物	にもつ	baggage	16E
物	ブツ、モツ、もの	thing	16E
騎	キ	rider	騎
騎兵	きへい	cavalry	16E
兵	ヘイ、ヒョウ	soldier	16E
苛	カ、いじ.める、さいな.む、いらだ.つ、からい、こまかい	torment; scold; chastise	苛
苛酷	かこく	harsh	16E
酷	コク	severe, intense, cruel, harsh	16E
歌	カ、うた、うた-う	song	歌
狂歌	きょうか	comic (satirical) tanka	16E
狂	キョウ、くる-う、くる-おしい	lunatic, mad	16E
河	カ、かわ	river	河
河馬	かば	hippopotamus	16E
馬	バ、うま、ま	horse	16E
奇	キ	strange, odd	奇
奇数	きすう	odd number	16E

数	スウ、ス、かず、かぞ-える	number, count	16E
崎	さき	cape, steep	崎
長崎	ながさき	Nagasaki	16E
長	チョウ、なが-い	long, senior	16E
椅	イ	chair	椅
椅子	いす	chair	16E
子	シ、ス、こ	child	16E

16F 説 CAMPHOR

ХО		説得		10B8
16F		せっとく		0‖4

Persuasive, "Festive", Fun-Loving Brothers were in a Taxing Situation that required Sorcery & Shedding Sharp Censorship

Non General Use character exchange, barter, person dispersing words 説

説	セツ、ゼイ、と-く	preach, explain	説
説得	せっとく	persuasion	16F
得*	トク、え-る、う-る	gain, potential	16F
祝	シュク、シュウ、いわ-う	celebration	祝
祝賀	しゅくが	celebrate	16F
賀	ガ	congratulations	16F
悦	エツ	joy	悦
悦楽	えつらく	enjoyment	16F
楽	ガク、ラク、たの-しい、たの-しむ	pleasure, music	16F
兄	ケイ、キョウ、あに	elder brother	兄
兄弟	きょうだい	brothers	16F
弟	テイ、ダイ、デ、おとうと	younger brother	16F

税	ゼイ	tax, tithe	税
税金	ぜいきん	tax	16F
金*	キン、コン、かね、かな	gold, money, metal	16F
況	キョウ	more so, situation	況
状況	じょうきょう	situation	16F
状	ジョウ	condition, letter	16F
呪	ジュ、シュ、シュウ、ズ、まじな.う、のろ.い、まじな.い、のろ.う	spell; curse; charm	呪
呪術	じゅじゅつ	magic; sorcery	16F
術	ジュツ	means, technique	16F
脱	ダツ、ぬ-ぐ、ぬ-げる	take off, shed, escape	脱
脱衣	だつい	undressing	16F
衣	イ、ころも	garment	16F
鋭	エイ、するど-い	sharp, keen	鋭
鋭利	えいりな	sharp, keen	16F
利	リ、き-く	profit, gain, effect	16F
閲	エツ	inspection	閲
検閲	けんえつ	censorship	16F
検	ケン	investigate	16F

16G 直 CAMPHOR

XO	直立	8C3
16G	ちょくりつ	1|2

The Erect Stethoscope of Morality Developed a Priceless Ornamental Colony outside the Law

Eye + needle and corner, fix with direct piercing stare 直

直	チョク、ジキ、ただ-ちに、なお-す、なお-る	direct, upright, fix	直
直立	ちょくりつ	erect	16G
立	リツ、リュウ、た-つ、た-てる	stand, rise, leave	16G
聴	チョウ、き-く	listen (carefully)	聴
聴心器	ちょうしんき	stethoscope	16G
心	シン、こころ	heart, feelings	16G
器*	キ、うつわ	vessel, utensil, skill	16G
徳	トク	virtue	徳
道徳	どうとく	morality	16G
道	ドウ、トウ、みち	way, road	16G
殖	ショク、ふ-える、ふ-やす	increase, enrich	殖
拓殖	たくしょく	colonize, develop	16G
拓	タク	reclaim, clear, rub	16G
値	チ、ね、あたい	price, value	値
値段	ねだん	price	16G
段	ダン	step, grade	16G
置	チ、お-く	put, place	置
置物	おきもの	ornament	16G
物	ブツ、モツ、もの	thing	16G
植	ショク、う-える、う-わる	plant	植

植民地	しょくみんち	colony	16G
民	ミン、たみ	people, populace	16G
地	チ、ジ	ground, land	16G
憲	ケン	law, constitution	憲
官憲	かんけん	officials; authorities	16G
官	カン	government, official	16G

Sic transit gloria mundi. As the old rocker's 長持 singing career was drawing to an end and 帳消 of his gigs in 東京 were frequent, he was forced into 就職 but managed to use his waning 影響 to score a sinecure as a television personality. With his flowing white hair and crumpled face, even after applying litres of 鯨油, he read 原稿 with some difficulty. Still, he survived in the murky 潮流 of TV Biz by using his strong sense of 自嘲 that found expression in an 奇数 of celebrated 狂歌 and 苛酷 practical jokes. He was known as the solitary 河馬 who was rumoured to use 呪術 and other 鋭利 practices for the 脱衣 of young songstresses. This is still under 検閲 of course! Eventually he did pay the 値段 for his lack of 道徳 so that even in the 植民地 it was reported that the ancient deviant had retired and that at present his only companion was a mangy old parrot.

17A 門 CAPUT MORTUUM

Tm	表門	9B19
17A	おもてもん	*

Ask to Open a Quiet Space in Kansai for Easy Listening near the Moist Gate

Pictograph of a gate with a double door 門

問	モン、と-う、と-い、とん	ask	問
詰問	きつもん	cross-examination	17A
詰	キツ、つ-める、つ-まる、つ-む	pack, packed, full	17A
開	カイ、ひら-く、ひら-ける、あ-く、あ-ける	open	開
公開	こうかい	open to the public	17A
公	コウ、おおやけ	public, fair, lord	17A
閑	カン	leisure, quiet	閑
閑却	かんきゃく	negligence; disregard	17A
却	キャク	(on the) contrary	17A
間	カン、ケン、あいだ、ま	space, gap	間
貸間	かしま	room to let; room for rent	17A
貸	タイ、か-す	lend, loan	17A
関	カン、せき	connection	関
関西	かんさい	Kansai (south-western half of Japan and Osaka)	17A
西	セイ、サイ、にし	west	17A
簡	カン	simple, brief	簡
簡易	かんい	simplicity; convenience; easiness; quasi-	17A
易	エキ、イ、やさ-しい	easy, change, divination	17A
聞	ブン、モン、き-く、き-こえる	hear, ask, listen	聞
逸聞	いつぶん	something unheard of	17A
逸	イツ	escape, go astray, fast, excel	17A

潤	ジュン、うるお-う、うるお-す、うる-む	moisten, enrich	潤
湿潤	しつじゅん	dampness	17A
湿	シツ、しめ-る、しめ-す	damp, moist, humid	17A
門	モン、かど	gate, door	門
表門	おもてもん	front gate	17A
表	ヒョウ、おもて、あらわ-す、あらわ-れる	show, surface, list	17A

17B 父 CAPUT MORTUUM

𝕋𝕞	雷親父	2A1
17B	かみなりおやじ	*

There is a Nasty Old Codger in the Boiler Room

Originally showing hand holding stick, rod of correction 父

父	フ、ちち	father	父
雷親父	かみなりおやじ	snarling old man; irascible old man	17B
雷	ライ、かみなり	thunder	17B
親	シン、おや、した-しい、した-しむ	intimate, parent	17B
釜	フ、かま	kettle; cauldron; iron pot	釜
釜場	かまば	boiler room	17B
場	ジョウ、ば	place	17B

17C 感 CAPUT MORTUUM

𝕋𝕞	感情	3 - 10

110

17C	かんじょう	*

Decrease Feelings of Regret

Chinese only unison, sharp weapon, trimming + mouth, all together 感

減	ゲン、へ-る、へ-らす	decrease	減
減少	げんしょう	decrease	17C
少	ショウ、すく-ない、すこ-し	a little, few	17C
感	カン	feeling	感
感情	かんじょう	feeling	17C
情	ジョウ、セイ、なさ-け	feeling, pity, fact	17C
憾	カン	regret	憾
遺憾な	いかん な	regrettable	17C
遺	イ、ユイ	leave, bequeath, lose	17C

17D 風 CAPUT MORTUUM

Tm	一風	2B3
17D	いっぷう	*

Eccentric riders on the Storm

Originally showing phoenix believed to ride the wind 風

風	フウ、フ、かぜ、かざ	wind, style	風
一風	いっぷう	eccentric	17D
一	イチ、イツ、ひと、ひと-つ	one	17D
嵐	ラン、あらし	storm	嵐
大嵐	おおあらし	raging storm	17D

大	ダイ、タイ、おお、おお-きい、おお-いに	big	17D

17E 泉 CAPUT MORTUUM

Tm	温泉	3 – 3
17E	おんせん	0|3

The Hot Spring Prost(r)ated in a Curved Line

Pictograph of water emerging from a hole in a rock/hillside 泉

泉	セン、いずみ	spring	泉
温泉	おんせん	hot spring	17E
温	オン、あたた-か、あたた-かい、あたた-まる、あたた-める	warm	17E
腺	セン	gland	腺
前立腺	ぜんりつせん	prostate gland	17E
前	ゼン、まえ	before, front	17E
立	リツ、リュウ、た-つ、た-てる	stand, rise, leave	17E
線	セン	line	線
曲線	きょくせん	curve	17E
曲*	キョク、ま-がる、ま-げる	bend, melody	17E

17F 矢 CAPUT MORTUUM

Tm	知合い	4A5
17F	しりあい	*

A Darting Fool Envies too much or too little Knowledge

Pictograph of an arrow 矢

矢	シ、や	arrow	矢
矢先	やさき	arrow head; brunt; target	17F
先	セン、さき	previous, precede, tip	17F
痴	チ	foolish	痴
白痴	はくち	idiot	17F
白	ハク、ビャク、しろ、しら、しろ-い	white	17F
嫉	シツ、そね.む、ねた.む、にく.む	jealous; envy	嫉
嫉妬	しっと	jealousy; envy	17F
妬	ト、ツ、ねた.む、そね.む、つも.る、ふさ.ぐ	jealous; envy	17F
知	チ、しる	know	知
知合い	しりあい	acquaintance	17F
合	ゴウ、ガッ、カッ、あ-う、あ-わす、あ-わせる	meet, join, fit	17F

17G 自 CAPUT MORTUUM

Tm	自然	3A
17G	しぜん	0|4

Smelly Nature, Sniff Sniff

Nose, self 自

臭	シュウ、くさ-い	smell, smack	臭
臭味	くさみ	smell, smack	17G
味	ミ、あじ、あじ-わう	taste, relish	17G

自	ジ、シ、みずか-ら	self	自
自然	しぜん	nature	17G
然	ゼン、ネン	duly, thus, so, but	17G
嗅	キュウ、か.ぐ	smell; sniff; scent	嗅
嗅覚	きゅうかく	sense of smell	17G
覚*	カク、おぼ-える、さ-ます、さ-める	remember, learn, experience	17G

Beware the green-eyed monster. Upon 詰問 Madame Sin admitted that 閑却 of 湿潤 near the 表門 of the 釜場 was a 遺憾な state of affairs. It was reported in the 大嵐 that the tabloids whipped up that an 一風 merchant in organic sprouts had complained about this affecting his 前立腺 when he was visiting her somewhat shady establishment at the 温泉. He was described as being an 白痴 who had shown signs of extreme 嫉妬 when he noticed that an 知合い had won the affections of one of Madame's employees. The viridian green 臭味 of envy: so different from the delicate fragrance of his beloved produce found in 自然!

18A 且 CINNABAR

古	且つ又	11C20
18A	かつまた	*

The Good Grandparents, Furthermore, Aimed to Help Investigate Obstructive Gangs that were Leasing Coarse Two-Mat rooms

Pictograph of cairn, piled up stones on top of others 且

宜	ギ、よろしい	good, right	宜
宜しく	よろしく	best regards	18A
祖	ソ	ancestor	祖
祖父母	そふぼ	grandparents	18A
父	フ、ちち	father	18A

母	ボ、はは	mother	18A
且	か-つ	furthermore, besides	且
且つ又	かつまた	moreover	18A
又	また	or again	18A
狙	ソ、ショ、ねら.う、ねら.い	aim at; sight; shadow; stalk	狙
狙撃	そげき	sniping	18A
撃	ゲキ、う-つ	strike, attack, fire	18A
助	ジョ、たす-ける、たす-かる、すけ	assist, help	助
扶助	ふじょ	aid	18A
扶	フ	help, support	18A
査	サ	investigate	査
捜査	そうさ	investigation	18A
捜	ソウ、さが-す	investigate	18A
阻	ソ、はば-む	obstruct, hinder	阻
険阻	けんそ な	steep	18A
険	ケン、けわ-しい	steep, severe, perilous	18A
組	ソ、く-む、くみ	group, assemble	組
組合	くみあい	union	18A
合	ゴウ、ガッ、カッ、あ-う、あ-わす、あ-わせる	meet, join, fit	18A
租	ソ	levy, tithe	租
租借	そしゃく	lease	18A
借	シャク、か-りる	borrow, rent	18A
粗	ソ、あら-い	coarse, rough	粗
粗末	そまつ	coarseness	18A
末	マツ、バツ、すえ	end, tip	18A

畳	ジョウ、たた-む、たたみ	mat, size, fold, pile, repeat	畳
二畳	にじょう	two-mat size	18A
二	ニ、ふた、ふた-つ	two	18A

18B 元 CINNABAR

| ![元] | 元来 | | 6A8 |
| 18B | がんらい | | 1\|1 |

If you Persevere, you can Cherish and bring to Completion the Original Laurels of the Crowning Institute

Person with the head exaggerated, upper part, prime part 元

頑	ガン	stubborn	頑
頑張る	がんばる	persevere	18B
張	チョウ、は-る	stretch	18B
玩	ガン、もてあそ-ぶ	play; take pleasure in; trifle with	玩
愛玩	あいがん	cherish	18B
愛	アイ	love	18B
完	カン	complete	完
完成	かんせい	completion	18B
成	セイ、ジョウ、な-る、な-す	become, make, consist	18B
元	ゲン、ガン、もと	originally, source	元
元来	がんらい	originally	18B
来	ライ、く-る、きた-る、きた-す	come	18B
冠	カン、かんむり	crown	冠
栄冠	えいかん	laurels	18B

栄*	エイ、さか-える、は-え、は-える	flourish	18B
院	イン	institute	院
医院	いいん	doctor's office (surgery); clinic; dispensary	18B
医	イ	doctor	18B

18C 介 CINNABAR

♁		介入	2B5
18C		かいにゅう	*

Does the World need Intervention

Casing, something in between, armour, shell 介?

界	カイ	area, boundary	界
世界	せかい	world	18C
世	セイ、セ、よ	world, society, age, generation	18C
介	カイ	mediate, shell	介
介入	かいにゅう	intervention	18C
入	ニュウ、い-る、い-れる、はい-る	to get in, to go in, to come in	18C

18D 歩 CINNABAR

♁		進歩	4C3
18D		しんぽ	*

Progressive and Frequent Negotiations Are Under Way

Originally doubling of foot, putting one foot in front of other 歩

117

歩	ホ、ブ、フ、ある-く、あゆ-む	walk	歩
進歩	しんぽ	progress	18D
進	シン、すす-む、すす-める	advance	18D
頻	ヒン	frequent, frown	頻
頻繁	ひんぱん	frequent, incessant	18D
繁	ハン	profuse, rich, complex	18D
渉	ショウ	cross over, liaise	渉
交渉	こうしょう	negotiations	18D
交	コウ、まじ-わる、まじ-える、ま-じる、ま-ざる、ま-ぜる	mix, exchange	18D
捗	チョク、ホ、はかど.る	make progress	捗
進捗	しんちょく	progress; underway	18D
進	シン、すす-む、すす-める	advance	18D

18E 南 CINNABAR

古	南極	2A3
18E	なんきょく	0|2

Dedicated to South Pole dancing

Warm side of the tent, south side? 南

献	ケン、コン	dedicate, present	献
献身	けんしん	dedication	18E

身	シン、み	body	18E
南	ナン、ナ、みなみ	south	南
南極	なんきょく	South Pole	18E
極*	キョク、ゴク、きわ-める、きわ-まる、きわ-み	extreme, pole	18

18F 予 CINNABAR

![glyph]	預金	4A5
18F	よきん	*

Booking a Wild Preface requires a Deposit

Weaving shuttle pushed to one side, prior action 予

予	ヨ	already, prior, I	予
予約	よやく	booking	18F
約	ヤク	promise, summarise, approximately	18F
野	ヤ、の	moor, wild	野
野性	やせい	wild	18F
性	セイ、ショウ	nature, sex	18F
序	ジョ	beginning, order	序
序文	じょぶん	preface	18F
文	ブン、モン、ふみ	writing, text	18F
預	ヨ、あず-ける、あず-かる	deposit, look after	預
預金	よきん	deposit	18F
金	キン、コン、かね、かな	gold, money, metal	18F

18G 角 CINNABAR

ㅂ	街角	4A8
18G	まちかど	0|1

When the Insect's Horns Touched the Scales, there was no Comment

Pictograph of a horn 角

角	カク、かど、つの	horn, angle	角
街角	まちかど	street corner	18G
街	ガイ、カイ、まち	road, town, area	18G
触	ショク、ふ-れる、さわ-る	feel, touch, contact	触
接触	せっしょく	contact	18G
接	セツ、つ-ぐ	contact, join	18G
衡	コウ	scales, yoke	衡
均衡	きんこう	balance	18G
均*	キン	level	18G
解	カイ、ゲ、と-く、と-かす、と-ける	unravel, explain, solve	解
解説	かいせつ	commentary	18G
説	セツ、ゼイ、と-く	preach, explain	18G

Brass knuckles and grey power. Aggrieved 祖父母 were conducting an 捜査 into the 険阻 decline of 扶助 for visiting 医院. They claimed that these 愛玩 consultations were the only reason why most of them 頑張る in their present conditions and that this political 介入 caused a lot of consternation. Their representatives were 交渉 with the government and 進歩 reports were issued on a regular basis with exemplary 献身. They called themselves the 南極 penguins as mobility was an issue and 予約 were always made in conveniently located public venues. 預金

were collected on every 街角 generating boisterous 解説 by besotted bloggers and veteran vloggers: first we take Tokyo, then we take Berlin!

19A 考 COPPER

♀		考案	2 – 1
19A		こうあん	*

Consider the Idea of being Tortured on the Rack

Originally bent figure + long hair, twisting water weed, old man 考

考	コウ、かんが-える	consider	考
考案	こうあん	idea	19A
案	アン	plan	19A
拷	ゴウ	torture, hit	拷
拷問台	ごうもんだい	the rack	19A
問	モン、と-う、と-い、とん	ask	19A
台	ダイ、タイ	platform, stand	19A

19B 半 COPPER

♀		半島	4A3
19B		はんとう	4‖6

Negotiations In the Middle of the Peninsula with Lakeside Accompaniment

Half a cow 半

判	ハン、バン	seal; stamp; judgment	判
談判	だんぱん	negotiations	19B
談	ダン	conversation, talk	19B
半	ハン、なか-ば	half, middle	半

半島	はんとう	peninsula	19B
島*	トウ、しま	island	19B
畔	ハン	ridge, edge	畔
湖畔	こはん	lakeside	19B
湖	コ、みずうみ	lake	19B
伴	ハン、バン、ともな-う	accompany	伴
伴奏	ばんそう	(musical) accompaniment	19B
奏*	ソウ、かな-でる	play, present, report	19B

19C 発 COPPER

♀		発表	2 - 7
19C		はっぴょう	*

Bow`s Announcement is an Abolition

Two planted feet shooting arrow from bow, dispatch 発

発	ハツ、ホツ	discharge, start, leave	発
発表	はっぴょう	announcement	19C
表	ヒョウ、おもて、あらわ-す、あらわ-れる	show, surface, list	19C
廃	ハイ、すた.れる、すた.る	abandon(ed), obsolete	廃
廃止	はいし	abolition	19C
止	シ、と-まる、と-める	stop	19C

19D 豆 COPPER

♀		豆腐	10G29
19D		とうふ	*

122

Blistering, Barking Smallpox Beans Clearly Enjoy Climbing
Heady mountains and Fighting Short spirits

Mono pedal table-cum-food vessel with contents 豆

膨	ボウ、ふく.らむ、ふく.れる	swell, expand	膨
火膨れ	ひぶくれ	blister	19D
火	カ、ひ、ほ	fire	19D
樹	ジュ	tree, stand	樹
樹皮	じゅひ	bark	19D
皮	ヒ、かわ	skin, leather	19D
痘	トウ	smallpox	痘
天然痘	てんねんとう	smallpox	19D
天	テン、あめ、あま	heaven, sky	19D
然	ゼン、ネン	duly, thus, so, but	19D
豆	トウ、ズ、まめ	beans, miniature	豆
豆腐	とうふ	tofu	19D
腐	フ、くさ-る、くさ-れる、くさ-らす	rot, decay, bad	19D
澄	チョウ、す-む、す-ます	clear, settle	澄
清澄	せいちょうな	clear	19D
清	セイ、ショウ、きよ-い、きよ-まる、きよ-める	pure, clean	19D
喜	キ、よろこ-ぶ	rejoice, happy	喜
喜劇	きげき	comedy	19D
劇	ゲキ	drama, intense	19D
登	トウ、ト、のぼ-る	climb	登
登山	とざん	mountaineering	19D
山	サン、やま	mountain	19D
頭	トウ、ズ、ト、あたま、かしら	head, counter for large animals	頭

核弾頭	かくだんとう	nuclear warhead	19D
核	カク	core, nucleus, nuclear	19D
弾	ダン、ひ-く、はず-む、たま	bullet, spring, play	19D
闘	トウ、たたか-う	fight	闘
闘志	とうし	fighting spirit	19D
志	シ、こころざ-す、こころざし	will, intent	19D
短	タン、みじか-い	short	短
短所	たんしょ	shortcoming	19D
所	ショ、ところ	place, situation	19D

19E 平 COPPER

| ♀ | | 平手 | | 3A6 |
| 19E | | ひらて | | * |

The Reputation of the Tsubo is in the Palm Of The Hand

Twisting water weed, small, flat, 2 scales 平

評	ヒョウ	criticism, comment	評
評判	ひょうばん	reputation	19E
判	ハン、バン	seal; stamp; judgment	19E
坪	つぼ	tsubo, square measure	坪
建坪	たてつぼ	floor space	19E
建	ケン、コン、た-てる、た-つ	build, erect	19E
平	ヘイ、ビョウ、たい-ら、ひら	flat, even, calm	平
平手	ひらて	palm of hand	19E
手	シュ、て、た	hand	19E

124

19F 言 COPPER

♀	言回し	4A3
19F	いいまわし	*

Unbelievable Words of Damning Praise

Originally mouth and sharp: articulate? 言

信	シン	trust, believe	信
威信	いしん	dignity	19F
威	イ	authority, threaten	19F
言	ゲン、ゴン、い-う、こと	word, say, speak	言
言回し	いいまわし	expression, phraseology	19F
回	カイ、エ、まわ-る、まわ-す	turn, rotate	19F
罰	バツ、バチ	penalty, punishment	罰
厳罰	げんばつ	severe punishment; rigorous measures	19F
厳	ゲン、ゴン、おごそ-か、きび-しい	severe, strict, solemn	19F
誉	ヨ、ほまれ	honour, fame, praise	誉
名誉	めいよ	honour; credit; prestige	19F
名	メイ、ミョウ、な	name, fame	19F

19G 走 COPPER

♀	奔走	4 - 3
19G	ほんそう	0‖14

Originally, the Plan was just Walking and Running

Frantic movement with the foot, running 走

起	キ、お-きる、お-こる、お-こす	arise, cause	起
起原	きげん	origin, beginning	19G
原	ゲン、はら	plain, origin	19G
趣	シュ、おもむき	gist, tendency	趣
趣向	しゅこう	scheme, plan, idea	19G
向*	コウ、む-く、む-ける、む-かう、む-こう	face towards, beyond	19G
徒	ト、あだ	follower, futility	徒
徒歩	とほ	walking	19G
歩	ホ、ブ、フ、ある-く、あゆ-む	walk	19G
走	ソウ、はし-る	run	走
奔走	ほんそう	running about, efforts	19G
奔*	ホン	run	19G

You're my wife now. Papa Lazarou's mind was on torturous 考案 and painful 談判 under 伴奏 whilst The Circus was being prepared for the grand 発表: would the 廃止 of polygamy be immanent? May they have 豆腐 with organic sprouts for lunch and get 火膨れ on their feet because this is no 喜劇! He put his wives' rings on the 平手 of his greasy hand and contemplated 厳罰 against all wowsers who threatened the 名誉 of his extended family. He was sure that with some 奔走 he could realise his superb 趣向. All of them would be rounded up and put in the cage before being hosed down with cold water by the little people!

20A 亜 CORAL

↳	亜熱帯	2C8
20A	あねったい	0|2

Subtropical Nightmare

Underground dwelling, crooked, hunchback 亜

亜	ア	next, sub-, Asia	亜
亜熱帯	あねったい	subtropics	20A
熱	ネツ、あつ-い	heat	20A
帯	タイ、お-びる、おび	wear, zone	20A
悪	アク、オ、わる-い	bad, hate	悪
悪夢	あくむ	nightmare	20A
夢*	ム、ゆめ	dream	20A

20B 主 CORAL

		主催	5A
20B		しゅさい	*

The Sponsor's Address was in need of a Shot of Round Trippy Pillars

Originally ornately stemmed burning oil lamp, master 主

主	シュ、ス、ぬし、おも	master, owner, main	主
主催	しゅさい	sponsorship	20B
催	サイ、もよお-す	organise, muster	20B
住	ジュウ、す-む、す-まう	reside, live	住
住所	じゅうしょ	address	20B
所	ショ、ところ	place, situation	20B
注	チュウ、そそ-ぐ	pour, note	注
注射	ちゅうしゃ	injection	20B
射	シャ、い-る	shoot	20B
往	オウ	go, gone, past	往
往復	おうふく	round trip	20B

復	フク	again, repeat	20B
柱	チュウ、はしら	column, pillar	柱
柱石	ちゅうせき	pillar	20B
石	セキ、シャク、コク、いし	stone, rock	20B

20C 身 CORAL

↳		身分	3 - 1
20C		みぶん	*

Show Gratitude when they Shoot Down your Status

Miscopied body instead of bow and arrow 身

謝	シャ、あやま-る	apologize, thank	謝
感謝	かんしゃ	gratitude	20C
感	カン	feeling	20C
射	シャ、い-る	shoot	射
射倒す	いたおす	shoot down	20C
倒	トウ、たお-れる、たお-す	fall, topple, invert	20C
身	シン、み	body	身
身分	みぶん	status	20C
分	ブン、フン、ブ、わ-ける、わ-かれる、わ-かる、わ-かつ	divide, minute, understand	20C

20D 秋 CORAL

↳		秋分	2B7
20D		しゅうぶん	*

Sad heart in Autumn

Rice plant + fire, dry autumn crop-fires caused by Foehn 秋

愁	シュウ、うれ-える、うれ-い	grief, sadness	愁
愁い顔	うれいがお	sad face	20D
顔	ガン、かお	face	20D
秋	シュウ、あき	autumn	秋
秋分	しゅうぶん	autumn equinox	20D
分	ブン、フン、ブ、わ-ける、わ-かれる、わ-かる、わ-かつ	divide, minute, understand	20D

20E 衣 CORAL

20E 並	衣桁 いこう		6A5 *

Awesome Baggy Garments Show Dependable (W)ebbing

Originally showing collar and sleeves, clothing 衣
Combining the early form of clothing and fur, fur clothing, outside, surface 表

畏	イ、おそ.れる、かしこま.る、かしこ、かしこ.し	fear; majestic; be apprehensive	畏
畏敬	いけい	reverence; awe; respect	20E
敬	ケイ、うやま-う	respect	20E
俵	ヒョウ、たわら	sack, bag	俵
土俵	どひょう	arena, esp. in sumo	20E
土	ド、ト、つち	earth	20E
衣	イ、ころも	garment	衣
衣桁	いこう	clothes rack	20E

桁	コウ、けた	beam; girder; spar; unit or column	20E
表	ヒョウ、おもて、あらわ-す、あらわ-れる	show, surface, list	表
黒表	こくひょう	blacklist	20E
黒	コク、くろ、くろ-い	black	20E
依	イ、エ	depend, as is	依
依存症	いぞんしょう	(alcohol, drug) dependence	20E
存	ソン、ゾン	exist, know, think	20E
症	ショウ	symptom, illness	20E
衰	スイ、おとろ-える	become weak, wither, ebb	衰
減衰	げんすい	attenuation; damping; decay	20E
減	ゲン、へ-る、へ-らす	decrease	20E

20F 米 CORAL

↳	新米	3
20F	しんまい	*

Perplexing Rice Riddles for Beginners

Pictograph of a rice plant 米

迷	メイ、まよ-う	be lost, perplexed	迷
低迷	ていめい	hanging low (over); low hanging; sluggish (e.g. economy)	20F
低	テイ、ひく-い、ひく-める、ひく-まる	low	20F
米	ベイ、マイ、こめ	rice, America	米

新米	しんまい	(1) new rice; (2) novice; beginner	20F
新	シン、あたら-しい、あら-た、にい	new	20F
謎	メイ、なぞ	riddle; puzzle; enigma; hint; tip	謎
謎解き	なぞとき	solution of a riddle	20F
解	カイ、ゲ、と-く、と-かす、と-ける	unravel, explain, solve	20F

20G 呂 CORAL

| | 風呂 | 4 - 6 |
| 20G | ふろ | * |

The Prince conducted Business in a Buddhist Bath

Former Jinmei character vertebrae, also joined blocks 呂

宮	キュウ、グウ、ク、みや	palace, shrine, prince	宮
神宮	じんぐう	shrine	20G
神	シン、ジン、かみ、かん、こう	god, spirit	20G
営	エイ、いとな-む	conduct, barracks	営
営業	えいぎょう	business	20G
業	ギョウ、ゴウ、わざ	profession, deed, karma	20G
侶	リョ、とも	companion; follower	侶
僧侶	そうりょ	Buddhist priest	20G
僧	ソウ	priest	20G
呂	リョ、ロ	spine; backbone	呂
風呂	ふろ	bath	20G
風	フウ、フ、かぜ、かざ	wind, style	20G

Spinning straw into gold. The stuff of 悪夢 engulfed both saints dwelling on 柱石 as those unfortunates living from one 注射 to the next. Remember your 身分 and give 感謝 and praise at the time of 秋分 because it is not you who is on the 黒表 for 依存症. Health infrastructure in 減衰 combined with an economic 低迷 were in need of a better 謎解き than finance minister Rumpelstiltskin could provide. He merely stated that we are all 僧侶 and nuns floating in a 風呂 of sin.

21A 死 CRUCIBLE

♉	早死に	2 - 5
21A	はやじに	*

Premature Death was Buried during a lethal Funeral

Originally variant of meatless bone, death + person 死

死	シ、し-ぬ	death	死
早死に	はやじに	die young/prematurely	21A
早	ソウ、サッ、はや-い、はや-まる、はや-める	early, fast, prompt	21A
葬	ソウ、ほうむ-る	bury	葬
葬式	そうしき	funeral	21A
式	シキ	ceremony, form	21A

21B 乗 CRUCIBLE

♉	乗り降り	4E2
21B 並	のりおり	0|1

Ann Recommends a Relaxing Ride on a Surplus

Originally person on top of a tree, climb a tree, mount 乗

Building + woman, referring to a woman resting quietly during menses 安

案	アン	plan	案
勧告案	かんこくあん	recommendation	21B
勧	カン、すす-める	encourage, advise	21B
告	コク、つ-げる	proclaim, inform	21B
安	アン、やす-い	restful, ease, cheap	安
慰安	いあん	solace, relaxation	21B
慰	イ、なぐさめ-る、なぐさ-む	comfort, console, amusement	21B
乗	ジョウ、の-る、の-せる	ride, mount, load	乗
乗り降り	のりおり	getting on and off	21B
降*	コウ、お-りる、お-ろす、ふ-る	fall, alight, descend	21B
剰	ジョウ	surplus, resides	剰
剰余	じょうよ	surplus	21B
余	ヨ、あま-る、あま-す	excess, ample, I	21B

21C 軍 CRUCIBLE

ʊ	空軍	4A8
21C	くうぐん	*

The Air Force was Commanded to Transport old Sparkie

Originally circle of carts, carts drawn into a circle, army 軍

軍	グン	military, army	軍
空軍	くうぐん	air force	21C
空	クウ、そら、あ-く、あ-ける、から	sky, empty	21C

揮	キ	wield, shake, command	揮
指揮	しき	command	21C
指	シ、ゆび、さ-す	finger, point	21C
運	ウン、はこ-ぶ	transport, luck, move	運
運動	うんどう	movement	21C
動	ドウ、うご-く、うご-かす	move	21C
輝	キ、かがや-く	sparkle, shine	輝
輝き	かがやき	light	21C

21D 与 CRUCIBLE

𝖴		与え主		2A4
21D		あたえぬし		*

Donors donated Photographs

Originally four hands, many interlocking hands, joint effort 与

与	ヨ、あた-える	give, convey, impart, involvement	与
与え主	あたえぬし	giver, donor	21D
主	シュ、ス、ぬし、おも	master, owner, main	21D
写	シャ、うつ-す、うつ-る	copy, transcribe	写
写真	しゃしん	photograph	21D
真	シン、ま	true, quintessence	21D

134

21E 受 CRUCIBLE

♉		受付	3 - 3
21E		うけつけ	*

She Nailed her Tuition behind the Reception

Hand reaching down 受

爪	ソウ、つめ	claw	爪
生爪	なまづめ	fingernail	21E
生	セイ、ショウ、い-きる、い-かす、い-ける、う-まれる、う-む	life, birth, grow	21E
授	ジュ、さず-ける、さず-かる	confer, teach	授
授業	じゅぎょう	tuition	21E
業	ギョウ、ゴウ、わざ	profession, deed, karma	21E
受	ジュ、う-ける、う-かる	receive	受
受付	うけつけ	reception	21E
付	フ、つ-ける、つ-く	attach, apply	21E

21F 反 CRUCIBLE

♉		反応	8 - 3
21F		はんのう*	*

The Selling of Fake Meals was in Reaction to a Return of a
Hanshin Signboard Up the Road

Cliff, phonetic turn over + hand 反

販	ハン		sell, trade	販

販売	はんばい	selling	21F
売	バイ、う-る、う-れる	sell	21F
仮	カ、ケ、かり	temporary, false	仮
仮	かりに	provisionally	21F
飯	ハン、めし	cooked, rice, food	飯
御飯	ごはん	cooked rice, meal	21F
御	ギョ、ゴ、おん	handle, drive, honourable, your	21F
反	ハン、ホン、タン、そ-る、そ-らす	oppose, anti, reverse	反
反応	はんのう*	reaction, response	21F
応	オウ	respond, react	21F
返	ヘン、かえ-す、かえ-る	return	返
返事	へんじ	reply	21F
事	ジ、ズ、こと	thing, matter, act	21F
阪	ハン、さか	heights; slope	阪
阪神	はんしん	Osaka and Kobe	21F
神	シン、ジン、かみ、かん、こう	god, spirit	21F
板	ハン、バン、いた	board, plate	板
看板	かんばん	signboard	21F
看	カン	watch	21F
坂	ハン、さか	slope	坂
坂道	さかみち	slope	21F
道	ドウ、トウ、みち	way, road	21F

21G 相 CRUCIBLE

		相談		4A7

| 21G | そうだん | | 1|5 |

Boxed Frost Damage sets the Ideological Discussion

Eye watching from behind the tree, careful observation 相

箱	はこ	box	箱
箱入り	はこいり	boxed	21G
入	ニュウ、い-る、い-れる、はい-る	to get in, to go in, to come in	21G
霜	ソウ、しも	frost	霜
霜害	そうがい	frost damage	21G
害	ガイ	harm, damage	21G
想	ソウ、ソ	idea, thought	想
思想	しそう	ideology	21G
思*	シ、おも-う	think	21G
相	ソウ、ショウ、あい	mutual, minister, aspect	相
相談	そうだん	discussion	21G
談	ダン	conversation, talk	21G

It's curtains dear boy. After the 葬式 of the tarento there was a 勧告案 suggesting that in order to find some 慰安 it was best to avoid 輝き and 運動. 写真 of the departed and some of his beloved 生爪 were available at the 受付. These were 販売 for considerable sums but as the smell of 御飯 wafted through the air the natural 反応 of the mourners was to head off to the dining room where playful 相談 on matters of 思想 were to be continued. Anyway, today was his best performance ever!

Chapter 4 Cancer

22A 真 DAY

⊕	真昼	4F7
22A	まひる	1|0

Discretely Compensate for Killing the Midday Pain

Originally person upside-down, (dead?), spirit, essence, truth 真

慎	シン、つつし-む	be discreet, refrain	慎
慎み深い	つつしみぶかい	discreet	22A
深	シン、ふか-い、ふか-まる、ふか-める	deep, deepen	22A
填	テン、いただき	fill in	填
補填	ほてん	compensate for	22A
補	ホ、おぎな-う	make good, stopgap	22A
鎮	チン、しず-める、しず-まる	calm, suppress, weight	鎮
鎮痛剤	ちんつうざい	painkiller	22A
痛	ツウ、いた-い、いた-む、いた-める	pain, painful	22A
剤	ザイ	medicine, drug	22A
真	シン、ま	true, quintessence	真
真昼	まひる	broad daylight, midday	22A
昼*	チュウ、ひる	daytime, noon	22A

22B 度 DAY

✛	程度	2 - 1
22B	ていど	*

The Degree of a Liquid Sentence is debatable

Measure various things with the hand, measurement 度

度	ド 、 ト 、 タク 、 たび	degree, times	度
程度	ていど	degree, extent	22B
程	テイ 、 ほど	degree, extent	22B
渡	ト 、 わた-る 、 わた-す	cross, handover	渡
言い渡す	いいわたす	sentence	22B
言	ゲン 、 ゴン 、 い-う 、 こと	word, say, speak	22B

22C 列 DAY

✛	列席	4A4
22C	れっせき	0|1

As a Rule, all Attending Heroines complained about Splitting headaches

Cut to the bone, set sequence for dismembering a carcass 列

例	レイ 、 たと-える	example, liken, precedent	例
条例	じょうれい	regulation, law, ordinance, rule	22C
条	ジョウ	clause, item, line	22C
列	レツ	row, line	列
列席	れっせき	attend, be present	22C
席*	セキ	seat, place	22C

烈	レツ		fierce, intense	烈
烈女	れつじょ		heroine	22C
女	ジョ、ニョ、ニョウ、おんな、め		woman	22C
裂	レツ、さ-く、さ-ける		split, rend, rip	裂
分裂	ぶんれつ		splitting	22C
分	ブン、フン、ブ、わ-ける、わ-かれる、わ-かる、わ-かつ		divide, minute, understand	22C

22D 眼 DAY

✛		千里眼	9 - 9
22D		せんりがん	0|5

Infinite Clairvoyance is in Decline but the Scarred Cultivated Silver Root had the Courtesy not to show a Grudge

Stop and stare, scrutinise (eye on legs) 眼

限	ゲン、かぎ-る		limit	限
無限	むげん		infinity	22D
無	ム、ブ、な-い		not, non, cease to be	22D
眼	ガン、ゲン、まなこ		eye	眼
千里眼	せんりがん		clairvoyant	22D
千*	セン、ち		thousand	22D
里	リ、さと		village, league	22D
退	タイ、しりぞ-く、しりぞ-ける		retreat, withdraw	退
衰退	すいたい		decline, degeneration	22D
衰	スイ、おとろ-える		become weak, wither, ebb	22D
痕	コン、あと		mark; footprint	痕

傷痕	きずあと	scar	22D
傷	ショウ、きず、いた-む、いた-める	wound, injury	22D
墾	コン	cultivate, reclaim	墾
開墾	かいこん	reclamation	22D
開	カイ、ひら-く、ひら-ける、あ-く、あ-ける	open	22D
銀	ギン	silver	銀
銀河	ぎんが	milky way	22D
河	カ、かわ	river	22D
根	コン、ね	root, base	根
屋根	やね	roof	22D
屋	オク、や	store, building	22D
懇	コン、ねんご-ろ	courtesy, cordiality, earnest wish	懇
懇談	こんだん	chat	22D
談	ダン	conversation, talk	22D
恨	コン、うら-む、うら-めしい	resent, regret	恨
遺恨	いこん	grudge	22D
遺	イ、ユイ	leave, bequeath, lose	22D

22E 旨 DAY

⊕	趣旨	5 – 4
22E	しゅし	*

The Fat Spirit Practised in giving Directions for Visiting the Temple

Something sweet that is spooned into the mouth, lingering 旨

脂	シ、あぶら	fat, grease, resin	脂
脂肪	しぼう	fat	22E
肪	ボウ	fat	22E
旨	シ、むね	tasty, good, gist	旨
趣旨	しゅし	spirit	22E
趣	シュ、おもむき	gist, tendency	22E
稽	ケイ、かんが.える、とど.める	think; consider	稽
稽古	けいこ	practice	22E
古	コ、ふる-い、ふる-す	old	22E
詣	ケイ、もう-でる	visit a temple	詣
初詣で	はつもうで	New Year's temple visit	22E
初	ショ、はじ-め、はじ-めて、はつ、うい、そ-める	beginning, first	22E
指	シ、ゆび、さ-す	finger, point	指
指図	さしず	directions	22E
図	ズ、ト、はか-る	map, drawing, plan	22E

22F 皿 DAY

⊕		灰皿	6C13
22F		はいざら	*

Saltwater Spas Gain from Trailing Ash of Fierce Bloodlines

Pictograph of a vessel 皿

塩	エン、しお	salt	塩
塩水	しおみず	saltwater	22F
水	スイ、みず	water	22F

温	オン、あたた-か、あたた-かい、あたた-まる、あたた-める	warm	温
温泉	おんせん	spa	22F
泉	セン、いずみ	spring	22F
益	エキ、やく	gain, profit, benefit	益
益々	ますます	increasingly	22F
皿	さら	dish, bowl, plate	皿
灰皿	はいざら	ashtray	22F
灰	カイ、はい	ashes	22F
猛	モウ	fierce, raging, brave	猛
猛烈	もうれつな	fierce	22F
烈	レツ	fierce, intense	22F
血	ケツ、ち	blood	血
血統	けっとう	lineage	22F
統	トウ、す-べる	supervise, lineage	22F

22G 進 DAY

✥	進呈	12F22
22G	しんてい	1|1

Who Reckoned that Piling Up Backbones for a Noisy Presentation Now Confirms the Upkeep of a Kindergarten; a Teary Stork perhaps?

Move with bird 進

誰	スイ、だれ	who; someone; somebody	誰

推	スイ、お-す	infer, push ahead	推
推算	すいさん	calculate, reckon, estimate	22G
算*	サン	calculate	22G
堆	タイ、ツイ、うずたか-い	piled high	堆
堆積	たいせき	accumulation	22G
積	セキ、つ-む、つ-もる	product, pile	22G
椎	ツイ、しい	oak; mallet	椎
脊椎	せきつい	spine; vertebral column	22G
脊	セキ、せ、せい	stature; height	22G
雑	ザツ、ゾウ	miscellany	雑
雑音	ざつおん	noise, static	22G
音	オン、イン、おと、ね	sound	22G
進	シン、すす-む、すす-める	advance	進
進呈	しんてい	presentation	22G
呈	テイ	present, offer	22G
唯	ユイ、イ、ただ	only, prompt (answer)	唯
唯今	ただいま	now	22G
今	コン、キン、いま	now	22G
確	カク、たし-か、たし-かめる	ascertain, firm	確
確認	かくにん	confirmation	22G
認	ニン、みと-める	recognise, appreciate	22G
維	イ	fasten, rope, support	維
維持	いじ	upkeep	22G
持	ジ、も-つ	hold, have, maintain	22G
稚	チ	young, immature	稚
幼稚園	ようちえん	kindergarten	22G

幼	ヨウ、おさな-い	infancy	22G
園	エン、その	garden, park	22G
催	サイ、もよお-す	organise, muster	催
催涙	さいるい	lachrymal	22G
涙	ルイ、なみだ	tear	22G
鶴	カク、つる	crane; stork	鶴

Ugly ducklings no more, possums! The 慎み深い charm of the bourgeoisie does not reveal itself without the help of 鎮痛剤 from 真昼 onwards and, at least to a large 程度, through elegant and heartfelt 言い渡す. All 列席 guests were eager to welcome the headmistress of the finishing school for graceful 烈女 and 千里眼 cos-players. Bubbly characters were engaged in joyful 懇談 and no dark 遺恨 were to be heard under that arched 屋根. Regular 稽古 in etiquette and strict 指図 in good deportment were the order of the day. The young pupils were becoming 益々 more proficient in walking upright whilst carrying 灰皿 filled with 塩水 on their heads. With a straight 脊椎, excellent 進呈 and cunning 推算 you will net the perfect husband ladies!

23A 丙 DECOCTION

+B	丙種	3 – 3
23A	へいしゅ	0|1

The genealogy of moral is a Third Grade Brand name of Illness

Large altar with sturdy legs 丙

丙	ヘイ	c, 3rd	丙
丙種	へいしゅ	class C; third class	23A
種	シュ、たね	seed, kind	23A
柄	ヘイ、がら、え	handle, pattern, power, nature	柄

銘柄	めいがら	brand	23A
銘	メイ	inscribe, sign	23A
病	ビョウ、ヘイ、や-む、やまい	illness	病
病床	びょうしょう	sickbed	23A
床*	ショウ、とこ、ゆか	bed, floor, alcove	23A

23B 式 DECOCTION

丰B	開会式	3 - 2
23B	かいかいしき	*

No Match without an Opening Ceremony Mopping it away

Carpenter's square and stake, measured intervals, order 式

試	シ、こころ-みる、ため-す	trial, test	試
試合	しあい	match	23B
合	ゴウ、ガッ、カッ、あ-う、あ-わす、あ-わせる	meet, join, fit	23B
式	シキ	ceremony, form	式
開会式	かいかいしき	opening ceremony	23B
開	カイ、ひら-く、ひら-ける、あ-く、あ-ける	open	23B
会	カイ、エ、あ-う	meet	23B
拭	ショク、シキ、ぬぐ.う、ふ.く	wipe; mop; swab	拭
払拭	ふっしょく	wiping out; sweeping away	23B
払	フツ、はら-う	pay, sweep away, rid	23B

23C 干 DECOCTION

＋B	干潟	6B13
23C	ひがた	*

It takes Sweat and Guts to Publish in Five Hovels near the Riverbank's Tideland

Forked thrusting weapon 干

汗	カン、あせ	sweat	汗
発汗	はっかん	sweating	23C
発	ハツ、ホツ	discharge, start, leave	23C
肝	カン、きも	liver, courage	肝
肝っ玉	きもったま	guts, pluck	23C
玉	ギョク、たま	ball, sphere, coin	23C
刊	カン	publish, engrave	刊
刊行	かんこう	publication	23C
行	コウ、ギョウ、アン、い-く、ゆ-く、おこな-う	go, conduct, column	23C
軒	ケン、のき	eaves, house, counter	軒
五軒	ごけん	five houses	23C
五	ゴ、いつ、いつ-つ	five	23C
岸	ガン、きし	bank, shore	岸
川岸	かわぎし	riverbank	23C
川	セン、かわ	river	23C
干	カン、ほ-す、ひ-る	dry, defence	干
干潟	ひがた	tidal flat, dry beach	23C

潟	かた	beach, lagoon	23C

23D 者 DECOCTION

⊞B	作者	10O15
23D	さくしゃ	2|3

A Capital Author Together with an Official Gambler Heated Up
the Book writer and Brought him to Boil while Both Hands were
holding Chopsticks

Originally box for storing kindling, odds and ends, plebs 者

都	ト、ツ、みやこ	capital, metropolis	都
首都	しゅと	capital	23D
首	シュ、くび	head, neck, chief	23D
者	シャ、もの	person	者
作者	さくしゃ	author	23D
作	サク、サ、つく-る	make	23D
緒	ショ、チョ、お	beginning, cord, clue, connection	緒
一緒	いっしょ	together	23D
一	イチ、イツ、ひと、ひと-つ	one	23D
署	ショ	government, office, sign	署
署員	しょいん	official	23D
員	イン	member, official	23D
賭	ト、か.ける、かけ	gamble; wager; bet	賭
賭場	とば	gambling hall	23D
場	ジョウ、ば	place	23D
暑	ショ、あつ-い	hot (weather)	暑

148

蒸し暑い	むしあつい		hot and humid, sultry	23D
蒸*	ジョウ、む-す、む-れる、む-らす		humid	23D
著	チョ、あらわ-す、いちじる-しい		notable, write-book	著
著者	ちょしゃ		author	23D
者	シャ、もの		person	23D
煮	シャ、に-る、に-える、に-やす		boil, cook	煮
煮立てる	にたてる		bring to boil	23D
立	リツ、リュウ、た-つ、た-てる		stand, rise, leave	23D
諸	ショ、もろ		various, many	諸
諸手	もろて		both hands	23D
手	シュ、て、た		hand	23D
箸	チョ、はし		chopsticks	箸

23E 充 DECOCTION

✛B		充分		6C6
23E		じゅうぶん		1‖1

The Tradition of having Enough Guns with Sulfuric Acid went out of Fashion in Education

New born baby with amniotic fluid 充

統	トウ、す-べる	supervise, lineage	統
伝統	でんとう	tradition	23E
伝*	デン、つた-わる、つた-える、つた-う	convey, transmit	23E

充	ジュウ、あ-てる	full, fill, provide	充
充分	じゅうぶん	enough	23E
分	ブン、フン、ブ、わ-ける、わ-かれる、わ-かる、わ-かつ	divide, minute, understand	23E
銃	ジュウ	gun	銃
小銃	しょうじゅう	gun	23E
小*	ショウ、ちい-さい、こ、お	small	23E
硫	リュウ	sulphur	硫
硫酸	りゅうさん	sulfuric acid	23E
酸	サン、す-い	acid, bitter	23E
流	リュウ、ル、なが-れる、なが-す	flow, stream	流
流行	りゅうこう	fashion	23E
行	コウ、ギョウ、アン、い-く、ゆ-く、おこな-う	go, conduct, column	23E
育	イク、そだ-つ、そだ-てる	raise, educate	育
教育	きょういく	education	23E
教	キョウ、おし-える、おそ-わる	teach	23E

23F 求 DECOCTION

+B	球広い	3A2
23F	たまひろい	*

The Caddy Desired Relief

Originally fur coat, desirable object 求

球	キュウ、たま	sphere, ball	球
球広い	たまひろい	caddy	23F

広	コウ、ひろ-い、ひろ-まる、ひろ-める、ひろ-がる、ひろ-げる	wide, spacious	23F
求	キュウ、もと-める	request, seek	求
希求	ききゅう	desire	23F
希	キ	desire, hope for, rare	23F
救	キュウ、すく-う	rescue, redeem	救
救援	きゅうえん	relief, rescue	23F
援	エン	help	23F

23G 出 DECOCTION

＋Ｂ		出演者	4B3
23G 並		しゅつえんしゃ	*

Clumsy Actors Exposed themselves on the Road

Descend, stop and start 路
Once written with foot and a line of containment, emerging foot 出

拙	セツ	bungling, clumsy, unskilful	拙
拙劣	せつれつ	clumsy, unskilful	23G
劣	レツ、おと-る	be inferior	23G
出	シュツ、スイ、で-る、だ-す	emerge, put out	出
出演者	しゅつえんしゃ	actor, performer	23G
演	エン	performance, play, presentation	23G
者	シャ、もの	person	23G

露	ロ、ロウ、つゆ	dew, reveal, small, Russia	露
露出	ろしゅつ	exposure	23G
出	シュツ、スイ、で-る、だ-す	emerge, put out	23G
路	ロ、じ	road, route	路
道路	どうろ	road	23G
道	ドウ、トウ、みち	way, road	23G

Biffo in Biholo. The 銘柄 of the 丙種 boxing 試合 between 払拭 "boom boom" Billy and 肝っ玉 Carl, the 発汗 "sweet pea", was nearly completed. In the 五軒 Arena near the 首都 a crooked 署員 argued that the bout should take place in the infamous 賭場 given the 蒸し暑い conditions. The 伝統 of the Gentleman's Game being so much in 流行 should provide 充分 reasons to stage it in that venue, he maintained. The punters have great 希求 for violent 救援 and would not wish to view a 出演者 that is so much 拙劣 and middle of the 道路: blood for the masses I say!

24A 副 DIGEST

𠂉	副業		4B6
24A	ふくぎょう		*

The Breadth of Happiness is but a Side-job of Wealth

Chinese only full wine jar and altar, blessed by the gods, fortunate 副

幅	フク、はば	width, scroll	幅
横幅	よこはば	breadth	24A
横	オウ、よこ	side, cross ways	24A
福	フク	good fortune	福
幸福	こうふく	happiness	24A

幸	コウ、さいわ-い、さち、しあわ-せ	happiness, luck	24A
副	フク	deputy, vice-, sub-	副
副業	ふくぎょう	side-job	24A
業	ギョウ、ゴウ、わざ	profession, deed, karma	24A
富	フ、フウ、と-む、とみ	wealth, riches	富
豊富	ほうふ	abundant, rich	24A
豊	ホウ、ゆたか	abundant, rich	24A

24B 送 DIGEST

⊥		放送	6 - 4
24B		ほうそう	*

Conflicting Dim Victories Sent Sharp Manuscripts Soaring

Royal we (Pluralis Majestatis) 送

藤	トウ、ふじ	wisteria	藤
葛藤	かっとう	conflict; complication; troubles; discord	24B
葛	カツ、くず、つづら	arrowroot; kudzu	24B
勝	ショウ、か-つ、まさ-る	win, surpass	勝
曇り勝ち	くもりがち	cloudy	24B
曇	ドン、くも-る	to cloud, dim, mar	24B
朕	チン	pluralis majestatis	朕
送	ソウ、おく-る	send	送

放送	ほうそう	broadcast	24B
放	ホウ、はな-す、はな-つ、はな-れる	release, emit	24B
騰	トウ	rise, leap	騰
暴騰	ぼうとう	sharp rise	24B
暴	ボウ、バク、あば-く、あば-れる	violence, expose	24B
謄	トウ	copy	謄
謄本	とうほん	manuscript	24B
本	ホン、もと	root, true, book, this	24B

24C 橋 DIGEST

⊔		陸橋	5C12
24C 並		りっきょう	*

Up and Down the Mountains and then Straight to the Overpass

Originally two horizontal lines indicating area below 下
Non General Use character tall, variant watchtower + person with
bent neck, arched 橋

上	ジョウ、ショウ、うえ、うわ、かみ、あ-げる、あ-がる、のぼ-る	up, top, over, go up	上
階上	かいじょう	upstairs	24C
階	カイ	story, grade, step	24C
下	カ、ゲ、した、しも、もと、さ-げる、さ-がる、くだ-る、くだ-す	base, under, lower	下
階下	かいか	downstairs	24C
階	カイ	story, grade, step	24C

峠	とうげ	mountain pass	峠
峠越え	とうげごえ	crossing a mountain pass	24C
越	エツ、こ-す、こ-える	cross, exceed, excel	24C
矯	キョウ、た-める	straighten, falsify	矯
矯め直す	ためなおす	correct	24C
直	チョク、ジキ、ただ-ちに、なお-す、なお-る	direct, upright, fix	24C
橋	キョウ、はし	bridge	橋
陸橋	りっきょう	overpass	24C
陸	リク	land	24C

24D 炎 DIGEST

| ᄂ | 気炎 | 3 - 4 |
| 24D | きえん | * |

Fiery Words made the Droplets Faint

Double flame, excessive fire/heat 炎

炎	エン、ほのお	inflammation, flame, blaze	炎
気炎	きえん	high spirits; big talking	24D
気	キ、ケ	spirit	24D
談	ダン	conversation, talk	談
奇談	きだん	strange story	24D

奇	キ		strange, odd	24D
淡	タン、あわ-い		pale, light, faint	淡
冷淡	れいたん		coolness; indifference	24D
冷	レイ、つめ-たい、ひ-える、ひ-や、ひ-やす		freeze, cold	24D

24E 快 DIGEST

⊥		快楽	2A7
24E		かいらく	*

Pleasure is the Solution

Pulled apart by water 快

快	カイ、こころよ-い	pleasant, cheerful	快
快楽	かいらく	pleasure	24E
楽	ガク、ラク、たの-しい、たの-しむ	pleasure, music	24E
決	ケツ、き-める、き-まる	decide, settle, collapse	決
解決	かいけつ	solution	24E
解	カイ、ゲ、と-く、と-かす、と-ける	unravel, explain, solve	24E

24F 録 DIGEST

⊥		記録	3D1
24F		きろく	*

Divesting Green Records

156

Liquid oozing from basket (from a crude wine press) 緑

剥	ハク、ホク、へ.ぐ、へず.る、む.く、む.ける、は.がれる	come off; peel; fade; discolour	剥
剥奪	はくだつ	divest of	24F
奪	ダツ、うば-う	snatch, captivate	24F
緑	リョク、ロク、みどり	green	緑
緑色	みどりいろ	green	24F
色	ショク、シキ、いろ	colour, sensuality	24F
録	ロク	record, inscribe	録
記録	きろく	record	24F
記	キ、しる-す	account, chronicle	24F

24G 童 DIGEST

⼧	児童	4A5
24G	じどう	*

Children's' Pupils Long For the Evening Bell

Slave standing on the ground carrying heavy sack 童

童	ドウ、わらべ	child	童
児童	じどう	children	24G
児	ジ、ニ	child	24G
瞳	トウ、ドウ、ひとみ	pupil	瞳
瞳孔	どうこう	pupil	24G
孔	コウ	hole, Confucius	24G

157

憧	ショウ、ドウ、あこが-れる	yearn after; long for; aspire to; admire; adore	憧
憧憬	しょうけい	yearn for	24G
憬	ケイ、あこが.れる	yearn for; aspire to; admire	24G
鐘	ショウ、かね	bell	鐘
晩鐘	ばんしょう	evening bell	24G
晩	バン	evening, late	24G

For whom the bell tolls. 幸福 and 豊富 contrasted sharply with these troubled times of 葛藤 and a 暴騰 in levels of hardship. Indeed, there have never been so many instances of 階下 versus 階上. Looking down from the 陸橋 it would be hard not to experience 冷淡 towards 気炎 members of a 快楽 seeking gaggle of nincompoops who advocated all kinds of 解決 to the realisation of the perfect 緑色 life. It be on 記録, however, that the 晩鐘 tolls for all 児童 who 憧憬 for the unbearable lightness of being.

25A 重 DISSOLUTION

🖵	重さ	6A3
25A	おもさ	*

The Heavy Labourer said that Animals and Bloated Humankind were on a Collision course

Person standing on the ground carrying heavy sack 重

重	ジュウ、チョウ、え、おも-い、かさ-ねる、かさ-なる	heavy, pile, -fold	重
重さ	おもさ	weight	25A
働	ドウ、はたら-く	work	働
労働者	ろうどうしゃ	labourer	25A
労	ロウ	labour, toil	25A

者	シャ、もの	person	25A
動	ドウ、うご-く、うご-かす	move	動
動物	どうぶつ	animal	25A
物	ブツ、モツ、もの	thing	25A
腫	シュ、ショウ、は.れる、は.れ、は.らす、く.む、はれもの	tumour; swelling	腫
腫瘍	しゅよう	tumour	25A
瘍	ヨウ、かさ	boil; carbuncle	25A
種	シュ、たね	seed, kind	種
人種	じんしゅ	humankind	25A
人	ジン、ニン、ひと	person	25A
衝	ショウ	collide, clash, road	衝
衝突	しょうとつ	collision	25A
突	トツ、つ-く	thrust, lunge, protrude	25A

25B 員 DISSOLUTION

☐		吏員	5 – 2
25B		りいん	*

The Official Bore the Loss and Ran Off with the Phonemes

Originally round kettle, persons gathered around 員

員	イン	member, official	員
吏員	りいん	official	25B
吏	リ	official	25B

負	フ、ま-ける、ま-かす、お-う	defeat, bear	負
抱負	ほうふ	aspiration; ambition; pretension	25B
抱	ホウ、だ-く、いだ-く、かか-える	embrace, hug, hold	25B
損	ソン、そこ-なう、そこ-ねる	loss, spoil, miss	損
損失	そんしつ	loss	25B
失	シツ、うしな-う	lose	25B
敗	ハイ、やぶ-れる	defeat	敗
敗走	はいそう	take flight; take to one's heels	25B
走	ソウ、はし-る	run	25B
韻	イン	rhyme, tone	韻
音韻	おんいん	phoneme	25B
音	オン、イン、おと、ね	sound	25B

25C 役 DISSOLUTION

⬚	兵役	11C14
25C	へいえき	0|3

Abandon Crotchety Military Service, Attack and Sterilize the Drilled Epidemic on the Custom-Designed Stairs of the Palatial Temple

Strike with axe, phonetic throw 役

投	トウ、な-げる	throw, cast	投
投げ出す	なげだす	abandon	25C
出	シュツ、スイ、で-る、だ-す	emerge, put out	25C

股	コ、また、もも	thigh; crotch; yarn; strand	股
股関節	こかんせつ	hip joint	25C
関	カン、せき	connection	25C
節	セツ、セチ、ふし	section, joint, period, point, tune, restrain	25C
役	ヤク、エキ	role, service, duty	役
兵役	へいえき	military service	25C
兵	ヘイ、ヒョウ	soldier	25C
撃	ゲキ、う-つ	strike, attack, fire	撃
攻撃	こうげき	attack	25C
攻	コウ、せ-める	attack	25C
殺	サツ、サイ、セツ、ころ-す	kill	殺
殺菌	さっきん	sterilize, disinfect	25C
菌*	キン	fungus, bacteria	25C
鍛	タン、きた-える	forge, train	鍛
鍛錬	たんれん	forge, train	25C
錬	レン	refine, train, drill	25C
疫	エキ、ヤク	epidemic	疫
疫病	えきびょう	epidemic	25C
病	ビョウ、ヘイ、や-む、やまい	illness	25C
設	セツ、もう-ける	establish, build	設
設計	せっけい	design	25C
計	ケイ、はか-る、はか-らう	measure	25C
段	ダン	step, grade	段
階段	かいだん	stairs	25C

161

階	カイ		story, grade, step	25C
殿	デン、テン、との、どの		palace, lord, Mr	殿
宮殿	きゅうでん		palace	25C
宮	キュウ、グウ、ク、みや		palace, shrine, prince	25C
刹	サツ、セツ		temple	刹
古刹	こさつ		ancient temple	25C
古	コ、ふる-い、ふる-す		old	25C

25D 幸 DISSOLUTION

⌨		射幸		2A11
25D		しゃこう		*

Speculation can be Rewarding

Originally reversal of calamity, happiness 幸

幸	コウ、さいわ-い、さち、しあわ-せ	happiness, luck	幸
射幸	しゃこう	speculation	25D
射	シャ、い-る	shoot	25D
報	ホウ、むく-いる	report, reward	報
報酬	ほうしゅう	reward	25D
酬	シュウ	reward, toast, reply	25D

25E 共 DISSOLUTION

⌨		洪水		6A7
25E		こうすい		*

In a Communist Harbour City we were Flooded with Respectful

Offers of Ridicule

Originally two hands offering a jewel, both, jointly together 共

共	キョウ、とも	together	共
共産主義	きょうさんしゅぎ	Communism	25E
産	サン、う-む、う-まれる、うぶ	birth, produce	25E
主	シュ、ス、ぬし、おも	master, owner, main	25E
義	ギ	righteousness	25E
港	コウ、みなと	harbour	港
港市	こうし	harbour city	25E
市	シ、いち	city, market	25E
洪	コウ	flood, vast	洪
洪水	こうすい	flood	25E
水	スイ、みず	water	25E
恭	キョウ、うやうや-しい	respectful	恭
恭順	きょうじゅん	obedience	25E
順	ジュン	sequence, compliance	25E
供	キョウ、ク、そな-える、とも	offer, attendant	供
提供	ていきょう	offer	25E
提	テイ、さ-げる	hold, carry, offer	25E
弄	ロウ、ル、いじく.る、ろう.する、いじ.る、ひねく.る	play with; tamper; trifle with	弄
愚弄	ぐろう	mockery; derision; ridicule	25E
愚	グ、おろ-か	foolish	25E

25F 錬 DISSOLUTION

	錬金術	3E6
25F	れんきんじゅつ	*

Rankan is Training in Alchemy

Sack, bundle, disperse, threads soften by boiling 練

欄	ラン	column, railing, space	欄
欄干	らんかん	railing	25F
干	カン、ほ-す、ひ-る	dry, defence	25F
練	レン、ね-る	refine, knead, train	練
訓練	くんれん	training	25F
訓	クン	instruct, advise	25F
錬	レン	refine, train, drill	錬
錬金術	れんきんじゅつ	alchemy	25F
金	キン、コン、かね、かな	gold, money, metal	25F
術	ジュツ	means, technique	25F

25G 宵 DISSOLUTION

	宵月	5D9
25G	よいずき	0|1

The Evening Moon, like Nitric Acid, Consumed the Portrait
Reducing it to its bare frame

Flesh of the body + variant of little, phonetic resemble, kids 肖

宵	ショウ、よい	evening	宵
宵月	よいずき	evening moon	25G

月*	ゲツ、ガツ、つき	moon	25G
硝	ショウ	nitre, gunpowder	硝
硝酸	しょうさん	nitric acid	25G
酸	サン、す-い	acid, bitter	25G
消	ショウ、き-える、け-す	extinguish, vanish, consume	消
消費	しょうひ	consumption	25G
費	ヒ、ついや-す、ついえ-る	spend	25G
肖	ショウ	be like, be lucky	肖
肖像	しょうぞう	portrait	25G
像	ゾウ	image	25G
削	サク、けず-る	pare, reduce	削
削除	さくじょ	deletion	25G
除	ジョ、ジ、のぞ-く	exclude, remove	25G

Send them to outer space. On the face of the earth the 重さ of 人種 resembles a 腫瘍 making it not unreasonable for Gaia to have the 抱負 that the entire race 敗走 to another planet: not a great 損失 to be sure! Human(un)kind is like an 疫病, a malignant force 攻撃 all flora & fauna and that might as well be 殺菌 before doing more harm. A fitting 報酬 for our careless 射幸 and lack of 恭順 whilst the 洪水 of homo sapiens takes everything and 提供 nothing. There is no 欄干 to cling to as we are engaged in the 錬金術 of destruction. The cruel light of the 宵月 will reflect on our boundless 消費 of natural resources and cast a shadow on the immanent 削除 of all earthlings.

26A 探 DISTILLATION

⬦	探究者	2

26A	たんきゅうしゃ		*

A watery hand Researched the Deep Sea

Originally chimney-like hole, deep part of the river 探

探	タン、さぐ-る、さが-す	search, probe	探
探究者	たんきゅうしゃ	researcher	26A
究	キュウ、きわ-める	investigate, extreme	26A
者	シャ、もの	person	26A
深	シン、ふか-い、ふか-まる、ふか-める	deep, deepen	深
深海	しんかい	deep sea	26A
海	カイ、うみ	sea	26A

26B 章 DISTILLATION

❖	憲章		3A4
26B	けんしょう		*

Commendations are Impeding the Charter

Tattooist's needle, identify slaves, mark, sign, badge 章

彰	ショウ	manifest, openly acknowledge	彰
表彰	ひょうしょう	commendation	26B
表	ヒョウ、おもて、あらわ-す、あらわ-れる	show, surface, list	26B
障	ショウ、さわ-る	hinder, block	障
障害	しょうがい	impediment	26B
害	ガイ	harm, damage	26B
章	ショウ	badge, chapter	章

憲章	けんしょう	charter	26B
憲	ケン	law, constitution	26B

26C 族 DISTILLATION

	家族	5 - 7
26C	かぞく	*

Rotating Facilities made the Sightseeing Family Pass out

Arrow under a streaming banner tied to a pole, mustering 族

旋	セン	rotate, turn	旋
旋回	せんかい	rotation	26C
回	カイ、エ、まわ-る、まわ-す	turn, rotate	26C
施	シ、セ、ほどこ-す	perform, charity	施
施設	しせつ	facilities	26C
設	セツ、もう-ける	establish, build	26C
遊	ユウ、ユ、あそ-ぶ	play, relax	遊
遊覧	ゆうらん	sightseeing	26C
覧	ラン	see, look	26C
族	ゾク	clan, family	族
家族	かぞく	family	26C
家	カ、ケ、いえ、や	house, specialist	26C
旅	リョ、たび	journey	旅
旅券	りょけん	passport	26C
券	ケン	ticket, pass, bond	28C

167

26D 羊 DISTILLATION

	羊飼い	9B17
26D	ひつじかい	*

Of Late Hot Details emerged of a Support team of Scandalous Shepherds frolicking in the Beautiful Clear Atlantic

Pictograph of a sheep 羊

遅	チ、おく-れる、おく-らす、おそ-い	tardy, slow, late	遅
遅咲き	おそざき	late-blooming	26D
咲	さ-く	blossom	26D
窯	ヨウ、かま	kiln, oven	窯
焼き窯	やきがま	kiln, oven	26D
焼	ショウ、や-く、や-ける	burn, roast	26D
詳	ショウ、くわ-しい	detailed	詳
未詳	みしょう	unknown; unidentified	26D
未	ミ	immature, not yet	38G
養	ヨウ、やしな-う	rear, support	養
給養	きゅうよう	maintaining; supplying	26D
給	キュウ	supply, bestow	26D
祥	ショウ	good fortune, omen	祥
不祥事	ふしょうじ	bad omen, scandal	26D
不	フ、ブ	not, un-, dis-	26D
事	ジ、ズ、こと	thing, matter, act	26D
羊	ヨウ、ひつじ	sheep	羊

羊飼い	ひつじかい	shepherd	26D
飼	シ、か-う	rear animals	26D
美	ビ、うつく-しい	beautiful, fine	美
賞美	しょうび	admiration; praise;	26D
賞	ショウ	prize, praise	26D
鮮	セン、あざ-やか	fresh, vivid, clear	鮮
鮮明	せんめい な	clear, vivid	26D
明	メイ、ミョウ、あ-かり、あか-るい、あか-るむ	clear, open, bright	26D
洋	ヨウ	ocean, western	洋
大西洋	たいせいよう	Atlantic	26D
大	ダイ、タイ、おお、おお-きい、おお-いに	big	26D
西	セイ、サイ、にし	west	26D

26E 径 DISTILLATION

| ❖ | 直情径行 | | 6 - 1 |
| 26E | ちょくじょうけいこう | | 1\|2 |

A Bashful Bulbous Apparition was Directed away with a Light Sutra

Warp threads of the loom, incomplete, bare, light 径

羞	シュウ、はじ.る、すすめ.る、は.ずかしい	feel ashamed	羞
羞恥	しゅうち	feel ashamed	26E
恥	チ、は-じる、はじ、は-じらう、は-ずかしい	shame	26E

茎	ケイ、くき	stalk, stem	茎
球茎	きゅうけい	bulb	26E
球	キュウ、たま	sphere, ball	26E
怪	カイ、あや-しい、あや-しむ	weird, suspicious	怪
怪談	かいだん	ghost story	26E
談	ダン	conversation, talk	26E
径	ケイ	path, direct	径
直情径行	ちょくじょうけいこう	impulsiveness	26E
直	チョク、ジキ、ただ-ちに、なお-す、なお-る	direct, upright, fix	26E
情	ジョウ、セイ、なさ-け	feeling, pity, fact	26E
行	コウ、ギョウ、アン、い-く、ゆ-く、おこな-う	go, conduct, column	26E
軽	ケイ、かる-い、かろ-やか	light, flippant	軽
軽食	けいしょく	snack	26E
食*	ショク、ジキ、く-う、く-らう、た-べる	food, eat	26E
経	ケイ、キョウ、へ-る	pass, sutra, longitude	経
経済	けいざい	economy	26E
済	サイ、す-む、す-ます	settle, finish	26E

26F 星 DISTILLATION

❖		出来星	2A4
26F		できぼし	*

Nouveau Riche bought three Grams of Drugs

Originally a trebling of sun and phonetic birth/life 星

星	セイ、ショウ、ほし	star	星
出来星	できぼし	upstart, nouveau riche	26F
出	シュツ、スイ、で-る、だ-す	emerge, put out	26F
来	ライ、く-る、きた-る、きた-す	come	26F
醒	セイ、さ-ます	awake; be disillusioned; sober up	醒
覚醒剤	かくせいざい	stimulant drugs	26F
覚	カク、おぼ-える、さ-ます、さ-める	remember, learn, experience	26F
剤	ザイ	medicine, drug	26F

26G 委 DISTILLATION

	国際捕鯨委員会	2A3
26G	こくさいほげいいいんかい	2|5

IWC: A-Trophy

Rice plant and woman, pliable 委

委	イ	committee; entrust to	委
国際捕鯨委員会	こくさいほげいいいんかい	International Whaling Commission; IWC	26G
国*	コク、くに	country, region	26G
際	サイ、きわ	occasion, edge, contact	26G

捕	ホ、と-らえる、と-らわれる、と-る、つか-まえる、つか-まる	seize, capture	26G
鯨	ゲイ、くじら	whale	26G
員	イン	member, official	26G
会	カイ、エ、あ-う	meet	26G
萎	イ、な、しお.れる、しな.びる、しぼ.む、な.える	wither; droop; lame	萎
萎縮	いしゅく	atrophy	26G
縮	シュク、ちぢ-む、ちぢ-まる、ちぢ-める	shrink, reduce	26G

Nasty Dutch skippers. Captain Van der Decken, well-known 探究者 into the mysteries of the 深海, decreed that the 憲章 of his disconcerting vessel was not an 障害 to do some 遊覧 and to visit a 旋回 restaurant with the 家族. Let us avoid all 不祥事 and confine ourselves to fulsome 賞美 of the fearsome 大西洋. Don't 羞恥 if that 怪談 of The Flying Dutchman terrifies you: the old boy was high on 覚醒剤 and, by the look of his 萎縮 crew, they also have been doing some heavy lifting for a couple of centuries!

27A 穴 DRAGON'S BLOOD

𝕊𝔇	穴埋め	4A2
27A	あなうめ	*

Crashing the Research as a Stopgap measure really Steals the show

Space opened up in the ground and covered, dwelling, hole 穴

突	トツ、つ-く	thrust, lunge, protrude	突
激突	げきとつ	crash, collision	27A
激	ゲキ、はげ-しい	violent, fierce, strong, intense	27A

究	キュウ、きわ-める	investigate, extreme	究
研究	けんきゅう	research	27A
研	ケン、と-ぐ	hone, refine	27A
穴	ケツ、あな	hole	穴
穴埋め	あなうめ	stopgap	27A
埋	マイ、う-める、う-まる、う-もれる	bury	27A
窃	セツ	steal, stealthy	窃
窃盗	せっとう	theft	27A
盗	トウ、ぬす-む	steal	27A

27B 択 DRAGON'S BLOOD

| 𝕯 | 選択 | 3A3 |
| 27B | せんたく | 3\|4 |

Choose a Marsh that is the Most Moist for your Destination

Originally take in hand and watch over file of prisoners, arrange 択

択	タク	choose, select	択
選択	せんたく	choice	27B
選*	セン、えら-ぶ	elect	27B
沢	タク、さわ	marsh, moisten, much, many, benefit	沢
沢山	たくさん	much, many	27B
山	サン、やま	mountain	27B
駅	エキ	station	駅
到着駅	とうちゃくえき	station of arrival; destination	27B
到	トウ	go, reach, arrive	27B

173

着	チャク、ジャク、き-る、き-せる、つ-く、つ-ける	arrive, wear	27B

27C 灰 DRAGON'S BLOOD

🔊	灰塗れ	2B3
27C	はいまみれ	*

King Ash handed over the Charcoal

Formerly hand and fire: fire that one can hold in the hand? 灰

灰	カイ、はい	ashes	灰
灰塗れ	はいまみれ	covered with ashes	27C
塗	ト、ぬ-る	plaster, coat, paint	27C
炭	タン、すみ	charcoal, coal	炭
炭鉱	たんこう	coalmine; coal pit	27C
鉱	コウ	mineral, ore	27C

27D 面 DRAGON'S BLOOD

🔊	暗黒面	2 - 3
27D	あんこくめん	*

Noodles' Seamy Side

Formerly face and covering, that which covers the face, mask 面

麺	メン、ベン、むぎこ	noodles; wheat flour	麺
麺類	めんるい	noodles	27D
類	ルイ	resemble, variety, sort	27D
面	メン、おも、おもて、つら	face, aspect, mask	面
暗黒面	あんこくめん	the dark or seamy side	27D

暗	アン、くら-い	dark, gloomy	27D
黒	コク、くろ、くろ-い	black	27D

27E 息 DRAGON'S BLOOD

🆂🅳		休息	2 – 2
27E		きゅうそく	0|5

A Breathing Child is Restful

Nose + heart = essence of life, breathing air 息

息	ソク、いき	breath, rest, child	息
休息	きゅうそく	rest	27E
休*	キュウ、やす-む、やす-まる、やす-める	rest	27E
憩	ケイ、いこ-い、いこ-う	rest	憩
憩い	いこい	rest, spell	27E

27F 波 DRAGON'S BLOOD

🆂🅳		波乗り	8A7
27F		なみのり	1||4

"Hasan Onibaba" Barked the Tired Surf Clothing assistant during the Wedding Reception on The Other Shore

Hand pulling the hide of an animal with the head still attached 波

破	ハ、やぶ-る、やぶ-れる	break, tear	破
破産	はさん	bankruptcy	27F
産	サン、う-む、う-まれる、うぶ	birth, produce	27F

175

婆	バ	old woman	婆
鬼婆	おにばば	witch, hag	27F
鬼	キ、おに	devil, demon, ghost	27F
皮	ヒ、かわ	skin, leather	皮
木の皮	きのかわ	bark	27F
木	ボク、モク、き、こ	tree, wood	27F
疲	ヒ、つか-れる、つか-らす	tire, exhaustion	疲
疲労	ひろう	fatigue	27F
労*	ロウ	labour, toil	27F
波	ハ、なみ	wave	波
波乗り	なみのり	surfing	27F
乗	ジョウ、の-る、の-せる	ride, mount, load	27F
被	ヒ、こうむ-る	sustain, cover, wear	被
被服	ひふく	clothing	27F
服	フク	clothes, yield, serve	27F
披	ヒ	open, disclose	披
披露宴	ひろうえん	(wedding) reception	27F
露	ロ、ロウ、つゆ	dew, reveal, small, Russia	27F
宴*	エン	banquet	27F
彼	ヒ、かれ、かの	he, that, distant goal	彼
彼岸	ひがん	equinox, other shore, goal	27F
岸	ガン、きし	bank, shore	27F

27G 非 DRAGON'S BLOOD

🆂	非行	7B18
27G	ひこう	*

A Tragic Haiku that Boycotts Sinful Seniors crashing through the Doors of Misdemeanours

Wings of a bird spreading apart as it is flies off 非

悲	ヒ、かな-しい、かな-しむ	sad	悲
悲劇	ひげき	tragedy	27G
劇	ゲキ	drama, intense	27G
俳	ハイ	amusement, actor	俳
俳句	はいく	haiku	27G
句	ク	phrase, clause	27G
排	ハイ	reject, expel, push, anti-	排
排斥	はいすい	boycott	27G
斥	セキ	repel, reject	27G
罪	ザイ、つみ	crime, sin	罪
罪深い	つみぶかい	sinful	27G
深	シン、ふか-い、ふか-まる、ふか-める	deep, deepen	27G
輩	ハイ	fellow, companion	輩
先輩	せんぱい	one's senior	27G
先	セン、さき	previous, precede, tip	27G
扉	ヒ、とびら	door, front page	扉
門扉	もんぴ	doors of a gate	27G
門	モン、かど	gate, door	27G
非	ヒ	not, un-, fault	非
非行	ひこう	misdemeanour	27G
行	コウ、ギョウ、アン、い-く、ゆ-く、おこな-う	go, conduct, column	27G

177

A wee bit peckish. The 窃盗 of 激突 Test Dummies did not alter the 到着駅 of 沢山 depressed foodies who were not only walking in sack cloths but were 灰塗れ as well. They all had emerged from 炭鉱 and 暗黒面 but were in good hope to find the perfect 麺類 and to take some 休息 at the Tampopo restaurant. They had experienced 疲労 and were afraid that the 鬼婆's promise would be fulfilled: thou shall have at the 披露宴 nothing but bad 俳句 to hear and be forced to fight famished 先輩 obstructing the 門扉 of the food barn!

28A 去 DRAM

⚠	過去	4A6
28A	かこ	*

Past Grammar is Contrary to the Ballast of the Law

Originally double lid on a rice container, consumption, gone? 去

去	キョ、コ、さ-る	go, leave, past	去
過去	かこ	the past	28A
過	カ、す-ぎる、す-ごす、あやま-つ、あやま-ち	pass, exceed, error	28A
法	ホウ、ハッ、ホッ	law	法
文法	ぶんぽう	grammar	28A
文	ブン、モン、ふみ	writing, text	28A
却	キャク	(on the) contrary	却
却下	きゃっか	rejection	28A
下	カ、ゲ、した、しも、もと、さ-げる、さ-がる、くだ-る、くだ-す	base, under, lower	28A

脚	キャク、キャ、あし	leg, foot	脚
脚荷	あしに	ballast	28A
荷	カ、に	load, burden	28A

28B 令 DRAM

| ▲ | 司令官 | 7F7 |
| 28B | しれいかん | * |

For Years the Commander Refrigerated the Consul in a Below Zero Wind Chime (Fatal)

Originally people summoned to hear the orders of their lord 令

齢	レイ	age	齢
年齢	ねんれい	age, years	28B
年	ネン、とし	year	28B
令	レイ	order, rule	令
司令官	しれいかん	commander	28B
司	シ	administer, official	28B
官	カン	government, official	28B
冷	レイ、つめ-たい、ひ-える、ひ-や、ひ-やす	freeze, cold	冷
冷蔵	れいぞう	refrigeration	28B
蔵	ゾウ、くら	storehouse, harbor	28B
領	リョウ	control, possess, chief, territory	領

領事	りょうじ	consul	28B
事	ジ、ズ、こと	thing, matter, act	28B
零	レイ	zero, tiny, fall	零
零下	れいか	below zero	28B
下	カ、ゲ、した、しも、もと、さ-げる、さ-がる、くだ-る、くだ-す	base, under, lower	28B
鈴	レイ、リン、すず	bell, chime	鈴
風鈴	ふうりん	wind chime	28B
風	フウ、フ、かぜ、かざ	wind, style	28B
命	メイ、ミョウ、いのち	life, order	命
命取り	いのちとり	fatal	28B
取	シュ、と-る	take control	28B

28C 医 DRAM

| △ | 産婦人科医 | | 2B9 |
| 28C | さんふじんかい | | * |

Greetings and Goodbye to Obstetricians and Gynaecologists

Formerly expressing to attack with alcohol (arrow + quiver + strike + wine jar) 医

挨	アイ	push open	挨
挨拶	あいさつ	greetings	28C
拶	サツ	be imminent	28C
医	イ	doctor; medicine	医
産婦人科医	さんふじんかい	obstetrician and gynaecologist	28C

産	サン、う-む、う-れる、うぶ	birth, produce	28C
婦	フ	woman, wife	28C
人	ジン、ニン、ひと	person	28C
科	カ	course, section	28C

28D 各 DRAM

	各駅	10A15
28D	かくえき	2‖8

Guests of Honour in Each Station Contacted & Bribed Cheesy Characters when they found that the Sum Of Money in the Short Cabinet had been Struck by Lightning

Descend, stop and start 各

客	キャク、カク	guest, visitor	客
賓客	ひんきゃく	guest of honour	28D
賓*	ヒン	guest, visitor	28D
各	カク、おのおの	each	各
各駅	かくえき	each station	28D
駅	エキ	station	28D
絡	ラク、から-む、から-まる	entwine, connect	絡
連絡	れんらく	contact	28D
連	レン、つら-なる、つら-ねる、つ-れる	accompany, row	28D
賂	ロ、まいな.い、まいな.う	bribe	賂
賄賂	わいろ	bribery	28D
賄	ワイ、まかな-う	bribe, provide, board	28D
酪	ラク	curd, dairy produce	酪
乾酪	かんらく	cheese	28D

乾	カン、かわ-く、かわ-かす	dry	28D
格	カク、コウ	standard, status	格
性格	せいかく	character	28D
性	セイ、ショウ	nature, sex	28D
額	ガク、ひたい	sum, plaque, frame, forehead	額
金額	きんがく	sum of money	28D
金	キン、コン、かね、かな	gold, money, metal	28D
略	リャク	abbreviate, outline	略
省略	しょうりゃく	abbreviate, omit	28D
省	セイ、ショウ、かえり-みる、はぶ-く	ministry, omit, examine	28D
閣	カク	cabinet, chamber	閣
内閣	ないかく	cabinet	28D
内	ナイ、ダイ、うち	inside	28D
落	ラク、お-ちる、お-とす	fall, drop	落
落雷	らくらい	be struck by lightning	28D
雷*	ライ、かみなり	thunder	28D

28E 追 DRAM

⚠	追放	2A5
28E	ついほう	*

Dream-beaver Dispatches Banishment

Pair of buttocks, phonetic chase 追

遣	ケン、つか-う、つか-わす	send, use, do	遣
派遣	はけん	dispatch	28E
派	ハ	faction, send	28E

追	ツイ、お-う	chase, pursue	追
追放	ついほう	banishment	28E
放	ホウ、はな-す、はな-つ、はな-れる	release, emit	28E

28F 代 DRAM

🔺	部屋代	3 – 1
28F	へやだい	*

Rent a Room but don't Stomach a Loan

Person + stake, phonetic replace, stand-in, exchange 代

代	ダイ、タイ、か-わる、か-える、よ、しろ	replace, world, generation, fee	代
部屋代	へやだい	room rent	28F
部	ブ	part, section, clan	28F
屋	オク、や	store, building	28F
袋	タイ、ふくろ	bag, pouch	袋
胃袋	いぶくろ	stomach	28F
胃	イ	stomach	28F
貸	タイ、か-す	lend, loan	貸
貸し金	かしきん	loan	28F
金	キン、コン、かね、かな	gold, money, metal	28F

28G 振 DRAM

🔺	妊娠	7C10
28G	にんしん	0|1

The Humiliated Earthquake was Waving her Pregnant Lips at the Rich Rural Community

Originally clam (now NGU character dragon) cutting grass, plants on field 振

辱	ジョク、はずかし-める	insult, humiliate	辱
恥辱	ちじょく	disgrace, humiliation	28G
恥	チ、は-じる、はじ、は-じらう、は-ずかしい	shame, ashamed	28G
震	シン、ふる-う、ふる-える	shake, tremble	震
地震	じしん	earthquake	28G
地	チ、ジ	ground, land	28G
振	シン、ふ-る、ふ-るう	wave, swing, air, manner, after	振
振動	しんどう	swing	28G
動	ドウ、うご-く、うご-かす	move	28G
娠	シン	pregnancy	娠
妊娠	にんしん	pregnancy	28G
妊	ニン	pregnant woman	28G
唇	シン、くちびる	lip(s)	唇
口唇	こうしん	lips	28G
口	コウ、ク、くち	mouth, opening	28G
濃	ノウ、こ-い	thick, deep, rich	濃
濃厚の	のうこうの	rich, intense	28G
厚*	コウ、あつ-い	thick, kind	28G
農	ノウ	farming	農
農村	のうそん	farm village, rural community	28G
村	ソン、むら	village	28G

Fluttering from pleasure to pleasure. To even consider 却下 of the 文法 of happiness is like hearing a 風鈴 in 零下 conditions.

Season's 挨拶 to euphoric 賓客, contented cats at 各駅 and other wonderful 性格. Let us 派遣 miracle workers striving towards 追放 of growling of the 胃袋 and paying of 部屋代. Time to end 恥辱 so that henceforth a powerful 振動 to 濃厚の gratification can be set in motion as vibrant as the 口唇 of a 妊娠.

Chapter 5 Leo

29A EARTH 祭

▽	夏祭	4 – 1
29A	なつまつり	1|3

Police the Summer Festival to prevent International Chafing

Hand placing meat on altar, worship 祭

察	サツ	judge, surmise, realise	察
警察	けいさつ	police	29A
警	ケイ	warn, approach	29A
祭	サイ、まつ-る、まつ-り	festival, worship	祭
夏祭	なつまつり	summer festival	29A
夏*	カ、ゲ、なつ	summer	29A
際	サイ、きわ	occasion, edge, contact	際
国際	こくさい	international	29A
国	コク、くに	country, region	29A
擦	サツ、す-る、す-れる	rub, chafe, brush	擦
擦り込む	すりこむ	rub in	29A
込	こ-む、こ-める	put in, be crowded	29A

29B 倍 EARTH

▽	倍加	6A4
29B	ばいか	*

The Jury was Partly Compensated by Cultivating a Doubling of Anatomy classes

Person and Chinese only spit 倍

陪	バイ	attend, accompany	陪
陪審	ばいしん	jury	29B
審	シン	judge, investigate	29B
部	ブ	part, section, clan	部
部分	ぶぶん	part	29B
分	ブン、フン、ブ、わ-ける、わ-かれる、わ-かる、わ-かつ	divide, minute, understand	29B
賠	バイ	compensate	賠
賠償	ばいしょう	compensation	29B
培	バイ、つちか-う	cultivate, grow	培
培養	ばいよう	cultivation	29B
養	ヨウ、やしな-う	rear, support	29B
償	ショウ、つぐな-う	recompense, redeem	29B
倍	バイ	double, -fold	倍
倍加	ばいか	doubling	29B
加	カ、くわ-える、くわ-わる	add, join	29B
剖	ボウ	divide, cutup	剖
解剖学	かいぼうがく	anatomy	29B
解	カイ、ゲ、と-く、と-かす、と-ける	unravel, explain, solve	29B
学	ガク、まな-ぶ	study	29B

29C 然 EARTH

▽	燃焼	3 – 6
29C	ねんしょう	*

Combustion of Coerced Composure

Roast dog meat 然

燃	ネン、も-える、も-やす、も-す	burn	燃
燃焼	ねんしょう	combustion	29C
焼	ショウ、や-く、や-ける	burn, roast	29C
圧	アツ	pressure	圧
威圧	いあつ	coercion	29C
威	イ	authority, threaten	29C
然	ゼン、ネン	duly, thus, so, but	然
泰然	たいぜん	composure	29C
泰	タイ	calm, serene, big, Thai	29C

29D 欠 EARTH

▽	炊事	14B5
29D	すいじ	0‖4

A Blowzy Drunken Thief Postured in Ibaraki as an Envious Order Cook when he Inquired about the Capital Arbitrary Weakness of Scanty Credit

Person yawning, wide open, vacant, lacking 欠

吹	スイ、ふ-く	blow, breathe out	吹
吹き倒す	ふきたおす	blow-down	29D
倒	トウ、たお-れる、たお-す	fall, topple, invert	29D

飲	イン、の-む	drink, swallow	飲
飲助	のみすけ	drunkard	29D
助	ジョ、たす-ける、たす-かる、すけ	assist, help	29D
盗	トウ、ぬす-む	steal	盗
盗人	ぬすびと*	thief	29D
人	ジン、ニン、ひと	person	29D
姿	シ、すがた	form, figure	姿
姿勢	しせい	posture	29D
勢	セイ、いきお-い	power, force	29D
茨	シ、いばら	briar; thorn	茨
茨城県	いばらきけん	Ibaraki Prefecture	29D
城	ジョウ、しろ	castle	29D
県	ケン	prefecture	29D
羨	セン、うらや-む	envious	羨
羨望	せんぼう	envy	29D
望	ボウ、モウ、のぞ-む	wish, hope, gaze	29D
次	ジ、シ、つ-ぐ、つぎ	next, follow	次
逓次	ていじ	in order, successively	29D
逓*	テイ	relay, in sequence	29D
炊	スイ、た-く	cook, boil	炊
炊事	すいじ	cooking	29D
事	ジ、ズ、こと	thing, matter, act	29D
諮	シ、はか-る	consult, inquire	諮
諮問	しもん	inquiry	29D
問	モン、と-う、と-い、とん	ask	29D
資	シ	capital, resources	資
資本	しほん	capital	29D

189

本	ホン、もと	root, true, book, this	29D
恣	シ、ほしいまま	selfish; arbitrary	恣
恣意	しい	selfishness; arbitrariness	29D
意	イ	mind, thought, will	29D
軟	ナン、やわ-らか、やわ-らかい	soft	軟
軟弱	なんじゃく	weakness	29D
弱	ジャク、よわ-い、よわ-る、よわ-まる、よわ-める	weak	29D
欠	ケツ、か-ける、か-く	lack	欠
欠乏	けつぼう	lack, scarcity, shortage, deficiency	29D
乏*	ボウ、とぼ-しい	meagre, scanty, scarce	29D
款	カン	friendship, clause, engrave	款
借款	しゃっかん	loan, credit	29D
借	シャク、か-りる	borrow, rent	29D

29E 比 EARTH

▽		比肩	9D21
29E		ひけん	1|1

All Harmonious Square Stairs leading to the Incomparable Insect Throne were of a Striking, Confusing beauty

People sitting next to each other 比

| 諧 | カイ、かな.う、やわ.らぐ | | harmony | 諧 |

190

俳諧	はいかい	haikai, a 17-syllable poem	29E
俳	ハイ	amusement, actor	29E
楷	カイ	square character style; correctness	楷
楷書	かいしょ	non-cursive kanji	29E
書	ショ、か-く	write	29E
皆	カイ、みな	all, everyone, full	皆
皆様	みなさま	everyone	29E
様*	ヨウ、さま	Esq.; way; manner; situation; polite suffix	29E
階	カイ	story, grade, step	階
階段	かいだん	stairs	29E
段	ダン	step, grade	29E
比	ヒ、くら-べる	compare, ratio	比
比肩	ひけん	comparison	29E
肩	ケン、かた	shoulder	29E
昆	コン	multitude, insect, descendants	昆
昆虫	こんちゅう	insect	29E
虫	チュウ、むし	insect, worm	29E
陛	ヘイ	majesty, throne	陛
陛下	へいか	majesty	29E

下	カ、ゲ、した、しも、もと、さ-げる、さ-がる、くだ-る、くだ-す	base, under, lower	29E
批	ヒ	criticise, strike, pass	批
批判	ひはん	criticism	29E
判	ハン、バン	seal; stamp; judgment	29E
混	コン、ま-じる、ま-ざる、ま-ぜる	mix, confusion	混
混乱	こんらん	confusion	29E
乱	ラン、みだ-れる、みだ-す	disorder, riot	29E

29F 号 EARTH

▽	番号	4B13
29F	ばんごう	*

Proud Call of Crafty Rotting Leaves

Originally tiger's call 号

誇	コ、ほこ-る	proud, boast	誇
誇り高い	ほこりたかい	proud; lordly	29F
高	コウ、たか-い、たか、たか-まる、たか-める	tall, high, sum	29F
号	ゴウ	number, call, sign	号
番号	ばんごう	number	29F
番	バン	turn, number, guard	29F
巧	コウ、たく-み	skill	巧
巧言	こうげん	flattery	29F
言	ゲン、ゴン、い-う、こと	word, say, speak	29F

朽	キュウ、く-ちる	decay, rot	朽
朽ち葉	くちば	dead leaves	29F
葉	ヨウ、は	leaf	29F

29G 有 EARTH

	所有者	6D9
29G	しょゆうしゃ	*

Essentially, Random Depravity Owes a debt to Indolent Bribery

Originally right hand holding a piece of meat 有

髄	ズイ	marrow	髄
真髄	しんずい	essence	29G
真	シン、ま	true, quintessence	29G
随	ズイ	random, follow	随
随筆	ずいひつ	random notes	29G
筆	ヒツ、ふで	writing brush	29G
堕	ダ	fall(en), degenerate	堕
堕落	だらく	depravity	29G
落	ラク、お-ちる、お-とす	fall, drop	29G
有	ユウ、ウ、ある	have, exist	有
所有者	しょゆうしゃ	owner	29G
所	ショ、ところ	place, situation	29G
者	シャ、もの	person	29G
惰	ダ	lazy, inert	惰
惰気	だき	indolence	29G
気	キ、ケ	spirit	29G
賄	ワイ、まかな-う	bribe, provide, board	賄
贈賄	ぞうわい	bribery	29G

贈	ゾウ、ソウ、おく-る	present, give	29G

Lords of the Rings. Surely you don't need to 擦り込む: at the 国際 event the strongly biased 陪審 might have striven to give 賠償 to aggrieved competitors but after barely disguised 威圧 tempers had reached 燃焼 point. The 恣意 of the decisions caused 羨望 so that many were pushing for an 諮問 and 皆様 had nothing but harsh 批判 for all this 混乱. The 誇り高い referees, however, were only interested in 巧言 and a considerable 番号 in the organisation showed disconcerting signs of 堕落 combined with 惰気 and a propensity for engaging in 贈賄. Emperor Theodosius, you're a legend!

30A 基 EBULLITION

🏃	基礎	6D12
30A	きそ	*

Base Moves were Flagged on the Checkerboard of Deceived Expectations

Non general use character "that", winnowing device, harvest, cycle of time 基

基	キ、もと、もとい	base	基
基礎	きそ	basis	30A
礎	ソ、いしずえ	foundation stone	30A
棋	キ	chess	棋
将棋	しょうぎ	chess	30A
将	ショウ	command, about to	30A
旗	キ、はた	flag	旗
国旗	こっき	national flag	30A
国	コク、くに	country, region	30A
碁	ゴ	Go (board game)	碁

碁盤	ごばん	checkerboard	30A
盤	バン	tray, board, bowl, plate	30A
欺	ギ、あざむ-く	cheat, deceive	欺
欺き取り	あざむきとり	defraud	30A
取	シュ、と-る	take control	30A
期	キ、ゴ	period, expect	期
期待	きたい	expectation	30A
待	タイ、ま-つ	wait	30A

30B 廷 EBULLUTION

🜨	法廷		3A1
30B	ほうてい		*

Tei the Gardener found himself in a Court of Law after stealing a Lifeboat

Chinese only artful, great, courtiers move to standing position on the ground 廷

庭	テイ、にわ	garden, courtyard	庭
庭園	ていえん	garden	30B
園	エン、その	garden, park	30B
廷	テイ	court, government office	廷
法廷	ほうてい	court of law	30B
法	ホウ、ハッ、ホッ	law	30B
艇	テイ	boat	艇
救命艇	きゅうめいてい	lifeboat	30B
救	キュウ、すく-う	rescue, redeem	30B
命	メイ、ミョウ、いのち	life, order	30B

195

30C 成 EBULLITION

	促成	4A1
30C	そくせい	*

Promoters in Castle Towns Sincerely desire Prosperity

Exact and trimming halberd 成

成	セイ、ジョウ、な-る、な-す	become, make, consist	成
促成	そくせい	growth, promotion	30C
促	ソク、うなが-す	urge, press	30C
城	ジョウ、しろ	castle	城
城下町	じょうかまち	castle town	30C
下	カ、ゲ、した、しも、もと、さ-げる、さ-がる、くだ-る、くだ-す	base, under, lower	30C
町	チョウ、まち	town	30C
誠	セイ、まこと	sincerity	誠
丹誠	たんせい	sincerity, diligence	30C
丹	タン	red, sincere	30C
盛	セイ、ジョウ、も-る、さか-る、さか-ん	prosper, heap, serve	盛
隆盛	りゅうせい	prosperity	30C
隆	リュウ	high, peak, prosper	30C

30D 官 EBULLITION

	警官	4A3

30D	けいかん	0|2

The Policeman grabbed a Hose as the Coffin caught fire in the Cinema

Roof + buttocks, phonetic work, sedentary activity 官

官	カン	government, official	官
警官	けいかん	policeman	30D
警	ケイ	warn, approach	30D
管	カン、くだ	pipe, control	管
蛇管	じゃかん	hose	30D
蛇	ジャ、ダ、へび	snake, serpent	30D
棺	カン	coffin	棺
棺おけ	かんおけ	coffin, casket	30D
館	カン	large building, hall	館
映画館	えいがかん	cinema	30D
映	エイ、うつ-る、うつ-す、は-える	reflect, shine	30D
画*	ガ、カク	picture, stroke	30D

30E 永 EBULLITION

永	永遠	3 – 4
30E	えいえん	0|2

When Swimming for Eternity, it's best to Recite Poems

Picture of the confluence of tributary and main river, originally long distance 永

泳	エイ、およ-ぐ	swim	泳
競泳	きょうえい	swimming race	30E

競*	キョウ、ケイ、きそ-う、せ-る	compete, vie for	30E
永	エイ、なが-い	long, lasting	永
永遠	えいえん	eternity	30E
遠	エン、オン、とお-い	distant	30E
詠	エイ、よ-む	poem, recite, compose	詠
詠歌	えいか	composition	30E
歌	カ、うた、うた-う	song	30E

30F 由 EBULLITION

| 肀 | | 由縁 | | 8D5 |
| 30F | | ゆえん | | * |

A Leading Report says that a Drawn-Out Whistle is the Way to make the Sky Scroll like Oil on water

Basket/ wine press, drops falling from basket, cause 由

袖	シュウ、そで	sleeve; wing (building); extension; give cold shoulder	袖
領袖	りょうしゅう	leader; chief; boss	30F
領	リョウ	control, possess, chief, territory	30F
届	とど-ける、とど-く	deliver, report	届
届け出る	とどけでる	notify	30F
出	シュツ、スイ、で-る、だ-す	emerge, put out	30F
抽	チュウ	pull, draw out	抽
抽出	ちゅうしゅつ	extraction	30F

出	シュツ、スイ、で-る、だ-す	emerge, put out	30F
笛	テキ、ふえ	flute, whistle	笛
汽笛	きてき	(steam) whistle	30F
汽	キ	steam	30F
由	ユ、ユウ、ユイ、よし	reason, means, way	由
由縁	ゆえん	relationship, reason, way	30F
縁	エン、ふち	relation(s), ties, fate, edge	30F
宙	チュウ	space, sky	宙
宇宙	うちゅう	space	30F
宇	ウ	eaves, roof, heaven	30F
軸	ジク	axle, shaft, scroll	軸
軸物	じくもの	scroll picture	30F
物	ブツ、モツ、もの	thing	30F
油	ユ、あぶら	oil	油
灯油	とうゆ	kerosene	30F
灯	トウ、ひ	light, lamp	30F

30G 是 EBULLITION

| | 是正 | 4A5 |
| 30G | ぜせい | 0\|1 |

A Tied-up finger in the Dyke is a Problem that needs Correction

Originally spoon kept on (proper) hook 是

| 提 | テイ、さ-げる | hold, carry, offer | 提 |
| 提携 | ていけい | cooperation, tie-up | 30G |

携*	ケイ、たずさ-える、たずさ-わる	carry, participate	30G
堤	テイ、つつみ	embankment	堤
堤防	ていぼう	levee, dyke	30G
防	ボウ、ふせ-ぐ	prevent, defend	30G
題	ダイ	subject, title	題
問題	もんだい	problem, issue	30G
問	モン、と-う、と-い、とん	ask	30G
是	ゼ	proper, this	是
是正	ぜせい	correction	30G
正	セイ、ショウ、ただ-しい、ただ-す、まさ	correct	30G

God's away on business. Sometimes 期待 are not met and there will be occasions when the 国旗 flutters less gloriously. The 救命艇 is sinking whilst the Children of Mammon repose themselves in the 庭園 of Babylon. Corrupt 法廷 bring 隆盛 to the Unrighteous but enhance 促成 of prisons for the poor. Bulky 警官 beat into the crowds as powerful 蛇管 spray everyone with foul liquids. A 詠歌 of pain and misery that goes on for 永遠. The 汽笛 of the Peace Train has been silenced a long time ago while the smell of 灯油 is wafting through the gutted buildings. A situation beyond 是正: 問題 without resolution like shattered hopes and broken 堤防.

31A 県 EFFERVESCENCE

EF		県庁	2A1
31A		けんちょう	*

Hang the head of that Perilous Prefecture

Originally joined threads/attach, severed head upside down in tree

県

懸	ケン、ケ、か-ける、か-かる	attach, hang, apply	懸
命懸け	いのちがけ	perilous	31A
命	メイ、ミョウ、いのち	life, order	31A
県	ケン	prefecture	県
県庁	けんちょう	prefectural office	31A
庁	チョウ	government, office, agency	31A

31B 具 EFFERVESCENCE

EF	台所道具		2A5
31B	だいどころどうぐ		*

Only Kitchen Utensils, I'm Afraid

Originally showing hands holding up a kettle, offer a utensil 具

具	グ	equip, means	具
台所道具	だいどころどうぐ	kitchen utensils	31B
台	ダイ、タイ	platform, stand	31B
所	ショ、ところ	place, situation	31B
道	ドウ、トウ、みち	way, road	31B
惧	ク、おそ.れる	fear; be afraid of; dread	惧
危惧	きぐ	apprehension	31B
危	キ、あぶ-ない、あや-うい、あや-ぶむ	dangerous	31B

31C 象 EFFERVESCENCE

EF	印象	2 - 1
31C	いんしょう	0|1

Hannibal's Elephants leave an Iconic Impression on the imagination

Pictograph of an elephant 象

像	ゾウ	image	像
聖像	せいぞう	sacred image, icon	31C
聖	セイ	saint, sage, sacred	31C
象	ショウ、ゾウ	elephant, image	象
印象	いんしょう	impression	31C
印*	イン、しるし	seal, sign, symbol	31C

31D 束 EFFERVESCENCE

EF	束の間	6 - 14
31D	つかのま	1||4

In Sharp Intense Moments the Unfriendly Imperial Edict is Maintained

Variant of east/tied sack with pole thrust through, bundle 束

辣	ラツ、から.い	bitter	辣
辛辣	しんらつ	bitter; sharp; acrimonious	31D
辛	シン、から-い	sharp, bitter	31D
速	ソク、はや-い、はや-める、すみ-やか	speed, fast	速
迅速	じんそく	quick, prompt, speedy	31D

迅*	ジン	fast, intense	31D
束	ソク、たば	bundle, manage	束
束の間	つかのま	moment	31D
間	カン、ケン、あいだ、ま	space, gap	31D
疎	ソ、うと-い、うと-む	distant, shun, coarse	疎
疎疎しい	うとうとしい	unfriendly	31D
勅	チョク	imperial edict	勅
勅語	ちょくご	imperial edict	31D
語	ゴ、かた-る、かた-らう	tell, speak, talk	31D
整	セイ、ととの-える、ととの-う	arrange	整
整備	せいび	maintenance	31D
備*	ビ、そな-える、そな-わる	equip, prepare	31D

31E 免 EFFERVESCENCE

EF	逸品	4F12
31E	いっぴん	0|2

One Evening she went Astray Studying Tax-exemptions

Women's genitals + crouching person, child birth, escape 免

晩	バン	evening, late	晩
今晩	こんばん	this evening	31E
今	コン、キン、いま	now	31E
逸	イツ	escape, go astray, fast, excel	逸
逸品	いっぴん	fine article	31E
品	ヒン、しな	goods, quality, kind	31E

勉	ベン		strive	勉
勉強	べんきょう		study	31E
強*	キョウ、ゴウ、つよ-い、つよ-まる、つよ-める、し-いる		strong	31E
免	メン、まぬか-れる		escape, avoid	免
免税	めんぜい		tax-exempt	31E
税	ゼイ		tax, tithe	31E

31F 区 EFFERVESCENCE

EF		区別		5B13
31F		くべつ		*

Europe was dealt a Distinctive Blow by a Pivotal Pioneer

Originally enclosure with three mouths, smaller enclosures Wards 区

欧	オウ		Europe, EU-	欧
欧州	おうしゅう		Europe	31F
州	シュウ、す		state, province	31F
区	ク		ward, section	区
区別	くべつ		distinction	31F
別	ベツ、わか-れる		split, differ, special	31F
殴	オウ、なぐ-る		hit, beat, assault	殴
殴打	おうだ		blow, assault	31F
打	ダ、う-つ		hit, strike	31F
枢	スウ		pivot, door	枢
中枢	ちゅうすう		centre, pivot	31F
中	チュウ、なか		middle, inside, China	31F
駆	ク、か-ける、か-る		gallop, spur on	駆

先駆者	せんくしゃ	pioneer	31F
先	セン、さき	previous, precede, tip	31F
者	シャ、もの	person	31F

31G 及 EFFERVESCENCE

EF	及第点	4C3
31G	きゅうだいてん	*

The Vampire Treated his Class Mate to an Extensive blood feast

Originally person + hand reaching out to seize 及

吸	キュウ、す-う	suck, inhale	吸
吸血鬼	きゅうけつき	vampire	31G
血	ケツ、ち	blood	31G
鬼	キ、おに	devil, demon, ghost	31G
扱	あつか-う	treat, handle, thresh	扱
取り扱い	とりあつかい	handling	31G
取	シュ、と-る	take control	31G
級	キュウ	rank, grade	級
同級生	どうきゅうせい	class mate	31G
同	ドウ、おな-じ	same	31G
生	セイ、ショウ、い-きる、い-かす、い-ける、う-まれる、う-む	life, birth, grow	31G

205

及	キュウ、およ-ぶ、およ-び、およ-ぼす	reach, extend, and	及
及第点	きゅうだいてん	pass mark	31G
第	ダイ	grade, order	31G
点	テン	point, mark	31G

More austerity anyone? Gonzo was subject to a 命懸け attack of 危惧 and loathing in addition to darkly disturbing 印象 after witnessing 辛辣 exchanges between 疎疎しい IMF economists and young impoverished Europeans. We strongly condemn any attempts to research and 勉強 ways to render yourself 免税. We reserve the right to launch fierce 殴打 on your living conditions which is a 中枢 piece of our policies in 欧州. Think of the Troika as a huge 吸血鬼 strangling your economies and sucking the lifeblood out of you and your destitute 同級生.

32A 央 ELEMENT

	震央	3A7
32A	しんおう	*

The Superior Shining Centre

Person with a yoke on the neck, restrained at the middle 央

英	エイ	superior, England	英
俊英	しゅんえい	excellence; genius	32A
俊	シュン	excellence, genius	32A
映	エイ、うつ-る、うつ-す、は-える	reflect, shine	映
映像	えいぞう	reflection; image; picture	32A

像	ゾウ	image	32A
央	オウ	centre	央
震央	しんおう	epicentre	32A
震	シン、ふる-う、ふる-える	shake, tremble	32A

32B 君 ELEMENT

④		君主	3A5
32B		くんしゅ	*

Lords are Flocking to the District

Hand holding stick to govern and mouth 君

君	クン、きみ	lord, you Mr	君
君主	くんしゅ	ruler, monarch	32B
主	シュ、ス、ぬし、おも	master, owner, main	32B
群	グン、む-れる、む-れ、むら	group, flock	群
群衆	ぐんしゅう	crowd, multitude	32B
衆	シュウ、シュ	multitude, populace	32B
郡	グン	county, district	郡
郡県	ぐんけん	counties and prefectures	32B
県	ケン	prefecture	32B

32C 更 ELEMENT

④		今更	4A4
32C		いまさら	*

I Belatedly experienced a Convenient Hardening Close Up

Originally, enforce + third rate, enforced change of guard 更

更	コウ、さら、ふ-ける、ふ-かす	anew, change, again, grow late	更
今更	いまさら	now, belatedly	32C
今	コン、キン、いま	now	32C
便	ベン、ビン、たよ-り	convenience, service, mail	便
郵便	ゆうびん	mail	32C
郵	ユウ	mail, relay station	32C
硬	コウ、かた-い	hard	硬
硬化	こうか	hardening	32C
化	カ、ケ、ば-ける、ば-かす	change, bewitch	32C
梗	コウ、キョウ、やまにれ	for the most part; close-up	梗
心筋梗塞	しんきんこうそく	heart attack	32C
心	シン、こころ	heart, feelings	32C
筋	キン、すじ	muscle, sinew, thread	32C
塞	サイ、ソク、とりで、ふさ-ぐ	close	32C

32D 昔 ELEMENT

𠀀		今昔	6 - 3
32D		こんじゃく	*

An Old Debt is not to be Mistaken with the Regrettable Step of Registering a Nationality

Originally sun/day and piling up, accumulating, the past 昔

昔	セキ、シャク、むかし	olden times, past	昔

今昔	こんじゃく	past and present	32D
今	コン、キン、いま	now	32D
借	シャク、か-りる	borrow, rent	借
借金	しゃっきん	debt	32D
金	キン、コン、かね、かな	gold, money, metal	32D
錯	サク	mix up, confuse	錯
錯誤	さくご	mistake	32D
誤	ゴ、あやま-る	mistake, mis-	32D
惜	セキ、お-しい、お-しむ	regret, be loath to	惜
惜し気	おしげ	regret	32D
気	キ、ケ	spirit	32D
措	ソ	place, dispose	措
措置	そち	step, action	32D
置	チ、お-く	put, place	32D
籍	セキ	register	籍
国籍	こくせき	nationality	32D
国	コク、くに	country, region	32D

32E 宿 ELEMENT

| ⊉ | | 宿題 | 2 - 2 |
| 32E | | しゅくだい | * |

Homework is Reduced to Shreds

Originally rush mat + building + person, resting 宿

宿	シュク、やど、やど-る、やど-す	lodge, shelter, house	宿
宿題	しゅくだい	homework	32E
題	ダイ	subject, title	32E

縮	シュク、ちぢ-む、ちぢ-まる、ちぢ-める	shrink, reduce	縮
縮小	しゅくしょう	reduction	32E
小	ショウ、ちい-さい、こ、お	small	32E

32F 全 ELEMENT

𝄐		安全	3 - 3
32F		あんぜん	0|2

Explore the completely Safe Fire Hydrant treatment

Jewel under cover, precious, perfect, whole, complete 全

詮	セン、そな-わる	discussion; methods called for; selection; result	詮
詮索	せんさく	inquiry into; enquiry into; prying (into); investigation; search	32F
索	サク	rope, search	32F
全	ゼン、まった-く	whole, completely	全
安全	あんぜん	safety	32F
安	アン、やす-い	restful, ease, cheap	32F
栓	セン	stopper plug, tap	栓
消火栓	しょうかせん	fire hydrant	32F
火*	カ、ひ、ほ	fire	32F
消	ショウ、き-える、け-す	extinguish, vanish, consume	32F

32G 不 ELEMENT

⟨glyph⟩	玉杯	3A6
32G	ぎょくはい	*

It is a Mistake to Deny Luna her Wine cup

Pictograph of a calyx 不

不	フ、ブ	not, un-, dis-	不
不覚	ふかく	imprudence, failure, mistake	32G
覚	カク、おぼ-える、さ-ます、さ-める	remember, learn, experience	32G
否	ヒ、いな	no, decline, deny	否
否定語	ひていご	negative	32G
定	テイ、ジョウ、さだ-める、さだ-まる、さだ-か	fix, establish	32G
語	ゴ、かた-る、かた-らう	tell, speak, talk	32G
杯	ハイ、さかずき	wine cup, cup(ful)	杯
玉杯	ぎょくはい	jade cup	32G
玉	ギョク、たま	ball, sphere, coin	32G

Ravens and mavens. According to 俊英 Dr Zahnstein the perfect 映像 of 群衆 funding consists of 郡県 sending large numbers of 郵便 pigeons even if 今更. The 借金 of generations 今昔 not only causes 惜し気 but also a 縮小 of financial 消火栓. This has become an urgent matter for conducting 詮索 into the multiple 不覚 of the 玉杯 mutual aid society. Cheers big ears!

33A 寒 EQUAL PARTS

⟨glyph⟩	寒村	4A13

33A 並	かんそん	*

No Chansons in Closed & Deserted Villages: The Final Issue of
Wintry Gloom

Old form phonetically expresses "become compact" and ice, winter
冬

Originally expressing binding of rushes to the wall of a house to
insulate against cold 寒

塞	サイ、ソク、とりで、ふさ-ぐ	close	塞
閉塞	へいそく	blockade	33A
閉	ヘイ、と-じる、と-ざす、し-める、し-まる	close, shut	33A
寒	カン、さむ-い	cold, midwinter	寒
寒村	かんそん	deserted village; poor village	33A
村	ソン、むら	village	33A
終	シュウ、お-わる、お-える	end, finish	終
終刊号	しゅうかんごう	final issue, last issue of a publication	33A
刊	カン	publish, engrave	33A
号	ゴウ	number, call, sign	33A
冬	トウ、ふゆ	winter	冬
冬枯れ	ふゆがれ	wintry desolation, poor business conditions	33A
枯	コ、か-れる、か-らす	wither, decay	33A

33B 建 EQUAL PARTS

dP	建物	3 - 1

33B		たてもの		*

Building Health is the Key

Movement of an erect brush 建

建	ケン、コン、た-てる、た-つ	build, erect	建
建物	たてもの	building	33B
物	ブツ、モツ、もの	thing	33B
健	ケン、すこ-やか	healthy	健
健康	けんこう	health	33B
康	コウ	peace, health	33B
鍵	ケン、かぎ	key	鍵
打鍵	だけん	key stroke	33B
打	ダ、う-つ	hit, strike	33B

33C 単 EQUAL PARTS

₫Ρ		簡単		5H12
33C		かんたん		*

The Simple Player had a Bestial Meditation about a Major War

Forked thrusting weapon 単

単	タン	simple, single, unit	単
簡単	かんたん	simple, brief	33C
簡	カン	simple, brief	33C
弾	ダン、ひ-く、はず-む、たま	bullet, spring, play	弾
弾き手	ひきて	player	33C
手	シュ、て、た	hand	33C
獣	ジュウ、けもの	beast	獣

鳥獣	ちょうじゅう	birds and wild animals, wildlife	33C
鳥	チョウ、とり	bird	33C
禅	ゼン	meditation	禅
座禅	ざぜん	meditation	33C
座	ザ、すわ-る	seat, sit, gather	33C
戦	セン、いく-さ、たたか-う	fight, war	戦
大戦	たいせん	major war	33C
大	ダイ、タイ、おお、おお-きい、おお-いに	big	33C

33D 帯 EQUAL PARTS

dP		熱帯魚	2B
33D		ねったいぎょ	0|1

Tropical Fish prefer to Stay in water

Cloth and belt with items attached to it 帯

帯	タイ、お-びる、おび	wear, zone	帯
熱帯魚	ねったいぎょ	tropical fish	33D
熱	ネツ、あつ-い	heat	33D
魚	ギョ、うお、さかな	fish	33D
滞	タイ、とどこお-る	stop, stagnate	滞
滞在	たいざい	sojourn, stay	33D
在*	ザイ、あ-る	exist, outskirts, suburbs	33D

33E 壮 EQUAL PARTS

dP		強壮	6D6

33E		きょうそう		*

His Majesty's Manly Make-up Disguised a womanly face,
according to a Working Scholar

Originally bed + samurai/male/ erect male organ 壮

荘	ソウ	villa, manor, solemn, majestic	荘
荘厳	そうごん	majesty	33E
厳	ゲン、ゴン、おごそ-か、きび-しい	severe, strict, solemn	33E
壮	ソウ	manly, strong, grand, fertile	壮
強壮	きょうそう	robustness	33E
強	キョウ、ゴウ、つよ-い、つよ-まる、つよ-める	strong	33E
粧	ショウ	adorn, makeup	粧
化粧	けしょう	make-up	33E
化	カ、ケ、ば-ける、ば-かす	change, bewitch	33E
装	ソウ、ショウ、よそお-う	wear, clothing, gear	装
変装	へんそう	disguise	33E
変	ヘン、か-わる、か-える	change, strange	33E
仕	シ、ジ、つか-える	serve, work, do	仕
仕方	しかた	way; method; means; resource; course	33E
方	ホウ、かた	side, way, square, direction, person	33E
士	シ	warrior, scholar, man	士
学士	がくし	university graduate	33E
学	ガク、まな-ぶ	study	33E

33F 召 EQUAL PARTS

dP	大詔	8 – 7
33F	たいしょう	0|1

An Inviting Showa Superman Summoned Swamp dwellers to Introduce the Illustrious Imperial Edict

Mouth + person bending as they answer their master's summons 召

招	ショウ、まね-く	invite, summon	招
招待	しょうたい	invitation	33F
待	タイ、ま-つ	wait	33F
昭	ショウ	bright, light	昭
昭和	しょうわ	Showa	33F
和*	ワ、オ、やわ-らぐ、やわ-らげる、なご-む、なご-やか	Japan, peace, soft	33F
超	チョウ、こ-える、こ-す	exceed, cross, super-	超
超人	ちょうじん	superman	33F
人	ジン、ニン、ひと	person	33F
召	ショウ、め-す	summon, partake, wear	召
召喚	しょうかん	summons	33F
喚	カン	shout, yell	33F
沼	ショウ、ぬま	swamp, marsh	沼
沼沢	しょうたく	swamp, marsh	33F
沢	タク、さわ	marsh, moisten, much, many, benefit	33F

216

紹	ショウ	introduce, inherit	紹
紹介	しょうかい	introduction	33F
介	カイ	mediate, shell	33F
照	ショウ、て-る、て-らす、て-れる	illuminate, shine	照
照明	しょうめい	illustration	33F
明	メイ、ミョウ、あ-かり、あか-るい、あか-るむ	clear, open, bright	33F
詔	ショウ、みことのり	imperial edict	詔
大詔	たいしょう	imperial edict	33F
大	ダイ、タイ、おお、おお-きい、おお-いに	big	33F

33G 井 EQUAL PARTS

dP		井戸	3 - 2
33G		いど	*

The Well-Tempered Perimeter

Pictograph of a well 井

井	セイ、ショウ、い	well	井
井戸	いど	well	33G
戸	コ、と	door	33G
丼	トン、タン、ショウ、セイ、どんぶり	bowl; bowl of food	丼
天丼	てんどん	tempura served over a bowl of rice	33G

天	テン、あめ、あま	heaven, sky	33G
囲	イ、かこ-む、かこ-う	surround	囲
周囲 しゅうい		perimeter	33G
周	シュウ、まわ-り	circumference, around	33G

Navel of the world. The 終刊号 of the Buggerallah Times was brought on by a combination of 冬枯れ and a steep decline of interest in rural 健康 issues. One final 打鍵 followed by a 簡単 reception marked the end of a proud local newspaper tradition. The small office would become the home of 鳥獣 and a variety of 熱帯魚 and possibly some swagmen looking for a place to 滞在. It goes without saying that poor 学士 and unsuccessful 化粧 artists also felt a strong desire to camp there. 沼沢 dwellers from far away as well as regional 超人 obeyed a secret 召喚 to seek out this mysterious spot without news: to a frog in a 井戸 the 周囲 of contentment is not very large.

34A 害 ESSENCE

| 牛 | 殺害 | 3 - 2 |
| 34A | さつがい | * |

In this Jurisdiction Murders are on Discount

Originally old (skull), inverted basket, cover head to smother? 害

轄	カツ	control, linchpin	轄
管轄	かんかつ	jurisdiction	34A
管	カン、くだ	pipe, control	34A
害	ガイ	harm, damage	害
殺害	さつがい	murder	34A
殺	サツ、サイ、セツ、ころ-す	kill	34A

218

割	カツ、わ-る、わり、わ-れる、さ-く	divide, rate	割
割引	わりびき	discount	34A
引	イン、ひ-く、ひ-ける	pull, draw	34A

34B 末 ESSENCE

╪		週末	2B2
34B		しゅうまつ	*

The Erasure of the Weekend

Tree with additional branches at the top, tip of tree 末

抹	マツ	erase, rub, paint	抹
抹殺	まっさつ	erasure	34B
殺	サツ、サイ、セツ、ころ-す	kill	34B
末	マツ、バツ、すえ	end, tip	末
週末	しゅうまつ	weekend	34B
週	シュウ	week	34B

34C 幾 ESSENCE

╪		幾つ	3A2
34C		いくつ	1‖5

How Many Kinky looms and Lawn Mowers make the cut

Short thread + variant of broad bladed halberd, loom 幾

幾	キ、いく	how many, how much	幾
幾つ	いくつ	how many?	34C
畿	キ、みやこ	capital; suburbs of capital	畿

近畿	きんき	Kinki (region around Osaka, Kyoto, Nara)	34C
近	キン、ちか-い	near	34C
機	キ、はた	loom, device, occasion	機
芝刈り機	しばかりき	lawn mower	34C
芝*	しば	lawn, turf	34C
刈*	か-る	reap, cut, shear	34C

34D 付 ESSENCE

中		仕付	5 – 9
34D		しつけ	*

Government Sources Tacked an Affiliated Ticket of Decay

Originally person + hand, reach out and give something to someone 付

府	フ	government centre, urban prefecture	府
政府筋	せいふすじ	government sources	34D
政	セイ、ショウ、まつりごと	government	34D
筋	キン、すじ	muscle, sinew, thread	34D
付	フ、つ-ける、つ-く	attach, apply	付
仕付	しつけ	tacking, basting	34D
仕	シ、ジ、つか-える	serve, work, do	34D
附	フ	attach	附
附属	ふぞく	affiliated	34D
属	ゾク	belong, genus	34D
符	フ	tally, sign	符
切符	きっぷ	ticket	34D

切	セツ、サイ、き-る、き-れる	cut	34D
腐	フ、くさ-る、くさ-れる、くさ-らす	rot, decay, bad	腐
腐敗	ふはい	decay, rot	34D
敗	ハイ、やぶ-れる	defeat	34D

34E 康 ESSENCE

| 𠂹 | 健康体 | 2A1 |
| 34E | けんこうたい | * |

Healthy Bodies are Banal

Hands holding pestle pounding cereals 康

康	コウ	peace, health	康
健康体	けんこうたい	healthy body	34E
健	ケン、すこ-やか	healthy	34E
体	タイ、テイ、からだ	body	34E
庸	ヨウ	ordinary, work	庸
凡庸	ぼんよう	banality	34E
凡	ボン、ハン	mediocre, common, roughly, in general	34E

34F 漢 ESSENCE

| 𠂹 | 漢字 | 6H7 |
| 34F | かんじ | * |

Circumspect Chinese Characters Lament Troublesome Work with Narrow Margins

Originally Han river gleaming like a flaming arrow 漢

謹	キン、つつし-む	circumspect	謹
謹厳	きんげん	seriousness	34F
厳	ゲン、ゴン、おごそ-か、きび-しい	severe, strict, solemn	34F
漢	カン	Han China, man	漢
漢字	かんじ	kanji	34F
字	ジ、あざ	letter, symbol	34F
嘆	タン、なげ-く、なげ-かわしい	lament, admire	嘆
嘆息	たんそく	sigh	34F
息	ソク、いき	breath, rest, child	34F
難	ナン、かた-い、むずか-しい	difficult, trouble	難
難民	なんみん	refugees	34F
民	ミン、たみ	people, populace	34F
勤	キン、ゴン、つと-める、つと-まる	work, duties	勤
出勤	しゅっきん	attendance	34F
出	シュツ、スイ、で-る、だ-す	emerge, put out	34F
僅	キン、わず-か	a wee bit	僅
僅差	きんさ	narrow margin	34F
差	サ、さ-す	difference, thrust	34F

34G 要 ESSENCE

芇		重要	3－2
34G		じゅうよう	*

Changing Important Manners

Originally two hands holding a waist, middle part, pivot, essential

要

遷	セン	move, change, shift	遷
左遷	させん	demotion; degradation	34G
左	サ、ひだり	left	34G
要	ヨウ、い-る	need, vital, pivot	要
重要	じゅうよう	important	34G
重	ジュウ、チョウ、え、おも-い、かさ-ねる、かさ-なる	heavy, pile, -fold	34G
腰	ヨウ、こし	hip, lower back, bearing	腰
物腰	ものごし	manner	34G
物	ブツ、モツ、もの	thing	34G

Waste not want not. Weekdays 殺害 are on 割引 but also in 週末 convenient 抹殺 can be arranged. It is surprising how lethal some 芝刈り機 can be: the number of hapless garden enthusiasts in the 近畿 region who met with a sticky end is quite high. According to 政府筋 an ambiguous whiff of 腐敗 hangs over the entire gardening business. What could have been a 切符 to creating 健康体 ended up being a labour of many 嘆息 and frustratingly 僅差. Can anyone have any doubt how 重要 a flourishing human removal business could be? Time for a 左遷 to compost laddie!

35A 民 EXTRACTION

⊟	移民	3 - 4
35A	いみん	*

Migrants are Hibernating in the Lower House

Needle in the eye, blind, slave, lowly people, commoners 民

民	ミン、たみ	people, populace	民
移民	いみん	migrant	35A
移	イ、うつ-る、うつ-す	transfer, move	35A
眠	ミン、ねむ-る、ねむ-い	sleep, sleepy	眠
冬眠	とうみん	hibernation	35A
冬	トウ、ふゆ	winter	35A
衆	シュウ、シュ	multitude, populace	衆
衆院	しゅういん	Lower House of the Diet	35A
院	イン	institute	35A

35B 勢 EXTRACTION

	勢力	4A4
35B	せいりょく	*

Power prefers to show Skulls with Variety and Feeling

Kneeling to plant a tree 勢

勢	セイ、いきお-い	power, force	勢
勢力	せいりょく	power	35B
力	リョク、リキ、ちから	strength, effort	35B
蓋	ガイ、おお-う、かさ、けだ-し、ふた	cover; lid; flap	蓋
頭蓋骨	ずがいこつ	skull	35B
頭	トウ、ズ、ト、あたま、かしら	head, counter for large animals	35B
骨	コツ、ほね	bone, frame	35B
芸	ゲイ	art, skill, plant	芸
演芸会	えんげいかい	an entertainment, variety show	35B

演	エン	performance, play, presentation	35B
会	カイ、エ、あ-う	meet	35B
熱	ネツ、あつ-い	heat	熱
熱心	ねっしん	fervour	35B
心	シン、こころ	heart, feelings	35B

35C 銭 EXTRACTION

⊟		金銭	6 - 13
35C		きんせん	*

Be Practical and cast away on a Shallow Jetty the Small Change of Prescribed Regret

Halberd cutting bone 浅

践	セン	step, act	践
実践的	じっせんてき	practical	35C
実	ジツ、み、みの-る	(bear) fruit, truth, reality	35C
的	テキ、まと	target, like, adjectival suffix	35C
浅	セン、あさ-い	shallow, light	浅
浅薄	せんぱく	shallowness	35C
薄	ハク、うす-い、うす- める、うす-まる、うす-らく	thin, weak, shallow, light	35C
桟	サン	spar, beam, frame	桟
桟橋	さんばし	jetty	35C
橋	キョウ、はし	bridge	35C
銭	セン、ぜに	sen, coin, money	銭

225

金銭	きんせん	money	35C
金	キン、コン、かね、かな	gold, money, metal	35C
箋	セン、ふだ	paper; label; letter; composition	箋
処方箋	しょほうせん	prescription for medicine	35C
処	ショ	deal with, place	35C
方	ホウ、かた	side, way, square, direction, person	35C
残	ザン、のこ-る、のこ-す	leave, cruel, harm	残
残念	ざんねん	regret	35C
念	ネン	thought, concern	35C

35D 即 EXTRACTION

	即刻	2C
35D	そっこく	*

Delegate Immediately

Originally taking one's place at the table, food + person 即

節	セツ、セチ、ふし	section, joint, period, point, tune, restrain	節
使節	しせつ	envoy, mission, delegation	35D
使	シ、つか-う	use, servant	35D
即	ソク	immediate, namely, accession	即
即刻	そっこく	immediately	35D
刻	コク、きざ-む	chop, mince, engrave	35D

35E 暁 EXTRACTION

🔄	暁星	2E13
35E	ぎょうせい	1|5

The light nature of Venus Burns Up quite easily

Chinese only high, trebling of earth 暁

暁	ギョウ、あかつき	dawn, light, event	暁
暁星	ぎょうせい	Venus, rarity	35E
星	セイ、ショウ、ほし	star	35E
焼	ショウ、や-く、や-ける	burn, roast	焼
焼き尽くす	やきつくす	burn up, consume, reduce to ashes	35E
尽*	ジン、つ-くす、つ-きる、つ-かす	use up, exhaust	35E

35F 川 EXTRACTION

🔄	川床	8C2
35F	かわどこ	3|0

Admonitory Words in Response to Provincial Riverbed Right-wingers regarding Pilgrimage & Pulsating Procedures

Originally showing water flowing between two banks 川

訓	クン	instruct, advise	訓
訓言	くんげん	admonitory speech, words of admonition	35F
言	ゲン、ゴン、い-う、こと	word, say, speak	35F

酬	シュウ	reward, toast, reply	酬
応酬	おうしゅう	exchange; return; (2) reply; riposte	35F
応	オウ	respond, react	35F
州	シュウ、す	state, province	州
州境	しゅうきょう	state boundary; provincial boundary	35F
境	キョウ、ケイ、さかい	boundary, border	35F
川	セン、かわ	river	川
川床	かわどこ	riverbed	35F
床	ショウ、とこ、ゆか	bed, floor, alcove	35F
派	ハ	faction, send	派
右派	うは	rightist faction	35F
右*	ウ、ユウ、みぎ	right	35F
巡	ジュン、めぐ-る	go around	巡
巡礼	じゅんれい	pilgrim, pilgrimage	35F
礼	レイ、ライ	courtesy, salute, bow	35F
脈	ミャク	vein, pulse	脈
山脈	さんみゃく	mountain range	35F
山	サン、やま	mountain	35F
順	ジュン	sequence, compliance	順
手順	てじゅん	process; procedure; sequence; protocol	35F
手	シュ、て、た	hand	35F

35G 的 EXTRACTION

⇄	的外れ		4C4
35G	まとはずれ		*

A Fishy Promise of Hooch was Off the Mark

White, conspicuous and pictograph of a ladle/scoop, setting apart, target 的

釣	チョウ、つ-る	fish, lure, change	釣
釣り場	つりば	fishing spot	35G
場	ジョウ、ば	place	35G
約	ヤク	promise, summarise, approximately	約
約束	やくそく	promise	35G
束	ソク、たば	bundle, manage	35G
酌	シャク、く-む	serve wine, ladle, scoop, drink	酌
晩酌	ばんしゃく	nightcap	35G
晩	バン	evening, late	35G
的	テキ、まと	target, like, adjectival suffix	的
的外れ	まとはずれ	off the mark	35G
外	ガイ、ゲ、そと、ほか、はず-す、はず-れる	outside, other, undo	35G

Extension du domaine de la lutte. The 衆院 seem to think that 移民 have 頭蓋骨 that teem with 勢力 and 熱心. The honourable members pretend that straight off the 桟橋 they are in need of 処方箋 and 金銭. Surely this perception should be 即刻 rejected so let us 焼き尽くす this and utter 訓言 instead. It is better to have a 手順 of 応酬 combined with rational consideration. When it is agreed that these notions are 的外れ we could all congregate at a good 釣り場 and cap it off with plenty of 晩酌.

Chapter 6 Virgo

36A 兆 FERMENTATION

🔔	前兆	6-6
36A	ぜんちょう	*

A Trillion Springy Peaches Defy you to Look Away

Cracks appearing on a heated turtle shell, divination 兆

兆	チョウ、きざ-す、きざ-し	sign, omen, trillion	兆
前兆	ぜんちょう	omen	36A
前	ゼン、まえ	before, front	36A
跳	チョウ、は-ねる、と-ぶ	spring, jump, leap	跳
跳ね返る	はなかえる	rebound	36A
返	ヘン、かえ-す、かえ-る	return	36A
桃	トウ、もも	peach	桃
桃色	ももいろ	pink	36A
色	ショク、シキ、いろ	colour, sensuality	36A
挑	チョウ、いど-む	challenge, defy	挑
挑戦	ちょうせん	challenge	36A
戦	セン、いく-さ、たたか-う	fight, war	36A
眺	チョウ、なが-める	gaze, look	眺
眺め	ながめ	view	36A
逃	トウ、に-げる、に-がす、のが-す、のが-れる	escape, evade, miss	逃

逃げ道	にげみち		escape route	36A
道	ドウ、トウ、みち		way, road	36A

36B 陸 FERMENTATION

⎈	陸海空	2 - 2
36B	りくかいくう	*

Terrestrial, Maritime & Aerial Friendships

Hill and mound (Chinese only), land 陸

陸	リク	land	陸
陸海空	りくかいくう	land, sea and air	36B
海	カイ、うみ	sea	36B
空	クウ、そら、あ-く、あ-ける、から	sky, empty	36B
睦	ボク、むつ-む	intimate; friendly; harmonious	睦
親睦	しんぼく	friendship	36B
親	シン、おや、した-しい、した-しむ	intimate, parent	36B

36C 戒 FERMENTATION

⎈	戒行	2 - 1
36C	かいぎょう	*

The Apparatus of Penance; kai, kai

Two hands holding a halberd, threat, commanding, punishing 戒

械	カイ		device	械
器械	きかい		apparatus	36C

231

器	キ、うつわ	vessel, utensil, skill	36C
戒	カイ、いまし-める	command, admonish	戒
戒行	かいぎょう	penance	36C
行	コウ、ギョウ、アン、い-く、ゆ-く、おこな-う	go, conduct, column	36C

36D 鏡 FERMENTATION

| ⊕ | 望遠鏡 | 2 – 1 |
| 36D | ぼうえんきょう | * |

Telescopic Frontiers

Non general use character finish, sound + bent figure 境

鏡	キョウ、がかみ	mirror	鏡
望遠鏡	ぼうえんきょう	telescope	36D
望	ボウ、モウ、のぞ-む	wish, hope, gaze	36D
遠	エン、オン、とお-い	distant	36D
境	キョウ、ケイ、さかい	boundary, border	境
国境	こっきょう	frontier	36D
国	コク、くに	country, region	36D

36E 包 FERMENTATION

| ⊕ | 小包み | 6A18 |
| 36E | こづつみ | 0\|4 |

Parcelmouth's Frothing Fickleness prevented Spore and Gun from Hugging

Originally embryo in womb 包

包	ホウ、つつ-む	wrap, envelop	包
小包み	こづつみ	parcel	36E
小	ショウ、ちい-さい、こ、お	small	36E
泡	ホウ、あわ	froth, bubble, foam	泡
泡立つ	あわだつ	froth, bubble, foam	36E
立	リツ、リュウ、た-つ、た-てる	stand, rise, leave	36E
飽	ホウ、あ-きる、あ-かす	tire, satiate	飽
飽き性	あきしょう	fickleness	36E
性	セイ、ショウ	nature, sex	36E
胞	ホウ	placenta, womb	胞
胞子	ほうし	spore	36E
子	シ、ス、こ	child	36E
砲	ホウ	gun, cannon	砲
大砲	たいほう	gun, cannon	36E
大	ダイ、タイ、おお、おお-きい、おお-いに	big	36E
抱	ホウ、だ-く、いだ-く、かか-える	embrace, hug, hold	抱
抱擁	ほうよう	embrace	36E
擁*	ヨウ	embrace, protect	36E

36F 利 FERMENTATION

		利益	3C7

233

36F	りえき	*

Pear shaped Profit like a golden Diarrhea

Reaping the harvest, pouring forth 利

利	リ、き-く	profit, gain, effect	利
利益	りえき	profit	36F
益	エキ、やく	gain, profit, benefit	36F
梨	リ、なし	pear tree	梨
山梨県	やまなしけん	Yamanashi Prefecture	36F
山	サン、やま	mountain	36F
県	ケン	prefecture	36F
痢	リ	diarrhea	痢
下痢	げり	diarrhea	36F
下	カ、ゲ、した、しも、もと、さ-げる、さ-がる、くだ-る、くだ-す	base, under lower	36F

36G 観 FERMENTATION

☨	観光	4 - 14
36G	かんこう	5‖5

It is Advisable to Abandon Sightseeing as a Pleasure

Chinese only heron 観

勧	カン、すす-める	encourage, advise	勧
勧告	かんこく	advice	36G
告	コク、つ-げる	proclaim, inform	36G

権	ケン、ゴン	right, authority, balance	権
棄権	きけん	abstention	36G
棄*	キ	abandon, renounce	36G
観	カン	watch, observe	観
観光	かんこう	sightseeing	36G
光*	コウ、ひか-る、ひかり	light, shine	36G
歓	カン	rejoice, merry	歓
歓楽	かんらく	pleasure	36G
楽	ガク、ラク、たの-しい、たの-しむ	pleasure, music	36G

Versus the grunt people. Portentous 前兆 and grave 挑戦: it is best to look for an 逃げ道 when trying to flee from stifling 親睦 and infuriating clichés. (Unless there is a need for 戒行 of course) It would be a wonderful thing to have an 器械 like a 望遠鏡 to spot these linguistic abominations from far away. Truisms make one 泡立つ at the mouth and reach for one's 大砲 to blow them out of the water. The use of those platitudes brings no 利益. Stop that verbal 下痢 is excellent 勧告 that will hopefully make users 棄権 those dreadful bromides forever!

37A 量 FILTRATION

33	重量		2
37A	じゅうりょう		*

Provisions increase your Weight

Originally heavy sack left on the ground 量

糧	リョウ、ロウ、かて	provisions, food	糧
食糧	しょくりょう	provisions	37A

食	ショク、ジキ、く-う、く-らう、た-べる	food, eat	37A
量	リョウ、はか-る	measure, quantity	量
重量	じゅうりょう	weight	37A
重	ジュウ、チョウ、え、おも-い、かさ-ねる、かさ-なる	heavy, pile, -fold	37A

37B 倫 FILTRATION

33	絶倫	6B11
37B	ぜつりん の	*

There is no Debate that a Chariot Stockade is Peerless, according to that Two-volume Dictionary

Chinese only arrange, align neatly (bamboo tablets bound together) 倫

論	ロン	argument, opinion	論
討論	とうろん	debate, discussion	37B
討	トウ、う-つ	attack	37B
輪	リン、わ	wheel, hoop	輪
車輪	しゃりん	vehicle wheel	37B
車	シャ、くるま	vehicle, chariot	37B
柵	サク	stockade; fence; weir; entwine around	柵
鉄柵	てっさく	iron railing	37B
鉄	テツ	iron, steel	37B
倫	リン	principles, ethics	倫
絶倫	ぜつりん の	matchless; unequalled; peerless	37B

絶	ゼツ、た-える、た-やす、た-つ	cease, sever, end	37B
冊	サツ、サク	book, volume	冊
二冊	にさつ	two volumes	37B
二	ニ、ふた、ふた-つ	two	37B
典	テン	code, rule, precedent	典
辞典	じてん	dictionary	37B
辞	ジ、や-める	word, decline, leave	37B

37C 義 FILTRATION

33		意義	4 - 7
37C		いぎ	*

Don't stand on Ceremony, Sacrifice Righteous Discussions

Sheep (praiseworthy) + I, consider oneself praiseworthy 義

儀	ギ	ceremony, rule, case	儀
儀式	ぎしき	ceremony	37C
式	シキ	ceremony, form	37C
犠	ギ	sacrifice	犠
犠牲	ぎせい	sacrifice	37C
牲	セイ	sacrifice	37C
義	ギ	righteousness	義
意義	いぎ	significance	37C
意	イ	mind, thought, will	37C
議	ギ	discussion	議
議論	ぎろん	discussion	37C
論	ロン	argument, opinion	37C

37D 布 FILTRATION

33	絹布	6A2
37D	けんぷ	*

Silk Decoration is the Commanding Horror Story in our Printed Rag

Hand beating cloth 布

布	フ、ぬの	cloth, spread	布
絹布	けんぷ	silk	37D
絹	ケン、きぬ	silk	37D
飾	ショク、かざ-る	decorate	飾
飾り物	かざりもの	decoration	37D
物	ブツ、モツ、もの	thing	37D
帥	スイ	commander	帥
将帥	しょうすい	commander	37D
将	ショウ	command, about to	37D
怖	フ、こわ-い	fear, afraid	怖
恐怖小説	きょうふしょうせつ	horror story	37D
恐	キョウ、おそ-れる、おそ-ろしい	fear, awe	37D
小	ショウ、ちい-さい、こ、お	small	37D
説	セツ、ゼイ、と-く	preach, explain	37D
刷	サツ、す-る	print, rub	刷
印刷所	いんさつしょ	printery	37D
印	イン、しるし	seal, sign, symbol	37D
所	ショ、ところ	place, situation	37D
巾	キン、はば	towel; hanging scroll; width	巾

| 雑巾 | ぞうきん | house-cloth; dust cloth; cleaning rag | 37D |
| 雑 | ザツ、ゾウ | miscellany | 37D |

37E 告 FILTRATION

| **33** | 広告 | 3B7 |
| 37E | こうこく | * |

She was Reprimanded after engaging in some Cruel Reforestation

Variant growing plant, phonetic proffer, proffer from the mouth 告

告	コク、つ-げる	proclaim, inform	告
訓告	くんこく	reprimand; admonition	37E
訓	クン	instruct, advise	37E
酷	コク	severe, intense, cruel, harsh	酷
残酷	ざんこく	cruelty	37E
残	ザン、のこ-る、のこ-す	leave, cruel, harm	37E
造	ゾウ、つく-る	make, build	造
造林	ぞうりん	(re)forestation	37E
林	リン、はやし	woods, forest	37E

37F 失 FILTRATION

| **33** | 失業 | 5 – 4 |
| 37F | しつぎょう | * |

The Disease of Unemployment can be Systematically Triggered and Reshuffled

Originally lose by slipping from the hand 失

| 疾 | シツ | illness, swiftly | 疾 |

疾患	しっかん	disease	37F
患	カン、わずら-う	disease, afflicted	37F
失	シツ、うしな-う	lose	失
失業	しつぎょう	unemployment	37F
業	ギョウ、ゴウ、わざ	profession, deed, karma	37F
秩	チツ	order, stipend	秩
秩序	ちつじょ	order, system	37F
序	ジョ	beginning, order	37F
鉄	テツ	iron, steel	鉄
引き金	ひきがね	trigger, gunlock	37F
引	イン、ひ-く、ひ-ける	pull, draw	37F
迭	テツ	alternate, rotate	迭
更迭	こうてつ	reshuffle	37F
更	コウ、さら、ふ-ける、ふ-かす	anew, change, again, grow late	37F

37G 変 FILTRATION

33		変遷	5A17
37G		へんせん	0|1

In a Strange Harbour Barbarians showed us Love's Successors

Originally Chinese only tied together, phonetic reverse 変

変	ヘン、か-わる、か-える	change, strange	変
変遷	へんせん	changes, transition	37G
遷	セン	move, change, shift	37G
湾	ワン	bay, gulf	湾
港湾	こうわん	harbour	37G
港	コウ、みなと	harbour	37G

240

蛮	バン	barbarian	蛮
蛮人	ばんじん	barbarian	37G
人	ジン、ニン、ひと	person	37G
恋	レン、こ-う、こい、こい-しい	love, beloved	恋
恋愛	れんあい	love	37G
愛	アイ	love	37G
跡	セキ、あと	trace, remains	跡
跡継ぎ	あとつぎ	successor, heir	37G
継*	ケイ、つ-ぐ	inherit, follow, patch, join	37G

Controversial Dialectics, innit? Measuring one's argumentative 重量 should include 食糧 of an intellectual nature such as 辞典, the quality of 討論 and at least 二冊 on the art of winning 議論. The latter is not without 意義 as a good ad hominem argument works like a 雑巾 wiping away potential defeat. Unfair perhaps but it is better to dish out 恐怖小説 than to receive them. If Hansel loses his way in a 造林 of contradictions, then even Gretchen's 訓告 will have little effect. The 残酷 of a sharp reductio ad absurdum is like pulling the 引き鉄 of a verbal shotgun. A tried and tested 秩序 of dubious rhetorical tricks will subdue the dull 蛮人 debaters and will ensure that your linguistic paradoxes will reach a safe 港湾.

38A 争 FIRE

△		戦争	4C5
38A 並		せんそう	*

Energetic Purification is a Steam Whistle for War

Hand reaching down to take hold of someone and restrain 争

Original representation of vapours rising from cooked rice 気

気	キ 、ケ	spirit	気
気鋭	きえい	spirited, energetic	38A
鋭	エイ 、するど-い	sharp, keen	38A
浄	ジョウ	pure, clean	浄
浄化	じょうか	purification	38A
化	カ 、ケ 、ば-ける 、ば-かす	change, bewitch	38A
汽	キ	steam	汽
汽笛	きてき	steam whistle	38A
笛	テキ 、ふえ	flute, whistle	38A
争	ソウ 、あらそ-う	conflict, vie	争
戦争	せんそう	war	38A
戦	セン 、いく-さ 、たたか-う	fight, war	38A

38B 以 FIRE

△		以内	2 – 1
38B		いない	*

The giant Within must Resemble the dwarf without

Originally person behind a plough 以

以	イ	starting point, means, use, through, because	以
以内	いない	within	38B
内	ナイ 、ダイ 、うち	inside	38B
似	ジ 、に-る	resemble	似
類似	るいじ	resemblance	38B
類	ルイ	resemble, variety, sort	38B

38C 砕 FIRE

△	砕氷船	5D12
38C	さいひょうせん	0|2

Within Limits Sloshed Men of Taste ought to be Graduated on an Icebreaker

Marked clothing indicating slave or soldier 砕

枠	わく	frame	枠
枠内	わくない	within limits	38C
内	ナイ、ダイ、うち	inside	38C
酔	スイ、よ-う	drunk, dizzy	酔
酔払い	よっぱらい	drunkard	38C
払	フツ、はら-う	pay, sweep away, rid	38C
粋	スイ	pure, essence, style	粋
粋人	すいじん	man of taste	38C
人	ジン、ニン、ひと	person	38C
卒	ソツ	soldier, end	卒
卒業	そつぎょう	graduation	38C
業	ギョウ、ゴウ、わざ	profession, deed, karma	38C
砕	サイ、くだ-く、くだ-ける	break, smash	砕
砕氷船	さいひょうせん	icebreaker	38C
氷*	ヒョウ、こおり、ひ	ice, hail, freeze	38C
船	セン、ふね、ふな	boat, ship	38C

38D 博 FIRE

△	博物館	5 - 10

243

38D	はくぶつかん	*

Rugs and Hanging Name Registers are on display in the Museum of Frivolity

Spread, big, extensive 博

敷	フ、し-く	spread, lay	敷
敷き物	しきもの	rug	38D
物	ブツ、モツ、もの	thing	38D
縛	バク、しば-る	bind	縛
縛り首	しばりくび	hanging	38D
首	シュ、くび	head, neck, chief	38D
簿	ボ	register, record(s)	簿
名簿	めいぼ	(name) register	38D
名	メイ、ミョウ、な	name, fame	38D
博	ハク、バク	extensive, spread, gain, gamble	博
博物館	はくぶつかん	museum	38D
物	ブツ、モツ、もの	thing	38D
館	カン	large building, hall	38D
薄	ハク、うす-い、うす-める、うす-まる、うす-らく	thin, weak, shallow, light	薄
軽薄	けいはく	frivolity	38D
軽	ケイ、かる-い、かろ-やか	light, flippant	38D

38E 奴 FIRE

△	奴隷	3 - 6

38E		どれい	*

One should Endeavour to Enslave one's Rage

Woman, compliance, work 奴

努	ド、つと-める	endeavour, try	努
努めて	つとめて	to the best of one's ability	38E
奴	ド	slave, servant, guy	奴
奴隷	どれい	slave	38E
隷	レイ	slave, prisoner	38E
怒	ド、いか-る、おこ-る	anger, rage	怒
怒鳴る	どなる	shout, bawl	38E
鳴	メイ、な-く、な-る、な-らす	cry, chirp, bark	38E

38F 良 FIRE

▲		良心	6D8
38F		りょうしん	2|7

Drifters like Taro's Son-in-Law heard the Good News about the Picture Gallery in good Conscience

Originally sieve selecting the good 良

浪	ロウ	wave, drift, waste	浪
浪人	ろうにん	drifter	38F
人	ジン、ニン、ひと	person	38F
郎	ロウ	man, husband	郎
太郎	たろう	Taro (name)	38F
太	タイ、タ、ふと-い、ふと-る	fat, big	38F

娘	むすめ	daughter, girl, young woman	娘
娘婿	むすめむこ	son-in-law	38F
婿*	セイ、むこ	son-in-law	38F
朗	ロウ、ほが-らか	clear, fine, cheerful	朗
朗報	ろうほう	good news	38F
報	ホウ、むく-いる	report, reward	38F
廊	ロウ	walk way	廊
画廊	がろう	picture gallery	38F
画	ガ、カク	picture, stroke	38F
良	リョウ、よ-い	good	良
良心	りょうしん	conscience	38F
心	シン、こころ	heart, feelings	38F

38G 航 FIRE

△		航空		3A4
38G		こうくう		*

Coal Mines Protest the Flight

Non general use character high, originally lashing boats together in a straight line 航

坑	コウ	mine, pit, hole	坑
炭坑	たんこう	coal mine	38G
炭	タン、すみ	charcoal, coal	38G
抗	コウ	resist, oppose	抗
抗議	こうぎ	protest	38G
議	ギ	discussion	38G
航	コウ	sail, voyage	航

航空	こうくう	flight	38G
空	クウ、そら、あ-く、あ-ける、から	sky, empty	38G

Neunundneunzig Luftballons. 気鋭 promoters of 戦争 usually put up a 類似 of peace to justify the purchase of 砕氷船 that, with a bit of creative accounting, always are 枠内 of the budget. Martial 粋人 rarely feel the need to attend 博物館 highlighting glorious exploits of the past or to consider the fate of a 縛り首 generalissimo. They 怒鳴る and try 努めて to praise mediocre pieces that are on display in the cold war 画廊. Those armchair warriors have no 良心 and think that it is 朗報 when, despite strong 抗議, the 航空 of yet another generation of drones is immanent.

39A 夫 FIRST MATTER

▽	夫君	5B6
39A 並	ふくん	*

Saints Offer Extensive Support to hair-pinned Husbands

Originally big male with an ornamental hairpin (sign of adulthood) 夫
Formerly mouth and standing person: person giving a verbal statement, presenting a report 呈

聖	セイ	saint, sage, sacred	聖
聖人	せいじん	saint; sage; holy man	39A
人	ジン、ニン、ひと	person	39A
呈	テイ	present, offer	呈
献呈	けんてい	presentation; dedication	39A
献	ケン、コン	dedicate, present	39A

程	テイ、ほど	degree, extent	程
行程	こうてい	distance; path length	39A
行	コウ、ギョウ、アン、い-く、ゆ-く、おこな-う	go, conduct, column	39A
扶	フ	help, support	扶
公的扶助	こうてきふじょ	public assistance	39A
公	コウ、おおやけ	public, fair, lord	39A
的	テキ、まと	target, like, adjectival suffix	39A
助	ジョ、たす-ける、たす-かる、すけ	assist, help	39A
夫	フ、フウ、おっと	husband, man	夫
夫君	ふくん	one's husband	39A
君	クン、きみ	lord, you Mr	39A

39B 則 FIRST MATTER

▽	原則		3 – 3
39B	げんそく		*

The Left Side Principles are Hard to Fathom

Originally notches in a kettle, scale 則

側	ソク、かわ	side	側
左側	ひだりがわ	left side	39B
左	サ、ひだり	left	39B
則	ソク	rule, model, standard	則
原則	げんそく	principle	39B
原	ゲン、はら	plain, origin	39B

測	ソク、はか-る	measure, fathom	測
測り難い	はかりがたい	hard to fathom	39B
難	ナン、かた-い、むずか-しい	difficult, trouble	39B

39C 兵 FIRST MATTER

▽		兵器	2 - 2
39C		へいき	*

Soldiers on the Shores of mass distraction

Axe being held with both hands 兵

兵	ヘイ、ヒョウ	soldier	兵
兵器	へいき	weapon	39C
器	キ、うつわ	vessel, utensil, skill	39C
浜	ヒン、はま	beach, shore	浜
浜辺	はまべ	beach, shore	39C
辺	ヘン、あた-り、べ	vicinity, boundary	39C

39D 票 FIRST MATTER

▽		投票	3A8
39D		とうひょう	*

Standard Voting Drifts Ashore

Originally leaping tongues of flame 票

標	ヒョウ	sign (post), mark	標
標準	ひょうじゅん	standard	39D
準	ジュン	level, conform, quasi-	39D

票	ヒョウ		vote, label, sign	票
投票	とうひょう		voting	39D
投	トウ、な-げる		throw, cast	39D
漂	ヒョウ、ただよ-う		float, drift, bob	漂
漂着	ひょうちゃく		drift ashore	39D
着	チャク、ジャク、き-る、き-せる、つ-く、つ-ける		arrive, wear	39D

39E 愛 FIRST MATTER

▽		渇愛	2 - 2
39E		かつあい	*

Aimee Craves for Ambiguity

Previously enveloped heart, completely covered. (convoluted etymology) 愛

愛	アイ	love	愛
渇愛	かつあい	thirst; craving; desire	39E
渇	カツ、かわ-く	thirst, parched	39E
曖	アイ、かげ-る	dark; not clear	曖
曖昧	あいまい	vague; ambiguous; unclear	39E
昧	マイ、くら-い	dark; foolish	39E

39F 旧 FIRST MATTER

▽		旧式	7D21
39F		きゅうしき	*

The Slandered Old Style Rice Crop evacuated Sinking Children and Molars from the Lagoon

Originally crested bird with cry of 'kyuu', simplification 旧

毀	キ、こぼ.つ、こわ.す、こぼ.れる、こわ.れる、そし.る、やぶ.る	break; destroy; be ruined	毀
毀損	きそん	damage; injury; waste	39F
損	ソン、そこ-なう、そこ-ねる	loss, spoil, miss	39F
旧	キュウ	old, past	旧
旧式	きゅうしき	old style	39F
式	シキ	ceremony, form	39F
稲	トウ、いね、いな	rice (plant)	稲
稲作	いなさく	rice crop	39F
作	サク、サ、つく-る	make	39F
陥	カン、おちい-る、おとしい-れる	collapse	陥
陥落	かんらく	fall; sinking; surrender	39F
落	ラク、お-ちる、お-とす	fall, drop	39F
児	ジ、ニ	child	児
児童	じどう	children	39F
童	ドウ、わらべ	child	39F
臼	キュウ、うす	mortar	臼
臼歯	きゅうし	molar	39F
歯	シ、は	tooth	39F
潟	かた	beach, lagoon	潟
潟湖	せきこ	lagoon	39F
湖	コ、みずうみ	lake	39F

39G 采 FIRST MATTER

▽	喝采	4 - 1
39G	かっさい	*

Harvesting Colourful Vegetables to General Acclamation

Take/gather/pluck, hand + tree/shrub 采

採	サイ、と-る	take, gather	採
採取	さいしゅ	harvesting	39G
取	シュ、と-る	take control	39G
彩	サイ、いろど-る	colour	彩
色彩	しきさい	colouring	39G
色	ショク、シキ、いろ	colour, sensuality	39G
菜	サイ、な	vegetable, rape	菜
野菜	やさい	vegetables	39G
野	ヤ、の	moor, wild	39G
采	サイ、と-る	dice; form; appearance; take; colouring; general's baton	采
喝采	かっさい	applause; acclamation; ovation; cheers	39G
喝	カツ	shout, scold	39G

When upon life's billows you are tempest tossed. Not only unfortunate 夫君 but also 聖人 who have fallen on hard times are sometimes in need of a measure of 的扶助 when the 行程 to financial security is a little longer than anticipated. The 原則 of a social safety net are not 測り難い as these are powerful 兵器 in the fight against poverty. Haste to the place where the wretched refuse of the teeming 浜辺 have 漂着. Be not 曖昧 in your intentions and try to slake the burning 渇愛 of the huddled masses be they tired 児童 or dirt poor dwellers of some awful 潟湖. Give freely of your 野菜 and do not hold back offerings from your vats of organic sprouts: a sure way to general 喝采!

40A 別 FIXATION

♀	誘拐	2 – 2
40A	ゆうかい	*

The Crook Kidnapped someone Special

Variant of bone 別

拐	カイ	deceive, kidnap, bend	拐
誘拐	ゆうかい	abduction; kidnapping	40A
誘	ユウ、さそ-う	invite, tempt, lead	40A
別	ベツ、わか-れる	split, differ, special	別
特別	とくべつ	special	40A
特	トク	special	40A

40B 林 FIXATION

♀	林間	5F15
40B 並	りんかん	*

A Historical Almanac of Forests, Woods & Bamboo Groves

Ideograph of trees 林
Trail of rice plants in an ordered regularly spaced row 歴

歴	レキ	history	歴
歴史	れきし	history	40B
史	シ	history, chronicler	40B
暦	レキ、こよみ	calendar, almanac	暦
西暦	せいれき	Anno Domini	40B
西	セイ、サイ、にし	west	40B

林	リン、はやし	woods, forest	林
林間	りんかん	in the forest	40B
間	カン、ケン、あいだ、ま	space, gap	40B
森	シン、もり	woods	森
森閑	しんかん	silence	40B
閑	カン	leisure, quiet	40B
竹	チク、たけ	bamboo	竹
竹束	たけたば	bamboo bundle	40B
束	ソク、たば	bundle, manage	40B

40C 最 FIXATION

♀		最大		4A4
40C 並		さいだい		*

Subcontracting "Photografiest" Photography in the name of Friendship

Originally warrior's helmet, attack + take 最
Originally pictograph of the right hand, again is borrowed meaning 又

又	また	or again	又
又請け	またうけ	subcontract	40C
請	セイ、シン、こ-う、う-ける	request, undertake	40C
最	サイ、もっと-も	most, -est	最
最大	さいだい	biggest	40C
大	ダイ、タイ、おお、おお-きい、おお-いに	biggest	40C
撮	サツ、と-る	pluck, take	撮
撮影	さつえい	photography	40C

影	エイ、かげ	shadow, light, image	40C
友	ユウ、とも	friend	友
友交	ゆうこう	friendship, companionship	40C
交	コウ、まじ-わる、まじ-える、ま-じる、ま-ざる、ま-ぜる	mix, exchange	40C

40D 吉 FIXATION

| ☿ | 妥結 | 3A8 |
| 40D | だけつ | 0\|2 |

Full Good Luck Packets Agree with joyfulness

Originally double-lidded container, plenty, good fortune 吉

詰	キツ、つ-める、つ-まる、つ-む	pack, packed, full	詰
詰め込む	つめこむ	cram	40D
込	こ-む、こ-める	put in, be crowded	40D
吉	キチ、キツ	good luck, joy	吉
不吉	ふきつ	bad omen	40D
不	フ、ブ	not, un-, dis-	40D
結	ケツ、むす-ぶ、ゆ-う、ゆ-わえる	bind, join, end	結
妥結	だけつ	agreement	40D
妥*	ダ	peaceful, tranquil	40D

40E 参 FIXATION

♀	参加	2 - 19
40E	さんか	*

Heartful Participation in a Cruel Tragedy

Originally attractive woman, kneeling with three ornamental hairpins 参

参	サン、まい-る	attend, go, be in love, be at a loss, 3	参
参加	さんか	participation	40E
加	カ、くわ-える、くわ-わる	add, join	40E
惨	サン、ザン、みじ-め	cruel, miserable	惨
惨劇	さんげき	tragedy	40E
劇	ゲキ	drama, intense	40E

40F 弓 FIXATION

♀	弓道	5B11
40F 並	きゅうどう	*

Archy's Seething passions increased the Cost of Living and Tightened supply of Funeral Flowers

Pictograph of a bow 弓
Chinese only not and water binding being undone, disperse 沸

弓	キュウ、ゆみ	bow	弓
弓道	きゅうどう	archery	40F
道	ドウ、トウ、みち	way, road	40F
沸	フツ、わ-く、わ-かす	boil, gush	沸

沸き立つ	わきたつ		seethe	40F
立	リツ、リュウ、た-つ、た-てる		stand, rise, leave	40F
費	ヒ、ついや-す、ついえ-る		spend	費
生活費	せいかつひ		cost of living	40F
生	セイ、ショウ、い-きる、い-かす、い-ける、う-まれる、う-む		life, birth, grow	40F
活	カツ		activity, life	40F
引	イン、ひ-く、ひ-ける		pull, draw	引
引締め	ひきしめ		tightening	40F
締	テイ、し-まる、し-める		bind, tighten, close	40F
弔	チョウ、とむら-う		mourn, funeral	弔
弔花	ちょうか		funeral flowers	40F
花	カ、はな		flower, blossom	40F

40G 豚 FIXATION

♀		豚肉	7D17
40G		ぶたにく	0|1

Edgy Takarazuka Soldier Girls Fell One By One as they Attempted their big Porky act

Flesh and pig 豚

縁	エン、ふち		relation(s), ties, fate, edge	縁

縁起	えんぎ	omen	40G
起	キ、お-きる、お-こる、お-こす	arise, cause	40G
塚	つか	mound, tumulus	塚
宝塚	たからづか	Takarazuka	40G
宝	ホウ、たから	treasure	40G
隊	タイ	corps, unit	隊
兵隊	へいたい	soldier	40G
兵	ヘイ、ヒョウ	soldier	40G
墜	ツイ	fall	墜
墜落	ついらく	fall	40G
落	ラク、お-ちる、お-とす	fall, drop	40G
逐	チク	chase, pursue	逐
逐一	ちくいち	one by one	40G
一	イチ、イツ、ひと、ひと-つ	one	40G
遂	スイ、と-げる	attain, finally	遂
未遂	みすい の	attempted	40G
未	ミ	immature, not yet	40G
豚	トン、ぶた	pig, pork	豚
豚肉	ぶたにく	pork	40G
肉*	ニク	meat, flesh	40G

Nothing to do with Sabine women! The 誘拐 was well-prepared and undertaken by a 特別 team who caught the obnoxious French author unawares and intoxicated in a 林間 where 森閑 reigned. They also took his 竹束 that contained notes about his potentially 最大 novel and some poorly executed 撮影. It was also 詰め込む with packets of cigarettes so there was an 妥結 to not to turn it into a 惨劇 if the captive was willing to consider 参加. After some time the Frenchman started to complain about 生活費, how expensive

弔花 were nowadays and of course the ever present monetary 引締め. His captors definitively got edgy when he started to demand large quantities of 豚肉 and 未遂 to convince them that much more alcohol was required. They refused, however, to let him watch 宝塚 DVDs: the cads!

41A 牙 FLOWERS OF SATURN

牙	象牙の塔	4B4
41A	ぞうげのとう	*

In the Ivory Tower Elegant Buds of Wickedness precede flowers of evil

Former ngu character picturing interlocking fangs 牙

牙	ガ、ゲ、きば	tusk; fang	牙
象牙の塔	ぞうげのとう	ivory tower	41A
象	ショウ、ゾウ	elephant, image	41A
塔	トウ	tower, monument	41A
雅	ガ	elegance, 'taste'	雅
優雅	ゆうが	elegance	41A
優	ユウ、やさ-しい、すぐ-れる	superior, gentle, actor	41A
芽	ガ、め	bud, sprout, shoot	芽
芽生える	めばえる	bud, sprout	41A
生	セイ、ショウ、い-きる、い-かす、い-ける、う-まれる、う-む	life, birth, grow	41A

邪	ジャ		wickedness	邪
邪悪	じゃあく		wickedness	41A
悪	アク、オ、わる-い		bad, hate	41A

41B 折 FLOWERS OF SATURN

折		折衷	5 - 1
41B		せっちゅう	*

After the Diagnosis was Compromised, the Philosopher Pledged to die a Sudden Death

Originally chop down trees, longstanding miscopy 折

断	ダン、た-つ、ことわ-る	cut, decline, warn, judge, be decisive	断
診断	しんだん	diagnosis	41B
診	シン、み-る	diagnose, examine	41B
折	セツ、お-る、おり、お-れる	bend, break, occasion	折
折衷	せっちゅう	compromise	41B
衷	チュウ	inner feelings	41B
哲	テツ	wisdom	哲
哲学	てつがく	philosophy	41B
学	ガク、まな-ぶ	study	41B
誓	セイ、ちか-う	pledge, vow, oath	誓
誓約	せいやく	pledge	41B
約	ヤク	promise, summarise, approximately	41B
逝	セイ、ゆ-く	die, passion, death	逝
急逝	きゅうせい	sudden death	41B
急	キュウ、いそ-ぐ	hurry, emergency, sudden	41B

41C 侯 FLOWERS OF SATURN

15		侯爵	3 – 2
41C		こうしゃく	0‖2

Marquis de Sade Throatily enjoys the Climate

Originally meet, greet, target range or archery 侯

侯	コウ	marquis, lord	侯
侯爵	こうしゃく	marquis	41C
爵*	シャク	baron	41C
喉	コウ、のど	throat; voice	喉
咽喉	いんこう	throat	41C
咽	イン、エン、エツ、むせ.ぶ、むせ.る、のど、の.む	throat; choked; smothered; stuffy	41C
候	コウ、そうろう	weather, sign, ask, polite suffix, serve	候
季候	きこう	climate	41C
季*	キ	season	41C

41D 述 FLOWERS OF SATURN

15		述語	4 – 5
41D 並		じゅつご	*

Prepare Operation Predicate and Fill in the Forms

Originally entrance of a primitive dwelling 入
Originally hand with bits (of glutinous rice) sticking to it 述

込	こ-む、こ-める	put in, be crowded	込
仕込	しこみ	training, stocking up, preparation	41D

仕	シ、ジ、つか-える	serve, work, do	41D
術	ジュツ	means, technique	術
手術	しゅじゅつ	operation	41D
手	シュ、て、た	hand	41D
述	ジュツ、の-べる	state, relate	述
述語	じゅつご	predicate	41D
語	ゴ、かた-る、かた-らう	tell, speak, talk	41D
入	ニュウ、い-る、い-れる、はい-る	to get in, to go in, to come in	入
記入	きにゅう	entry, filling in forms	41D
記	キ、しる-す	account, chronicle	41D

41E 司 FLOWERS OF SATURN

㥮	司会者	6 - 8
41E	しかいしゃ	*

Breeding Verbs Visited the Heir of the Imperial Master of Ceremonies

Originally mirror image of anus, sedentary work? 司

飼	シ、か-う	rear animals	飼
羊飼い	ひつじかい	shepherd	41E
羊	ヨウ、ひつじ	sheep	41E
詞	シ	word, part of speech	詞
動詞	どうし	verb	41E
動	ドウ、うご-く、うご-かす	move	41E
伺	シ、うかが-う	visit, seek, ask, hear	伺
伺い事	うかがいごと	inquiry	41E

事	ジ、ズ、こと	thing, matter, act	41E
嗣	シ	heir, succeed to	嗣
嗣子	しし	heir	41E
子	シ、ス、こ	child	41E
后*	コウ	empress, behind, later	后*
太后	たいこう	empress dowager; queen mother	41E
太	タイ、タ、ふと-い、ふと-る	fat, big	41E
司	シ	administer, official	司
司会者	しかいしゃ	master of ceremonies	41E
会	カイ、エ、あ-う	meet	41E
者	シャ、もの	person	41E

41F 倹 FLOWERS OF SATURN

| 𠆢 | | 倹約 | 5E14 |
| 41F | | けんやく | * |

After a Frugal Experience, the Inspector Insured the Sword Dance

Originally two talking persons examining horses, discuss 倹

倹	ケン	thrifty, frugal	倹
倹約	けんやく	frugality	41F
約	ヤク	promise, summarise, approximately	41F
験	ケン、ゲン	examine	験
経験	けいけん	experience	41F
経	ケイ、キョウ、へ-る	pass, sutra, longitude	41F
検	ケン	investigate	検

検査員	けんさいん	inspector	41F
査	サ	investigate	41F
員	イン	member, official	41F
険	ケン、けわ-しい	steep, severe, perilous	険
保険	ほけん	insurance	41F
保	ホ、たも-つ	preserve, maintain	41F
剣	ケン、つるぎ	sword, bayonet	剣
剣舞	けんぶ	sword dance	41F
舞	ブ、ま-う、ま-い	dance, flit	41F

41G 倉 FLOWERS OF SATURN

忟	創造	2B7
41G	そうぞう	*

The Wounded Warehouse Suddenly Created Goods

Cover, preserving + door, that which is covered behind a door 倉

倉	ソウ、くら	warehouse, sudden	倉
倉荷	くらに	warehouse goods	41G
荷	カ、に	load, burden	41G
創	ソウ	start, wound	創
創造	そうぞう	creation	41G
造	ゾウ、つく-る	make, build	41G

Chambermaids and Libertines. Although 邪悪 can appear to have 優雅 this is neither a 哲学 of the boudoir nor a proper 診断 of Weltschmerz. The Divine 侯爵 rasped his 咽喉 and stated that strict 仕込 of the fair Juliette was in order: the 述語 can never be subject but 動詞 frequently transform a simple 羊飼い into a refined 司会者! Painful 経験 made Shamela the wicked creature that tried to seduce poor 検査員 Booby with lurid talk of adult 倉荷 and the 創造 of festivities during the 120 days of Sodom!

42A 復 FURNACE

⊟	復習	5 - 5
42A	ふくしゅう	*

Again I Revise my Personal History as I Cover my Belly

Chinese only go back, food Chinese only container of reversible shape + inversed foot 復

複	フク	double, again	複
複雑	ふくざつ	complexity	42A
雑	ザツ、ゾウ	miscellany	42A
復	フク	again, repeat	復
復習	ふくしゅう	revision	42A
習	シュウ、なら-う	learn, train	42A
履	リ、は-く	wear (feet), walk, footwear, act	履
履歴	りれき	personal history	42A
歴	レキ	history	42A
覆	フク、おお-う、くつがえ-す、くつがえ-る	overturn, cover	覆
転覆	てんぷく	overturn	42A
転	テン、ころ-がる、ころ-げる、ころ-がす、ころ-ぶ	rotate, roll, tumble	42A
腹	フク、はら	belly, guts	腹
腹立ち	はらだち	anger	42A
立	リツ、リュウ、た-つ、た-てる	stand, rise, leave	42A

42B 果 FURNACE

	果汁	6A7
42B	かじゅう	*

Candy Floss and Fruit Juice remained in the Lexicon after the Naked Section Head had Flown the Coop

Originally fruit on a tree, replaced by rice field, abundant crop, outcome 果

菓	カ	fruit, cake	菓
綿菓子	わたがし	candy floss	42B
綿	メン、わた	cotton, cotton wool	42B
子	シ、ス、こ	child	42B
果	カ、は-たす、は-てる、は-て	fruit, result, carry out	果
果汁	かじゅう	fruit juice	42B
汁	ジュウ、しる	juice, soup, liquid	42B
彙	イ、はりねずみ	same kind; classify	彙
語彙	ごい	vocabulary; lexicon; lexis; terminology	42B
語	ゴ、かた-る、かた-らう	tell, speak, talk	42B
裸	ラ、はだか	naked, bare	裸
裸身	らしん	nudity	42B
身	シン、み	body	42B
課	カ	section, lesson, levy	課
課長	かちょう	section head	42B
長	チョウ、なが-い	long, senior	42B
巣	ソウ、す	nest	巣
巣立つ	すだつ	leave nest	42B

| 立 | リツ、リュウ、た-つ、た-てる | stand, rise, leave | 42B |

42C 必 FURNACE

| | | 必然 | 5A4 |
| 42C | | ひつぜん の | * |

Dense Secretion of Nectar must Necessarily be Cherished

Originally halberd/lance between two poles (to prevent break) 必

密	ミツ	dense, secret	密
密度	みつど	density	42C
度	ド、ト、タク、たび	degree, times	42C
泌	ヒツ、ヒ	flow, secrete	泌
分泌	ぶんぴつ	secretion	42C
分	ブン、フン、ブ、わ-ける、わ-かれる、わ-かる、わ-かつ	divide, minute, understand	42C
蜜	ミツ	honey; nectar; molasses	蜜
蜂蜜	はちみつ	honey	42C
蜂	ホウ、はち	bee; wasp; hornet	42C
必	ヒツ、かなら-ず	necessarily	必
必然	ひつぜん の	inevitable	42C
然	ゼン、ネン	duly, thus, so, but	42C
秘	ヒ、ひ-める	(keep) secret	秘
秘蔵	ひぞう	treasure, cherish	42C
蔵	ゾウ、くら	storehouse, harbor	42C

267

42D 志 FURNACE

⊟⊷▭	意志	4 – 4
42D 並	いし	*

The Resolute Will is strong in the 10,000 Yen sun & steel Magazine

Pictograph of an extended finger 一
Emerging plant, movement of the heart, intent 志

一	イチ、イツ、ひと、ひと-つ	one	一
一筋	ひとすじ	one long straight object, earnest, resolute, intent	42D
筋	キン、すじ	muscle, sinew, thread	42D
志	シ、こころざ-す、こころざし	will, intent	志
意志	いし	will	42D
意	イ	mind, thought, will	42D
壱	イチ	one	壱
壱万円	いちまんえん	10,000 Yen	42D
万	マン、バン	ten thousand, myriad	42D
円	エン、まる-い	round, yen	42D
誌	シ	record, journal	誌
雑誌	ざっし	magazine	42D
雑	ザツ、ゾウ	miscellany	42D

42E 佳 FURNACE

⊟⊷▭	絶佳	7E18
42E	ぜっか	*

Bluffing Hangers-On Closed off the Country's Superb Horizontal Shopping Street

Non general use character edge/angle/jewel, raised earthen paths 佳

崖	ガイ、がけ	cliff; bluff; precipice	崖
断崖	だんがい	palisade; cliff	42E
断	ダン、た-つ、ことわ-る	cut, decline, warn, judge, be decisive	42E
掛	か-ける、か-かる、かかり	be connected, apply, hang, depend, cost	掛
掛かり人	かかりびと	hanger-on	42E
人	ジン、ニン、ひと	person	42E
封	フウ-ホウ	close off, fief	封
封鎖	ふうさ	blockade, freeze (assets)	42E
鎖	サ、くさり	close, shut, chain	42E
邦	ホウ	country, Japan	邦
連邦	れんぽう	commonwealth; federation of states	42E
連	レン、つら-なる、つら-ねる、つ-れる	accompany, row	42E
佳	カ	beautiful, good	佳
絶佳	ぜっか	superb	42E
絶	ゼツ、た-える、た-やす、た-つ	cease, sever, end	42E
涯	ガイ	shore, edge	涯
天涯	てんがい	horizon	42E
天	テン、あめ、あま	heaven, sky	42E
街	ガイ、カイ、まち	road, town, area	街
商店街	しょうてんがい	shopping street	42E
商	ショウ、あきな-う	trade, deal, sell	42E

269

店	テン、みせ	store, premises	42E

42F 加 FURNACE

[⊡]		添加	3G4
42F		てんか	*

Congratulations on the Additional Bookshelves

Add strength to an argument by adding one's own words 加

賀	ガ	congratulations	賀
年賀状	ねんがじょう	new year card	42F
年	ネン、とし	year	42F
状	ジョウ	condition, letter	42F
加	カ、くわ-える、くわ-わる	add, join	加
添加	てんか	addition	42F
添	テン、そ-える、そ-う	accompany, add	42F
架	カ、か-ける、か-かる	build, span, frame	架
書架	しょか	bookshelf	42F
書	ショ、か-く	write	42F

42G 胃 FURNACE

[⊡]		胃酸	3A12
42G		いさん	*

A Silky Spinal Cordial of Gastric Acid

Pictograph of the stomach and (underneath) flesh of the body 胃

絹	ケン、きぬ	silk	絹
絹布	けんぷ	silk; silk cloth	42G

布	フ、ぬの	cloth, spread	42G
脊	セキ、せ、せい	stature; height	脊
脊髄	せきずい	spinal cord	42G
髄	ズイ	marrow	42G
胃	イ	stomach	胃
胃酸	いさん	stomach acid; gastric acid	42G
酸	サン、す-い	acid, bitter	42G

Let's burn the midnight oil. Is your 腹立ち pure within the bewildering 複雑 of your feelings? No doubt that accurate 語彙 makes all the difference in highlighting the 裸身 and rawness of emotions. Don't indulge in sentimental 綿菓子 and refrain from 秘蔵 those 必然 conspiracy theories peddled in cheap 雑誌. Focus on the 意志 instead so that you may achieve your goals which are, as ever, just after the 天涯 and beyond the next 商店街. Cherish your 書架 and welcome the 添加 of new knowledge. It's better to wear the 絹布 skullcap of the learned than to suffer 胃酸 of the ignorant.

Chapter 7 Libra

43A 居 GLASS

古		住居		3A2
43A		じゅうきょ		*

We Sat Down and Made a Dwelling at the Base of a Mountain

Slumped figure and old, so staying immobile, in one place 居

据	す-える、す-わる	set, place, sit	据
据え付け	すえつけ	installation	43A
付	フ、つ-ける、つ-く	attach, apply	43A
居	キョ、い-る	be, reside	居
住居	じゅうきょ	dwelling	43A
住	ジュウ、す-む、す-まう	reside, live	43A
裾	キョ、すそ	cuff; hem; foot of mountain	裾
裾野	すその	foot or base of a mountain; foothills	43A
野	ヤ、の	moor, wild	43A

43B 臣 GLASS

古		大臣		4D7
43B		だいじん		*

The Pretty Princess punched a Seaside Minister in the Kidneys

Eye, wide eyed alertness, guard, servant, subject 臣

姫	ひめ	princess, lady, little, pretty	姫
姫宮	ひめみや	princess	43B
宮	キュウ、グウ、ク、みや	palace, shrine, prince	43B
臨	リン、のぞ-む	face, verge on, attend, command	臨
臨海	りんかい	seaside	43B
海	カイ、うみ	sea	43B
臣	シン、ジン	retainer, subject	臣
大臣	だいじん	minister	43B
大	ダイ、タイ、おお、おお-きい、おお-いに	big	43B
腎	ジン	kidney	腎
腎臓	じんぞう	kidney	43B
臓	ゾウ	entrails, viscera	43B

43C 勇 GLASS

古		蛮勇	2 - 1
43C		ばんゆう	*

Brutish Bravery Seethes Savagely

Originally expressing break through and strength 勇

勇	ユウ、いさ-む	courage; cheer up; be in high spirits; bravery; heroism	勇
蛮勇	ばんゆう	foolhardiness; recklessness; savage valour; brute courage	43C
蛮	バン	barbarian	43C
湧	ユウ、ヨウ、わ-く	boil; ferment; seethe; uproar; breed	湧

湧水	ゆうすい	spring water	43C
水	スイ、みず	water	43C

43D 易 GLASS

古		貿易	2A5
43D		ぼうえき	*

Easy Trade Bestows divine Boons

Originally big-eyed lizard + rays of the sun, iridescent, change 易

易	エキ、イ、やさ-しい	easy, change, divination	易
貿易	ぼうえき	trade	43D
貿	ボウ	trade, exchange	43D
賜	シ、たまわ-る	bestow	賜
賜物	たまもの*	gift, boon	43D
物	ブツ、モツ、もの	thing	43D

43E 妖 GLASS

古		妖精	5 - 4
43E		ようせい	*

Fertile Fairies Smilingly Dismissed Flowery Fellow Travelers

Originally referred to a type of thistle (bamboo + person with bowed head) 妖

沃	ヨウ、ヨク、オク、そそ.ぐ	fertility	沃
肥沃	ひよく	fertile	43E
肥	ヒ、こ-える、こえ、こ-やす、こ-やし	fatten, enrich	43E

妖	ヨウ、あや-しい、なまめ-く	attractive	妖
妖精	ようせい	fairy	43E
精	セイ、ショウ	spirit, vitality, refine, detail	43E
笑	ショウ、わら-う、え-む	laugh, smile	笑
笑殺	しょうさつ	laughing off; dismissing with a laugh	43E
殺	サツ、サイ、セツ、ころ-す	kill	43E
咲	さ-く	blossom	咲
咲き誇る	さきほこる	to be in fullness of bloom	43E
誇	コ、ほこ-る	proud, boast	43E
添	テン、そ-える、そ-う	accompany, add	添
添乗	てんじょう	accompanying; escorting	43E
乗	ジョウ、の-る、の-せる	ride, mount, load	43E

43F 尚 GLASS

古		高尚	8B19
43F		こうしょう	1|7

At that Time a Lofty Political Palm Compensated more than Conventional Dining Hall Praise

Originally smoke rising out of the window of a house, height 尚

当	トウ、あ-たる、あ-てる	apply, hit, mark, appropriate, this	当
当時	とうじ	at that time; in those days	43F

275

時	ジ、とき	time	43F
尚	ショウ	furthermore, esteem	尚
高尚	こうしょう	loftiness	43F
高	コウ、たか-い、たか、たか-まる、たか-める	tall, high, sum	43F
党	トウ	party, faction	党
政党	せいとう	political party	43F
政	セイ、ショウ、まつりごと	government	43F
掌	ショウ	control, palm(hand)	掌
掌中	しょうちゅう	in one's hand	43F
中	チュウ、なか	middle, inside, China	43F
償	ショウ、つぐな-う	recompense, redeem	償
弁償	べんしょう	compensation	43F
弁	ベン	speech, know, valve	43F
常	ジョウ、つね、とこ	usual, always	常
常例	じょうれい	convention	43F
例	レイ、たと-える	example, liken, precedent	43F
堂	ドウ	hall, temple	堂
食堂	しょくどう	dining hall	43F
食	ショク、ジキ、く-う、く-らう、た-べる	food, eat	43F
賞	ショウ	prize, praise	賞
賞賛	しょうさん	praise, admire	43F
賛*	サン	praise	43F

43G 窓 GLASS

古		窓口		2A3

43G	まどぐち	*

How much is the Total Amount for that grill in the Window?

Pictograph of a window with grille 窓

総	ソウ	whole, total	総
総額	そうがく	total amount	43G
額	ガク、ひたい	forehead	43G
窓	ソウ、まど	window	窓
窓口	まどぐち	window	43G
口	コウ、ク、くち	mouth, opening	43G

Desire makes everything blossom. What would be the best location for a Proustian 住居: at the 裾野 or at the 臨海? As far as the 腎臓 are concerned a setting with 湧水 would be most favourable. It would also be a 賜物 if some lovely 妖精 were to be found frolicking in the shadow of young girls 咲き誇る. Of course, it definitively needs to contain a sumptuous 食堂 where a select committee of culture vultures may heap 賞賛 on the charming and 高尚 host. In addition, a 窓口 of appearances should not be lacking where the aesthete like a pharaoh may receive the 総額 of public adoration.

44A 墓 GLUE OF THE WISE

	墓地	8A11
44A	ぼち	0‖4

Retina is Yearning for Evenings when Groping Recruits Desert Tents and Graveyards

Non general use character not, sun among many plants is setting, covered 墓

膜	マク	membrane	膜
網膜	もうまく	retina	44A

網*	モウ、あみ	net, network	44A
慕	ボ、した-う	yearn, adore, dear	慕
慕心	ぼしん	yearning	44A
心	シン、こころ	heart, feelings	44A
暮	ボ、く-れる、く-らす	live, sunset, end	暮
夕暮れ	ゆうぐれ	evening	44A
夕	セキ、ゆう	evening	44A
模	モ、ボ	copy, model, mould	模
模索	もさく	groping	44A
索	サク	rope, search	44A
募	ボ、つの-る	gather, raise, enlist, grow intense	募
募集	ぼしゅう	recruitment	44A
集*	シュウ、あつ-まる、あつ-める、つど-う	gather, collect	44A
漠	バク	vague, vast, desert	漠
砂漠	さばく	desert	44A
砂	サ、シャ、すな	sand, gravel, grain	44A
幕	マク、バク	curtain, tent, act	幕
天幕	てんまく	curtain, tent	44A
天	テン、あめ、あま	heaven, sky	44A
墓	ボ、はか	grave	墓
墓地	ぼち	graveyard	44A
地	チ、ジ	ground, land	44A

44B 亭 GLUE OF THE WISE

亭	料亭	2 - 1

44B	りょうてい	*

This Restaurant is famous for its Power Cuts

Simplification of tall, building + nail, phonetic stop/stay 亭

亭	テイ	pavilion, inn	亭
料亭	りょうてい	restaurant	44B
料	リョウ	materials, measure, charge	44B
停	テイ	stop	停
停電	ていでん	power cut	44B
電	デン	electricity	44B

44C 協 GLUE OF THE WISE

⑤	日本放送協会	3A1
44C	にっぽんほうそうきょうかい	*

Channel Ten might be Wacky, but I am Forced to say that I strongly prefer NHK

Trebling of strength and ten, expressing many; strength of many persons, cooperate 協

脇	キョウ、わき	armpit; the other way; another place; flank	脇
小脇	こわき	under one's arm; (in) the armpit	44C
小	ショウ、ちい-さい、こ、お	small	44C
脅	キョウ、おびや-かす、おど-す、おど-かす	threaten, coerce	脅
脅迫	きょうはく	threat; menace; coercion; terrorism	44C

279

迫	ハク、せま-る	press, draw near	44C
協	キョウ	cooperate	協
日本放送協会	にっぽんほうそうきょうかい； にほんほうそうきょうかい	Japan National Broadcasting Company; NHK	44C
日	ニチ、ジツ、ひ、か	sun, day	44C
本	ホン、もと	root, true, book, this	44C
放	ホウ、はな-す、はな-つ、はな-れる	release, emit	44C
送	ソウ、おく-る	send	44C
会	カイ、エ、あ-う	meet	44C

44D 属 GLUE OF THE WISE

⛎		付属		3A8
44D		ふぞく		*

The cultural Attaché Voiced Impure Sounds of Expectation

Variant of tail + ngu character caterpillar 属

属	ゾク	belong, genus	属
付属	ふぞく	attached	44D
付	フ、つ-ける、つ-く	attach, apply	44D
濁	ダク、にご-る、にご-す	impure, turbid, voiced	濁
濁音	だくおん	voiced sound	44D
音	オン、イン、おと、ね	sound	44D
嘱	ショク	request, entrust	嘱
嘱望	しょくぼう	expectation	44D
望	ボウ、モウ、のぞ-む	wish, hope, gaze	44D

44E 保 GLUE OF THE WISE

∽	保険	2 - 5
44E	ほけん	*

Your Reward is to be Insured

Originally mother carrying a child in a blanket 保

褒	ホウ、ほ-める	praise, reward	褒
褒美	ほうび	praise, reward	44E
美	ビ、うつく-しい	beautiful, fine	44E
保	ホ、たも-つ	preserve, maintain	保
保険	ほけん	insurance	44E
険	ケン、けわ-しい	steep, severe, perilous	44E

44F 責 GLUE OF THE WISE

∽	債権者	5A5
44F	さいけんしゃ	*

A Pickled Creditor Achieved to shift the Intended Blame

Taper, phonetic demand, money which can be demanded promptly 責

漬	つ-ける、つ-かる	pickle, soak	漬
漬物	つけもの	pickles	44F
物	ブツ、モツ、もの	thing	44F
債	サイ	debt, loan	債
債権者	さいけんしゃ	creditor	44F
権	ケン、ゴン	right, authority, balance	44F

者	シャ、もの	person	44F
績	セキ	achievement, spin	績
業績	ぎょうせき	achievement	44F
業	ギョウ、ゴウ、わざ	profession, deed, karma	44F
積	セキ、つ-む、つ-もる	product, pile	積
積もり	つもり	intention	44F
責	セキ、せ-める	liability, blame	責
自責	じせき	self-reproach	44F
自	ジ、シ、みずか-ら	self	44F

44G 俊 GLUE OFTHE WISE

𠆢	俊才	3D5
44G	しゅんさい	*

Dropping Acid Entices sheer Excellence

Chinese only linger/dawdle, stop/start + self and legs 俊

酸	サン、す-い	acid, bitter	酸
酸性	さんせい	acidity	44G
性	セイ、ショウ	nature, sex	44G
唆	サ、そそのか-す	entice, incite	唆
教唆	きょうさ	incitement	44G
教	キョウ、おし-える、おそ-わる	teach	44G
俊	シュン	excellence, genius	俊
俊才	しゅんさい	genius	44G
才	サイ	talent, year of age	44G

A pendulum between pain and boredom. There are sometimes
夕暮れ when the 慕心 to have dinner in a decent 料亭 becomes so

strong that it is like a culinary 脅迫. It almost feels as having an anthill 小脇: so many 嘱望 but so few 付属 reputable establishments! Are there then no 褒美 for the palate and is there no 保険 against insipid starchy fare? The lack of 業績 in the culture of taste and conviviality is disheartening and I may have to settle for some humble 漬物. At least its 酸性 is refreshing whilst the quest continues to find the hidden Kitchen Princess or elusive 俊才 of fine cuisine.

45A 犯 GOLD

✒		犯人	3 – 2
45A		はんにん	*

Inundation of Criminal Models

Pictograph of a slumped figure 犯

氾	ハン、ひろ.がる	spread out; wide	氾
氾濫	はんらん	overflowing; flood; inundation	45A
濫	ラン	flood, overdo, wanton	45A
犯	ハン、おか-す	crime, violate, commit, assault	犯
犯人	はんにん	criminal	45A
人	ジン、ニン、ひと	person	45A
範	ハン	model, norm, limits	範
軌範	きはん	model, example	45A
軌	キ	track, rut, way	45A

45B 片 GOLD

✒		片手	4 – 7
45B 並		かたて	*

The One Hand Publisher's Thesis Made Waves

Tree cut in half, thin piece 片
Formerly depicting an intricately patterned collar, (complex) writing 文

片	ヘン、かた	one side, piece	片
片手	かたて	one hand	45B
手	シュ、て、た	hand	45B
版	ハン	print, board	版
出版者	しゅっぱんしゃ	publisher	45B
出	シュツ、スイ、で-る、だ-す	emerge, putout	45B
者	シャ、もの	person	45B
文	ブン、モン、ふみ	writing, text	文
学位論文	がくいろんぶん	thesis, dissertation	45B
学	ガク、まな-ぶ	study	45B
位	イ、くらい	rank, extent	45B
論	ロン	argument, opinion	45B
紋	モン	(family) crest, pattern	紋
波紋	はもん	ripples, repercussions	45B
波	ハ、なみ	wave	45B

45C 那 GOLD

⌀		旦那		2C6
45C 並		だんな		*

Husbands are sometimes Rare commodities

Specially interwoven cloth, rare 希

City where furs where worn, ancient barbarian kingdom 那

那	ナ	what?	那
旦那	だんな	husband	45C
旦	タン	daybreak; dawn; morning	45C
希	キ	desire, hope for, rare	希
希少	きしょう	rare, scarce	45C
少	ショウ、すく-ない、すこ-し	a little, few	45C

45D 爆 GOLD

⌖	爆発	2A1
45D	ばくはつ	*

Tyrants Explode like fire

Expose rice to the sun 爆

暴	ボウ、バク、あば-く、あば-れる	violence, expose	暴
暴君	ぼうくん	tyrant	45D
君	クン、きみ	lord, you Mr	45D
爆	バク	burst, explode	爆
爆発	ばくはつ	explosion	45D
発	ハツ、ホツ	discharge, start, leave	45D

45E 悠 GOLD

⌖	悠然	4C6

45E 並	ゆうぜん		*

Each Item is to be Studied with a Calm heart on a cool Slab of Stone

Brushing specks of dirt off clothes, elegant 修
Formerly hand striking person with a stick and tree, something straight, line 条

条	ジョウ	clause, item, line	条
各条	かくじょう	each item, each clause	45E
各	カク、おのおの	each	45E
修	シュウ、シュ、おさ-める、おさ-まる	practice, master	修
修業	しゅうぎょう	study	45E
業	ギョウ、ゴウ、わざ	profession, deed, karma	45E
悠	ユウ	compose, distant, long time, ample	悠
悠然	ゆうぜん	calmly	45E
然	ゼン、ネン	duly, thus, so, but	45E
枚	マイ	sheet, counter	枚
一枚岩	いちまいいわ	monolith, large slab of rock	45E
一	イチ、イツ、ひと、ひと-つ	one	45E
岩	ガン、いわ	rock, crag	45E

45F 貫 GOLD

⌀	貫通	2 - 1
45F	かんつう	*

Heart-piercing Customary Penetration

Originally two shells/units of money threaded on a string 貫

慣	カン、な-れる、な-らす	become used to	慣
習慣	しゅうかん	habit, custom	45F
習	シュウ、なら-う	learn, train	45F
貫	カン、つらぬ-く	pierce	貫
貫通	かんつう	penetration	45F
通	ツウ、ツ、とお-る、とお-す、かよ-う	pass, way, commute	45F

45G 妊 GOLD

⌀	妊婦	4A10
45G	にんぷ	*

Lusty made an Appointment to collect the Rent from a Pregnant Woman

Person + spindle, burden borne by a person, duty 任

淫	イン、ひた.す、ほしいまま、みだ.ら、みだ.れる、みだり	lewdness; licentiousness	淫
淫欲	いんよく	lust	45G
欲	ヨク、ほっ-する、ほ-しい	greed, desire	45G
任	ニン、まか-せる、まか-す	duty, entrust	任
任命	にんめい	appointment	45G
命	メイ、ミョウ、いのち	life, order	45G
賃	チン	wages, fee	賃
家賃	やちん	rent	45G
家	カ、ケ、いえ、や	house, specialist	45G
妊	ニン	pregnant, swollen	妊

妊婦	にんぷ	pregnant woman	45G
婦	フ	woman, wife	45G

Who's a clever tyrant? "Après nous le 氾濫" is an appropriate 軌範 of how to cope verbally with a major disaster and it's unfortunate 波紋. On the 片手 an ordinary 旦那 can try to formulate a bon mot but on the other hand it would be fair to say that 暴君 often have better lines. They arguably might have more time for 修業 and would be able to 悠然 devote themselves to more interesting pursuits. Still, to have a 習慣 of delivering witty retorts combined with a 淫欲 for life trumps any 任命 with a teacher of rhetoric (or with his 妊婦).

46A 示 GRADE OF FIRE

示 (drawn)	宗教	5F8
46A	しゅうきょう	1‖3

Nothing Remains Displayed in this Lofty Nara Religion

Altar with drops of blood/wine 示

踪	ソウ、ショウ、あと	remains; clue; footprint	踪
失踪	しっそう	disappearance	46A
失	シツ、うしな-う	lose	46A
示	ジ、シ、しめ-す	show	示
展示	てんじ	display	46A
展*	テン	unfold	46A
崇	スウ	lofty, noble, revere	崇
崇拝	すうはい	worship	46A
拝*	ハイ、おが-む	worship, respectful	46A
奈	ナ、いかん	nara; what?	奈
奈良県	ならけん	Nara Prefecture (Kinki area)	46A

良	リョウ、よ-い	good	46A
県	ケン	prefecture	46A
宗	シュウ、ソウ	religion, main	宗
宗教	しゅうきょう	religion	46A
教	キョウ、おし-える、おそ-わる	teach	46A

46B 築 GRADE OF FIRE

	建築	2A3
46B	けんちく	*

Build your Fear on a tree top

Hand striking instrument 築

築	チク、きず-く	build	築
建築	けんちく	building	46B
建	ケン、コン、た-てる、た-つ	build, erect	46B
恐	キョウ、おそ-れる、おそ-ろしい	fear, awe	恐
恐怖	きょうふ	fear	46B
怖	フ、こわ-い	fear, afraid	46B

46C 矛 GRADE OF FIRE

	矛先	4A8
46C	ほこさき	*

In the Morning Mist he Dutifully performed Judo and practised with a Spear point

Barbed lance 矛

霧	ム、きり		mist, fog	霧

289

朝霧	あさぎり	morning mist	46C
朝	チョウ、あさ	court, morning	46C
務	ム、つと-める	(perform) duty	務
義務	ぎむ	duty	46C
義	ギ	righteousness	46C
柔	ジュウ、ニュウ、やわ-らか、やわ-らかい	soft, gentle, weak	柔
柔道	じゅうどう	judo	46C
道	ドウ、トウ、みち	way, road	46C
矛	ム、ほこ	halberd, lance, spear	矛
矛先	ほこさき	spear point	46C
先	セン、さき	previous, precede, tip	46C

46D 鳥 GRADE OF FIRE

| 𠂤 | | 候鳥 | 4C11 |
| 46D 並 | | こうちょう | * |

Birds of Passage Prepare and Ratify their Mating Calls

Pictograph of a bird 鳥
Chinese only hawk, phonetic level, possibly settled on a level 准

鳥	チョウ、とり	bird	鳥
候鳥	こうちょう	bird of passage, migratory bird	46D
候	コウ、そうろう	weather, sign, ask, polite suffix, serve	46D
準	ジュン	level, conform, quasi-	準
準備	じゅんび	preparation	46D

備	ビ、そな- える、そな-わる	equip, prepare	46D
准	ジュン	quasi-, conform, permit	准
批准	ひじゅん	ratification	46D
批	ヒ	criticise, strike, pass	46D
鳴	メイ、な-く、な- る、な-らす	cry, chirp, bark	鳴
求愛鳴き	きゅうあいなき	mating call	46D
求	キュウ、もと-める	request, seek	46D
愛	アイ	love	46D

46E 渦 GRADE OF FIRE

| 🌀 | 渦巻き | 4A4 |
| 46E | うずまき | * |

The Root of Evil is a Vortex of Errors swirling in a Cauldron

Bone/vertebrae, flexibility, ease of movement 渦

禍	カ	calamity	禍
禍根	かこん	root of evil	46E
根	コン、ね	root, base	46E
渦	カ、うず	whirlpool, eddy	渦
渦巻き	うずまき	eddy, vortex	46E
巻	カン、ま-く、ま-き	roll, reel, volume	46E
過	カ、す-ぎる、す-ごす、 あやま-つ、あやま-ち	pass, exceed, error	過
言い過ぎ	いいすぎ	exaggeration	46E
言	ゲン、ゴン、い-う、こと	word, say, speak	46E
鍋	カ、なべ	pot; pan; kettle	鍋

291

大鍋	おおなべ	cauldron	46E
大	ダイ、タイ、おお、おお-きい、おお-いに	big	46E

46F 輸 GRADE OF FIRE

	輸出	4
46F	ゆしゅつ	*

Cure the Instructor by Exporting Pleasure

Chinese only affirmation, originally convey, boat + cap off, phonetic transfer 輸

癒	ユ	cure, heal, vent	癒
治癒	ちゆ	cure	46F
治	ジ、チ、おさ-める、おさ-まる、なお-る、なお-す	govern, rule, cure	46F
諭	ユ、さと-す	instruct, admonish	諭
教諭	きょうゆ	instructor	46F
教	キョウ、おし-える、おそ-わる	teach	46F
輸	ユ	transport, send	輸
輸出	ゆしゅつ	export	46F
出	シュツ、スイ、で-る、だ-す	emerge, putout	46F
愉	ユ	joy, pleasure	愉
愉快	ゆかい	pleasure	46F
快	カイ、こころよ-い	pleasant, cheerful	46F

46G 能 GRADE OF FIRE

𠃌	大熊座	4 - 2
46G	おおぐまざ	0|1

Ursa Major shows an Efficient Attitude of Dismissal

Pictograph of a bear, ability "abearability" 能

熊	ユウ、くま	bear	熊
大熊座	おおぐまざ	Ursa Major (constellation)	46G
大	ダイ、タイ、おお、おお- きい、おお-いに	big	46G
座	ザ、すわ-る	seat, sit, gather	46G
能	ノウ	ability, can, Noh	能
能率	のうりつ	efficiency	46G
率*	ソツ、リツ、ひき-いる	rate, command	46G
態	タイ	appearance, intent	態
態度	たいど	attitude	46G
度	ド、ト、タク、たび	degree, times	46G
罷	ヒ	cease, leave, go	罷
罷免	ひめん	dismissal	46G
免	メン、まぬか-れる	escape, avoid	46G

Of murky midnight ride the air sublime. The 失踪 of a 宗教 based on 恐怖 resembles the 朝霧 gradually dissipating under the rays of the rising sun: the 矛先 of reason revoking the 求愛鳴き of the ominous 候鳥? The chthonic 大鍋 as the equivalent of the 禍根 and dark 愉快 that is to find a 治癒 through the 能率 and rational 態度 of the Olympians? Such a 罷免 of the dreaded left path is premature. Defy Persephone and her witches at your own risk!

47A 禁 GRANATE

禁煙	2 - 1
47A	きんえん	*

The Nape of the Neck appeals to Non-Smokers

Altar + forest phonetic. Abstain, abstain for religious reasons 禁

襟	キン、えり	collar, neck, heart	襟
襟首	えりくび	nape of the neck	47A
首	シュ、くび	head, neck, chief	47A
禁	キン	ban, forbid	禁
禁煙	きんえん	no smoking	47A
煙	エン、けむ-る、けむり、けむ-い	smoke	47A

47B 制 GRANATE

規制	2 - 1
47B	きせい	2|0

Made in Systematic Japan

Originally prune a tree, order 制

製	セイ	manufacture	製
日本製	にほんせい	made in Japan	47B
日	ニチ、ジツ、ひ、か	sun, day	47B
本	ホン、もと	root, true, book, this	47B
制	セイ	system, control	制
規制	きせい	regulation, control	47B
規*	キ	standard, measure	47B

47C 武 GRANATE

	武者	5A8
47C 並	むしゃ	*

Two Virtuous Warriors offered Twenty Monthly Payments

Two fingers 二
Advance on foot with a halberd 武

二	ニ、ふた、ふた-つ	two	二
無二	むに	peerless, matchless	47C
無	ム、ブ、な-い	not, non, cease to be	47C
仁	ジン、ニ	virtue, benevolence, man	仁
仁者	じんしゃ	man of virtue, humanitarian	47C
者	シャ、もの	person	47C
武	ブ、ム	military, warrior	武
武者	むしゃ	warrior	47C
者	シャ、もの	person	47C
弐	ニ	two	弐
弐拾	にじゅう	twenty	47C
拾	シュウ、ジュウ、ひろ-う	pickup, gather, ten	47C
賦	フ	levy, tribute, ode	賦
月賦	げっぷ	monthly payment	47C
月	ゲツ、ガツ、つき	moon	47C

47D 余 GRANATE

	余暇	7A4
47D	よか	2|6

295

On the Slope of a Slowly Cleansed Future Nondescript Lacquering is Leisurely falling over

Cover + wooden cross frame, roomy ample 余

斜	シャ、なな-め	slanting, diagonal	斜
傾斜	けいしゃ	inclination, slant, slope	47D
傾	ケイ、かたむ-く、かたむ-ける	incline, dedicate	47D
徐	ジョ	slowly, gradually	徐
徐々に	じょじょに	slowly	47D
除	ジョ、ジ、のぞ-く	exclude, remove	除
掃除	そうじ	cleaning	47D
掃	ソウ、は-く	sweep	47D
途	ト	road, way	途
前途	ぜんと	future	47D
前	ゼン、まえ	before, front	47D
叙	ジョ	describe, confer	叙
叙術	じょじゅつ	description	47D
術	ジュツ	means, technique	47D
塗	ト、ぬ-る	plaster, coat, paint	塗
漆塗り	うるしぬり	lacquering	47D
漆	シツ、うるし	lacquer, varnish	47D
余	ヨ、あま-る、あま-す	excess, ample, I	余
余暇	よか	leisure	47D
暇*	カ、ひま	leisure, free time	47D

47E 舎 GRANATE

击	田舎	2 - 1
47E	いなか*	*

Abandoned Countryside

Originally mouth/breathe + ample, easily, relax 舎

捨	シャ、す-てる	abandon	捨
捨て子	すてご	foundling	47E
子	シ、ス、こ	child	47E
舎	シャ	house, quarters	舎
田舎	いなか*	countryside	47E
田	デン、た	rice field	47E

47F 識 GRANATE

击	常識	3 - 2
47F	じょうしき	*

It's Common Sense to let Staff wear Textiles

The marker that produces words, intelligence, knowledge 識

識	シキ	knowledge	識
常識	じょうしき	common sense	47F
常	ジョウ、つね、とこ	usual, always	47F
職	ショク	employment, job	職
職員	しょくいん	staff	47F
員	イン	member, official	47F
織	ショク、シキ、お-る	weave	織
織物	おりもの	textiles	47F
物	ブツ、モツ、もの	thing	47F

47G 屯 GRANATE

𠦊	屯営	4A4
47G	とんえい	*

In the Orderly Barracks Stupidity reaps Pure Profit

Originally sprouting plant + bud 屯

頓	トン、とみ-に	suddenly; immediately; in a hurry	頓
整頓	せいとん	orderliness; tidying up; arranging neatly	47G
整	セイ、ととの-える、ととの-う	arrange	47G
屯	トン	barracks, camp, post	屯
屯営	とんえい	barracks	47G
営	エイ、いとな-む	conduct, barracks	47G
鈍	ドン、にぶ-い、にぶ-る	blunt, dull	鈍
鈍才	どんさい	stupidity	47G
才	サイ	talent, year of age	47G
純	ジュン	pure	純
純益	じゅんえき	pure profit	47G
益	エキ、やく	gain, profit, benefit	47G

Demise of the fleshpots. No drinking, 禁煙, no revealing parts other than the 襟首: surely all this 規制 is going too far. Where can a 仁者 find some entertainment around here? There are more than 弐拾 venues but they seem to be of the 無二 organic sprouts variety. The 掃除 of this once thriving district defies 叙述 and in the 前途 there will be instead only little 漆塗り shops left. There probably is more fun in the 田舎 where 常識 prevails in those matters and were well-trained 職員 are available. The recently created 整頓 of this place is dismaying and I blame it all on the 鈍才 of those righteous city councillors!

48A 因 GUM

🔧G	因果関係	4 – 3
48A	いんがかんけい	*

Deglutition of Kindness can Cause Marriage

Big man + enclosure, prisoner, cause of imprisonment? 因

咽	イン、エン、エツ、むせ.ぶ、むせ.る、のど、の.む	throat; choked	咽
咽下	えんげ; えんか	swallowing; deglutition	48A
下	カ、ゲ、した、しも、もと、さ-げる、さ-がる、くだ-る、くだ-す	base, under, lower	48A
恩	オン	favour, kindness	恩
恩返し	おんがえし	return favour	48A
返	ヘン、かえ-す、かえ-る	return	48A
因	イン、よ-る	cause, be based on, depend on	因
因果関係	いんがかんけい	cause-and-effect	48A
果	カ、は-たす、は-てる、は-て	fruit, result, carry out	48A
関	カン、せき	connection	48A
係	ケイ、かか-る、かかり	involvement	48A
姻	イン	marriage	姻
婚姻	こんいん	marriage	48A

| 婚 | コン | | marriage | 48A |

48B 耕 GUM

⛏G		耕作	5F14
48B 並		こうさく	*

Farming Feeble Minded Cattle on a Station can be a Criminal Case

Chinese only plough, or serrated wood 耕
Pictograph of a cow's head and horns 牛

耕	コウ、たがや-す	till, plough	耕
耕作	こうさく	farming	48B
作	サク、サ、つく-る	make	48B
耗	モウ、コウ	waste, decrease	耗
心神耗弱	しんしんもうじゃく	feeble minded	48B
心	シン、こころ	heart, feelings	48B
神	シン、ジン、かみ、かん、こう	god, spirit	48B
弱	ジャク、よわ-い、よわ-る、よわ-まる、よわ-める	weak	48B
牛	ギュウ、うし	cow	牛
牛舎	ぎゅうしゃ	cow shed; cattle barn	48B
舎	シャ	house, quarters	48B
牧	ボク、まき	pasture	牧
牧場	ぼくじょう	station, farm, ranch	48B
場	ジョウ、ば	place	48B

件	ケン	affair, case, matter	件
刑事事件	けいじじけん	criminal case	48B
刑	ケイ	punish	48B
事	ジ、ズ、こと	thing, matter, act	48B

48C 偉 GUM

🔗		偉人	5B4
48C		いじん	*

A Different Southern Latitude Kan give you Greater Hygiene

Chinese only leather/hide, originally patrol, move all around 偉

違	イ、ちが-う、ちが-える	differ	違
相違	そうい	difference	48C
相	ソウ、ショウ、あい	mutual, minister, aspect	48C
緯	イ	horizontal, weft	緯
緯度	いど	latitude	48C
度	ド、ト、タク、たび	degree, times	48C
韓	カン	Korea	韓
韓国	かんこく	South Korea	48C
国	コク、くに	country, region	48C
偉	イ、えら-い	great, grand	偉

偉人	いじん	hero, prodigy	48C
人	ジン、ニン、ひと	person	48C
衛	エイ	guard, protect	衛
衛生	えいせい	hygiene	48C
生	セイ、ショウ、い-きる、い-かす、い-ける、う-まれる、う-む	life, birth, grow	48C

48D 曽 GUM

🔔G	僧院	6G2
48D	そういん	*

Increasingly, Lower Ranked Priests Started to Hate Donations from unpleasant Great-Grandmothers

Originally build up, steam from a rice cooker 曽

増	ゾウ、ま-す、ふ-える、ふ-やす	increase, build up	増
増大	ぞうだい	increase	48D
大	ダイ、タイ、おお、おお-きい、おお-いに	big	48D
層	ソウ	stratum, layer	層
下層	かそう	lower classes	48D
下	カ、ゲ、した、しも、もと、さ-げる、さ-がる、くだ-る、くだ-す	base, under, lower	48D
僧	ソウ	priest	僧
僧院	そういん	monastery, temple	48D
院	イン	institute	48D

憎	ゾウ、にく-む、にく-い、にく-らしい、にく-しみ	hate(ful)	憎
憎悪	ぞうお	malice, hatred	48D
悪	アク、オ、わる-い	bad, hate	48D
贈	ゾウ、ソウ、おく-る	present, give	贈
寄贈	きぞう	donation	48D
寄	キ、よ-る、よ-せる	draw near, send, visit	48D
曽	ソ、ソウ、かつ-て、すなわ-ち	formerly; once; before	曽
曽祖母	そうそぼ	great-grandmother	48D
祖	ソ	ancestor	48D
母	ボ、はは	mother	48D

48E 綿 GUM

♪G	綿雪	2 - 3
48E	わたゆき	*

The Woodblock Print featured Large Snowflakes

White, threads, and cloth/cotton 綿

錦	キン、にしき	brocade	錦
錦絵	にしきえ	coloured woodblock print	48E
絵	カイ、エ	picture	48E
綿	メン、わた	cotton, cotton wool	綿
綿雪	わたゆき	large snowflakes	48E
雪	セツ、ゆき	snow	48E

48F 句 GUM

🔗G	文句	7E18
48F	もんく	*

In the Last Part of the Month the complaining Chrysanthemum was seized, held in Custody and Dutifully "Clogged" to Death

Mouth + cover/wrap/encircle, intertwining words, phrase 句

句	ジュン	ten-day period	句
下旬	げじゅん	last part of month	48F
下	カ、ゲ、した、しも、もと、さ-げる、さ-がる、くだ-る、くだ-す	base, under, lower	48F
句	ク	phrase, clause	句
文句	もんく	words, complaint	48F
文	ブン、モン、ふみ	writing, text	48F
菊	キク	chrysanthemum	菊
残菊	ざんぎく	late chrysanthemums	48F
残	ザン、のこ-る、のこ-す	leave, cruel, harm	48F
拘	コウ	seize, adhere to	拘
拘引	こういん	arrest, custody	48F
引	イン、ひ-く、ひ-ける	pull, draw	48F
勾	コウ、かぎ	be bent; slope; capture	勾
勾引	こういん	arrest; custody; abduction	48F
引	イン、ひ-く、ひ-ける	pull, draw	48F
駒	ク、こま	pony; horse; pawn (chess)	駒
駒下駄	こまげた	wooden clogs; komageta	48F

下	カ、ゲ、した、しも、もと、さ-げる、さ-がる、くだ-る、くだ-す	base, under, lower	48F
駄	ダ	pack-horse, poor quality	48F
殉	ジュン	dutiful death	殉
殉死	じゅんし	dutiful death	48F
死	シ、し-ぬ	death	48F

48G 逆 GUM

ゐ_G	遡行	5B7
48G	そこう	*

Going against the Current, the Treacherous Model Rejected the charges and Boycotted the Lawsuit

From inverted variant of big man, opposite normal, going backwards 逆

遡	ソ、さかのぼ-る	go upstream; retrace the past	遡
遡行	そこう	going upstream	48G
行	コウ、ギョウ、アン、い-く、ゆ-く、おこな-う	go, conduct, column	48G
逆	ギャク、さか、さか-らう	reverse, oppose	逆
反逆	はんぎゃく	treason	48G
反	ハン、ホン、タン、そ-る、そ-らす	oppose, anti, reverse	48G
塑	ソ	model, figurine	塑
塑像	そぞう	figure, figurine	48G
像	ゾウ	image	48G
斥	セキ	repel, reject	斥

排斥	はいせき	boycott	48G
排	ハイ	reject, expel, push, anti-	48G
訴	ソ、うった-える	sue, appeal	訴
訴訟事件	そしょうじけん	lawsuit	48G
訟	ショウ	accuse, sue	48G
事	ジ、ズ、こと	thing, matter, act	48G
件	ケン	affair, case, matter	48G

Stiff upper lip in the face of adversity. When Candide 恩返し by entering into a 婚姻 of convenience with the 心神耗弱 Cunegonde he decided to go into 耕作 and experience the 相違 between "Ein 偉人 Leben" and the mental 衛生 of hard work. To make amends for his colourful past there was going to be an 増大 of 寄贈 to the 下層 and the start of a series of 錦絵. It would show the tale of his 勾引 in the 下旬 and the spectacular escape on 駒下駄. Pangloss advised that any 文句 were unwarranted and that 訴訟事件 were unnecessary as it would be 反逆 to doubt that this outcome was merely the best of all possible worlds!

49A 厄 GYPSUM

♈		災厄	2 - 19
49A		さいやく	1|13

Calamity Jane is a Danger

Cliff, bending figure, danger 厄

厄	ヤク	misfortune, disaster	厄
災厄	さいやく	calamity	49A
災*	サイ、わざわ-い	calamity	49A
危	キ、あぶ-ない、あや-うい、あや-ぶむ	dangerous	危

危険	きけん		danger	49A
険	ケン、けわ-しい		steep, severe, perilous	49A

49B 契 GYPSUM

![symbol]		契約	3 – 5
49B		けいやく	0|1

I Pledge to Receive Immaculate virgins

Originally tally, right, proper 契

契	ケイ、ちぎ-る	pledge, join	契
契約	けいやく	contract	49B
約	ヤク	promise, summarise, approximately	49B
喫	キツ	ingest, receive	喫
喫茶店	きっさてん	café	49B
茶*	チャ、サ	tea	49B
店	テン、みせ	store, premises	49B
潔	ケツ、いさぎよ-い	clean, pure	潔
潔白	けっぱくな	immaculate	49B
白	ハク、ビャク、しろ、しら、しろ-い	white	49B

49C 券 GYPSUM

![symbol]		拳銃	3 – 4
49C		けんじゅう	*

Hand me a Pistol and New Banknotes

307

Originally expressing notched pledge 券

手	シュ、て、た	hand	手
手金	てきん	deposit	49C
金	キン、コン、かね、かな	gold, money, metal	49C
拳	ケン、こぶし	fist	拳
拳銃	けんじゅう	pistol	49C
銃	ジュウ	gun	49C
券	ケン	ticket, pass, bond	券
新券	しんけん	new banknote	49C
新	シン、あたら-しい、あら-た、にい	new	49C

49D 雄 GYPSUM

⅄		雄犬	6D11
49D		めすいぬ	1|4

The Excited Male Dog in that Japanese Ballad made a Comprehensive Recovery before Taking Off

Bird with forearm Chinese only, phonetic fine/showy bird, male bird 雄

奮	フン、ふる-う	be excited, stir	奮
興奮	こうふん	get excited	49D
興*	コウ、キョウ、おこ-る、おこ-す	rise, raise, interest	49D
雄	ユウ、お、おす	male, powerful	雄
雄犬	めすいぬ	male dog	49D
犬	ケン、いぬ	dog	49D

璃	リ	glassy	璃
操浄瑠璃	あやつりじょうるり	old name for Bunraku	49D
操	ソウ、みさお、あやつ-る	handle, chastity	49D
浄	ジョウ	pure, clean	49D
瑠	ル	lapis lazuli	49D
羅	ラ	gauze, net, include	羅
網羅的	もうらてき	comprehensive	49D
網	モウ、あみ	net, network	49D
的	テキ、まと	target, -like, adjectival suffix	49D
奪	ダツ、うば-う	snatch, captivate	奪
奪回	だっかい	recovery	49D
回	カイ、エ、まわ-る、まわ-す	turn, rotate	49D
離	リ、はな-れる、はな-す	separate, leave	離
離陸	りりく	take-off	49D
陸	リク	land	49D

49E 豊 GYPSUM

ⵖ	豊胸		2 - 6
49E	ほうきょう		*

Voluptuous Full Breasts

Originally showing food vessel and edible plant, full, plenty 豊

艶	エン、あで-やか、つや	glossy; lustre; glaze; polish; charm; colourful; captivating	艶
妖艶	ようえん	voluptuous	49E
妖	ヨウ、あや-しい、なまめ-く	attractive	49E

豊	ホウ、ゆたか	abundant, rich	豊
豊胸	ほうきょう	full breasts	49E
胸	キョウ、むね、むな	chest, breast, heart	49E

49F 講 GYPSUM

| 𐂷 | 講義 | 6 - 11 |
| 49F | こうぎ | 0\|3 |

He Drained his Mental Readiness with a Second Attempt at a Lecture in Praise of Buying

Non general use character large amount, accumulation, two baskets piled up 講

溝	コウ、みぞ	ditch, channel	溝
下水溝	げすいこう	drain	49F
水	スイ、みず	water	49F
下	カ、ゲ、した、しも、もと、さ-げる、さ-がる、くだ-る、くだ-す	base, under, lower	49F
構	コウ、かま-える、かま-う	build, mind	構
心構え	こころがまえ	mental readiness	49F
心	シン、こころ	heart, feelings	49F
再	サイ、サ、ふたた-び	again, twice, re-	再
再挙	さいきょ	second attempt	49F
挙*	キョ、あ-げる、あ-がる	offer, raise, act, perform	49F
講	コウ	lecture	講

講義	こうぎ	lecture	49F
義	ギ	righteousness	49F
称	ショウ	name, praise	称
自称	じしょう	self-styled; would-be; calling one self	49F
自	ジ、シ、みずか-ら	self	49F
購	コウ	buy	購
購買	こうばい	buying	49F
買	バイ、か-う	buy	49F

49G 並 GYPSUM

| ⊻ | 杉並木 | 4A3 |
| 49G | すぎなみき | 0\|1 |

A Ghostly Music Score Passed in the Avenue of Cedars

Doubling of standing person, row/line, rank along side 並

霊	レイ、リョウ、たま	spirit, soul	霊
幽霊	ゆうれい	ghost	49G
幽	ユウ	dark, obscure, faint, lonely	49G
譜	フ	notation, genealogy	譜
楽譜	がくふ	musical score	49G
楽	ガク、ラク、たの-しい、たの-しむ	pleasure, music	49G
普	フ	widely, generally	普
普通	ふつう	ordinary	49G

311

通	ツウ、ツ、とお-る、とお-す、かよ-う	pass, way, commute	49G
並	ヘイ、なみ、なら-べる、なら-ぶ、なら-びに	row, line, rank with, ordinary	並
杉並木	すぎなみき	avenue of cedars	49G
杉*	すぎ	cryptomeria, cedar	49G
木	ボク、モク、き、こ	tree, wood	49G

Public or private sector? It would be a 災厄 if the 契約 for special 喫茶店 were secured with just a fistful of 新券 and followed up by the pointing of a 拳銃. A 網羅的 review is required after which an all-embracing 奪回 of the industry should be attempted. It transpired that the top 雄犬 is also involved in establishments where 豊胸 are a non-negotiable condition for work. Indeed, this 自称 lord of the 下水溝 does not mind giving 講義 on how to do your 購買 by making offers that very few would want to refuse: the 幽霊 of winter past plays from a haunting 楽譜 in praise of 普通 madness.

Chapter 8 Scorpio

50A 玄 HOUR

⊠	玄妙	11A10
50A	げんみょう	*

It was a Saving Grace that a Childish Magical Bowstring Magnetised the Rich Mysterious Life Stock on Starboard

Short thread suitable for twisting, very small, hard to see 玄

蓄	チク、たくわ-える	accumulate, store	蓄
貯蓄	ちょちく	savings	50A
貯	チョ	store, save	50A
慈	ジ、いつく-しむ	love, pity, affection	慈
慈善	じぜん	charity	50A
善	ゼン、よ-い	good, virtuous	50A
幼	ヨウ、おさな-い	infancy	幼
幼児	ようじ	infant; baby; child	50A
児	ジ、ニ	child	50A
幻	ゲン、まぼろし	illusion, magic	幻
幻術	げんじゅつ	magic	50A
術	ジュツ	means, technique	50A
弦	ゲン、つる	(bow)string	弦
弓弦	ゆみずる	bowstring	50A
弓	キュウ、ゆみ	bow	50A
磁	ジ	magnet, porcelain	磁
磁石	じしゃく	magnet	50A
石	セキ、シャク、コク、いし	stone, rock	50A

滋	ジ	luxuriant, rich, strengthen, enliven	滋
滋養	じよう	nourishment	50A
養	ヨウ、やしな-う	rear, support	50A
幽	ユウ	dark, obscure, faint, lonely	幽
幽玄	ゆうげん	mystery	50A
玄	ゲン	occult, black	玄
玄妙	げんみょう	mystery	50A
妙	ミョウ	exquisite, strange, mystery	50A
畜	チク	livestock	畜
牧畜	ぼくちく	livestock/cattle raising	50A
牧	ボク、まき	pasture	50A
舷	ゲン、ふなばた	gunwale	舷
右舷	うげん	starboard	50A
右	ウ、ユウ、みぎ	right	50A

50B 留 HOUR

⊠		留守番	4F15
50B		るすばん	*

Even Yanagi, the Caretaker, is Trading in Lapis Lazuli

Horse's bit, control 留

柳	リュウ、やなぎ	willow	柳
留	リュウ、ル、と-める、と-まる	stop, fasten	留
留守番	るすばん	caretaker	50B
守	シュ、ス、まも-る、もり	protect, keep	50B

314

番	バン	turn, number, guard	50B
貿	ボウ	trade, exchange	貿
貿易業	ぼうえきぎょう	trading	50B
易	エキ、イ、やさ-しい	easy, change, divination	50B
業	ギョウ、ゴウ、わざ	profession, deed, karma	50B
瑠	ル	lapis lazuli	瑠
瑠璃色	るりいろ	lapis lazuli blue; bright blue; azure	50B
璃	リ	glassy	50B
色	ショク、シキ、いろ	colour, sensuality	50B

50C 忍 HOUR

⊠		忍耐	2 - 2
50C		にんたい	*

Appreciate Patience

Blade, phonetic bear, bear something painful in the heart? 忍

認	ニン、みと-める	recognise, appreciate	認
認識	にんしき	cognition	50C
識	シキ	knowledge	50C
忍	ニン、しの-ぶ、しの-ばせる	endure, stealth	忍
忍耐	にんたい	patience	50C
耐	タイ、た-える	endure, bear	50C

50D 刻 HOUR

⊠		時刻	5A4
50D		じこく	*

It is Time to Investigate those Cupboard Skeletons of Relevant

Nuclear Weapons

Jinmei character zodiac hog, variant of pig, phonetic carve 刻

刻	コク、きざ-む	chop, mince, engrave	刻
時刻	じこく	time, hour	50D
時	ジ、とき	time	50D
劾	ガイ	investigate (wrongdoing)	劾
弾劾	だんがい	impeachment	50D
弾	ダン、ひ-く、はず-む、たま	bullet, spring, play	50D
骸	ガイ、カイ、むくろ	bone; body; corpse	骸
骸骨	がいこつ	skeleton	50D
骨	コツ、ほね	bone, frame	50D
該	ガイ	relevance, the said-	該
該当	がいとう	relevance	50D
当	トウ、あ-たる、あ-てる	apply, hit, mark, appropriate, this	50D
核	カク	core, nucleus, nuclear	核
核兵器	かくへいき	nuclear weapon	50D
兵	ヘイ、ヒョウ	soldier	50D
器	キ、うつわ	vessel, utensil, skill	50D

50E 垂 HOUR

✕	雨垂れ	4A2
50E	あまだれ	0‖3

Despicable Sleepy Mail Relayed like Rain Drops

Originally ground + plant with leaves hanging down to ground 垂

唾	ダ、タ、つば、つばき	saliva; sputum	唾

唾棄	だき	contemptuous; despicable	50E
棄	キ	abandon, renounce	50E
睡	スイ	sleep	睡
睡眠	すいみん	sleep	50E
眠	ミン、ねむ-る、ねむ-い	sleep, sleepy	50E
郵	ユウ	mail, relay station	郵
郵便局	ゆうびんきょく	post office	50E
便	ベン、ビン、たよ-り	convenience, service, mail	50E
局*	キョク	office, section, end, circumstances	50E
垂	スイ、た-れる、た-らす	suspend, hang down	垂
雨垂れ	あまだれ	rain drops	50E
雨*	ウ、あめ、あま	rain	50E

50F 護 HOUR

✕		弁護士	3
50F		べんごし	*

Lawyers Obtain clients like Satan Harvests souls

Crested bird in hand, phonetic make dizzy, snare with words 護

護	ゴ	defend, protect	護
弁護士	べんごし	lawyer	50F
弁	ベン	speech, know, valve	50F
士	シ	warrior, scholar, man	50F
獲	カク、え-る	obtain, gain, seize	獲
獲物	えもの	prey	50F

物	ブツ、モツ、もの	thing	50F
穫	カク	harvest	穫
収穫	しゅうかく	harvest	50F
収	シュウ、おさ-める、おさ-まる	obtain, store, supply	50F

50G 巻 HOUR

⧖		鉢巻	2D3
50G		はちまき	*

Communist Blocked Headbands featured a silver hammer and sickle

Hands rolling rice + curled or bent body 巻

圏	ケン	range, sphere, zone	圏
共産圏	きょうさんけん	Communist Bloc	50G
共	キョウ、とも	together	50G
産	サン、う-む、う-まれる、うぶ	birth, produce	50G
巻	カン、ま-く、ま-き	roll, reel, volume	巻
鉢巻	はちまき	headband	50G
鉢	ハチ、ハツ	bowl, pot, skull	50G

Expulsion of the triumphant beast. At the time of that 幼児's birth there were portents of 幽玄 and 幻術 and although the 留守番 did not drink he was drunk for a week firmly refusing to leave the 瑠璃色 chamber. Even the wandering marabout with his vast 認識 nearly lost 忍耐 as the 骸骨 was about to strike the 時刻. Unquiet 睡眠 and 雨垂れ dark and gruesome 弁護士 seeking 獲物 they may devour: a 収穫 of erring souls that wildly roam groaning under cruelly spiked 鉢巻.

51A 異 IRON

♔	異人	3 - 3
51A	いじん	*

Old Grey Haired Aliens are like Winged Dragons

Person putting on a mask, different, strange appearance 異

戴	タイ、いただ-く	be crowned with; live under (a ruler); receive	戴
戴白	たいはく	old people; becoming grey haired	51A
白	ハク、ビャク、しろ、しら、しろ-い	white	51A
異	イ、こと	differ, strange	異
異人	いじん	alien, foreigner	51A
人	ジン、ニン、ひと	person	51A
翼	ヨク、つばさ	wing	翼
翼竜	よくりゅう	pterodactyl	51A
竜	リュウ、たつ	dragon	51A

51B 編 IRON

♔	編集 者	3A6
51B	へんしゅうしゃ	*

The Editor prided himself on his Universal Prejudice

Originally doorplate, door + bound writing tablets 編

編	ヘン、あ-む	edit, knit, book	編
編集者	へんしゅうしゃ	editor	51B
集	シュウ、あつ-まる、あつ-める、つど-う	gather, collect	51B
者	シャ、もの	person	51B
遍	ヘン	widely, everywhere	遍
普遍性	ふへんせい	universality	51B
普	フ	widely, generally	51B
性	セイ、ショウ	nature, sex	51B
偏	ヘン、かたよ-る	incline, bias	偏
偏見	へんけん	prejudice	51B
見	ケン、み-る、み-える、み-せる	look, see, show	51B

51C 域 IRON

🜚	領域	7B16
51C	りょういき	*

The Trouble with Delicate Pirates is that in 2 Years their Authority over a Domain is Extinct

Walk and halberd, originally walking one lap, Chinese only multiple of time 域

惑	ワク、まど-う	be confused	惑
迷惑	めいわく	trouble	51C
迷	メイ、まよ-う	be lost, perplexed	51C
繊	セン	fine, slender	繊
繊細	せんさい	fine, delicate	51C

320

細	サイ、ほそ-い、ほそ-る、こま-か、こま-かい	slender, fine	51C
賊	ゾク	rebel, plunder, injure	賊
海賊	かいぞく	pirate	51C
海	カイ、うみ	sea	51C
歳	サイ-セイ	year	歳
二歳	にさい	two years' old	51C
二	ニ、ふた、ふた-つ	two	51C
威	イ	authority, threaten	威
威力	いりょく	authority,	51C
力	リョク、リキ、ちから	strength, effort	51C
域	イキ	area, limits	域
領域	りょういき	domain	51C
領	リョウ	control, posses, chief, territory	51C
滅	メツ、ほろ-びる、ほろ-ぼす	destroy	滅
絶滅	ぜつめつ	extinction	51C
絶	ゼツ、た-える、た-やす、た-つ	cease, sever, end	51C

51D 宇 IRON

| ♔ | 宇頂天 | 3A13 |
| 51D | うちょうてん | * |

Taro experienced moments of Ecstasy in the Laundry

Originally roof that completely covers, firmament/heaven 宇

芋	いも	potato	芋
里芋	さといも	taro	51D
里	リ、さと	village, league	51D

宇	ウ	eaves, roof, heaven	宇
宇頂天	うちょうてん	ecstasy	51D
頂	チョウ、いただ-く、いただき	receive, top, crown	51D
天	テン、あめ、あま	heaven, sky	51D
汚	オ、けが-す、けが-れる、けが-らわしい、よご-す、よご-れる、きたな-い	dirt, dishonour	汚
汚れ物	よごれもの	laundry	51D
物	ブツ、モツ、もの	thing	51D

51E 煩 IRON

	煩悩	4 - 1
51E	ぼんのう	*

Oligopoly of Distribution is the Apex of Carnal Desire

Person with exaggerated head 煩

寡	カ	few, minimum, widow	寡
寡占	かせん	oligopoly	51E
占	セン、し-める、うらな-う	divine, occupy	51E
頒	ハン	distribute, divide	頒
頒布	はんぷ	distribution	51E
布	フ、ぬの	cloth, spread	51E
頂	チョウ、いただ-く、いただき	receive, crown, top	頂
頂点	ちょうてん	apex	51E
点	テン	point, mark	51E

322

煩	ハン、ボン、わずら-う、わずら-わす	trouble, pain, torment	煩
煩悩	ぼんのう	carnal desire	51E
悩	ノウ、なや-む、なや-ます	worry, distress, tease	51E

51F 貴 IRON

♔	貴重	3 – 5
51F	きちょうな	*

Neglect of Precious Scrap Value

Shell/money and non general use character gather, basket 貴

遺	イ、ユイ	leave, bequeath, lose	遺
遺漏	いろう	omission, negligence, oversight	51F
漏	ロウ、も-る、も-れる、も-らす	lose	51F
貴	キ、たっと-い、とうと-い、たっと-ぶ、とうと-ぶ	precious, revered	貴
貴重	きちょうな	precious	51F
重	ジュウ、チョウ、え、おも-い、かさ-ねる、かさ-なる	heavy, pile, -fold	51F
潰	カイ、エ、つぶ.す、つぶ.れる、つい.える	crush; smash; break; dissipate	潰
潰し値段	つぶしねだん	scrap value	51F
値	チ、ね、あたい	price, value	51F
段	ダン	step, grade	51F

51G 監 IRON

⛀	監視	6A9
51G	かんし	*

It was Observed that In View of Abusive Sightseeing the Warship would sail away with the Students

Originally person bending over to stare at water in bowl 監

監	カン	supervise, watch	監
監視	かんし	observation	51G
視	シ	see, look, regard	51G
鑑	カン、かんがみる	take note, heed	鑑
鑑みて	かんがみて	in view of	51G
濫	ラン	flood, overdo, wanton	濫
濫用	らんよう	abuse	51G
用	ヨウ、もち-いる	use	51G
覧	ラン	see, look	覧
巡覧	じゅんらん	tour, sightseeing	51G
巡	ジュン、めぐ-る	go around	51G
艦	カン	warship	艦
軍艦	ぐんかん	warship	51G
軍	グン	military, army	51G
藍	ラン、あい	indigo	藍
出藍	しゅつらん	outshining one's teacher	51G
出	シュツ、スイ、で-る、だ-す	emerge, put out	51G

For those who've come across the seas. Some 異人 are harmless but most are as fierce as 翼竜, according to disreputable 編集者 of tabloids and broadsheets light on news but heavy on 偏見. They always cause 迷惑, don't heed 威力and rage like 海賊 stealing even 里芋 and 汚れ物 from poor villages in the countryside. In addition, there is boundless 煩悩 and the 頒布 of all kinds of illegal substances and 貴重 commodities. More 監視 by the authorities is urgently required 鑑みて this widespread 濫用 of privileges because after all, despite those asylum seekers, Nauru is a fabulous place for 巡覧!

52A 憂 JUNIPER

ℭ		憂愁	2 - 1
52A		ゆうしゅう	1|3

Grief is a superior Actor

Originally head/heart + upturned foot, walk slowly, phonetic sad 憂

憂	ユウ、うれ-える、うれ-い、う-い	grief, sorrow	憂
憂愁	ゆうしゅう	grief, gloom	52A
愁	シュウ、うれ-える、うれ-い	grief, sadness	52A
優	ユウ、やさ-しい、すぐ-れる	superior, gentle, actor	優
男優	だんゆう	actor	52A
男*	ダン、ナン、おとこ	man, male	52A

52B 適 JUNIPER

ℭ		適性	5 - 2
52B		てきせい	*

An Heir with a legal Aptitude was Exposed to Dripping Hostility

Chinese only base/starting point, (emperor and mouth/say) 適

嫡	チャク	legitimate heir	嫡
嫡子	ちゃくし	legal heir	52B
子	シ、ス、こ	child	52B
適	テキ	suitable, fit, go	適
適性	てきせい	aptitude	52B
性	セイ、ショウ	nature, sex	52B
摘	テキ、つ-む	pluck, pick, extract	摘
摘発	てきはつ	exposure	52B
発	ハツ、ホツ	discharge, start, leave	52B
滴	テキ、しずく、したた-る	drop, drip	滴
水滴	すいてき	water drop	52B
水	スイ、みず	water	52B
敵	テキ、かたき	match, enemy	敵
敵意	てきい	hostility	52B
意	イ	mind, thought, will	52B

52C 敢 JUNIPER

	勇敢	2C3
52C	ゆうかん	*

Solemn Strictness and tragic Bravery

Originally pulling something out of a container, make-or-break effort? 敢

敢	カン	daring, tragic	52C
厳	ゲン、ゴン、おごそ-か、きび-しい	severe, strict, solemn	厳
森厳	しんげん な	solemn	52C
森	シン、もり	woods	52C

敢	カン	daring, tragic	敢
勇敢	ゆうかん	bravery, valour	52C
勇	ユウ、いさ-む	courage	52C

52D 尺 JUNIPER

		尺八	4A3
52D		しゃくはち	0|2

Shakuhachi gives a Sturdy Interpretation of Words and Rice

Span of the hand, measure 尺

尺	シャク	measure, foot	尺
尺八	しゃくはち	shakuhachi (eight shaku instrument)	52D
八*	ハチ、や、やっ-つ、よう	eight	52D
丈	ジョウ、たけ	length, stature, measure	丈
丈夫	じょうぶ	sturdy, robust	52D
夫	フ、フウ、おっと	husband, man	52D
訳	ヤク、わけ	translation, meaning	訳
通訳	つうやく	interpreting	52D
通	ツウ、ツ、とお-る、とお-す、かよ-う	pass, way, commute	52D
釈	シャク	explain, release	釈
解釈	かいしゃく	interpretation	52D
解	カイ、ゲ、と-く、と-かす、と-ける	unravel, explain, solve	52D

327

52E 将 JUNIPER

⑤	将来	2D5
52E	しょうらい	*

Beefy Bounty hunters meet in the Future

Originally offer meat to a superior, (on a litter?) 将

奨	ショウ	urge, encourage	奨
奨励金	しょうれいきん	bounty	52E
励	レイ、はげ-む、はげ-ます	encourage, strive	52E
金	キン、コン、かね、かな	gold, money, metal	52E
将	ショウ	command, about to	将
将来	しょうらい	future	52E
来	ライ、く-る、きた-る、きた-す	come	52E

52F 亡 JUNIPER

⑤	文盲	7 - 9
52F	もんもう	*

Death is neither Illiterate nor Forgetful, Gazing Mournfully at the Deluded and Extremely Busy

Originally person no longer able to be seen, escaping 亡

亡	ボウ、モウ、な-い	die, escape, lose	亡
死亡	しぼう	death	52F
死	シ、し-ぬ	death	52F
盲	モウ	blind	盲

文盲	もんもう	illiteracy	52F
文	ブン、モン、ふみ	writing, text	52F
忘	ボウ、わす-れる	forget, leave behind	忘
忘れ勝ち	わすれがち	forgetful	52F
勝	ショウ、か-つ、まさ-る	win, surpass	52F
望	ボウ、モウ、のぞ-む	wish, hope, gaze	望
渇望	かつぼう	craving; longing; thirsting	52F
渇	カツ、かわ-く	thirst, parched	52F
喪	ソウ、も	mourn, loss, death	喪
阻喪	そそう	loss of spirit; dejection	52F
阻	ソ、はば-む	obstruct, hinder	52F
妄	モウ、ボウ	irrational, rash	妄
妄想	もうそう	delusion	52F
想	ソウ、ソ	idea, thought	52F
忙	ボウ、いそが-しい	busy	忙
多忙な	たぼうな	very busy	52F
多	タ、おお-い	many	52F

52G 宅 JUNIPER

𝒢	自宅	2B2
52G	じたく	*

Commit Your House; Itaku, Jitaku

Roof and growing plant, 'taken root' 宅

託	タク	entrust, commit	託
委託	いたく	commission	52G

329

委	イ	committee, entrust to	52G
宅	タク	house, home	宅
自宅	じたく	one's own house	52G
自	ジ、シ、みずか-ら	self	52G

Pass into the city of woe. The experience of 憂愁 combined with prolonged 摘発 to 敵意 requires 勇敢 and 森厳 resolve to deal with this. Be 丈夫 and go for an 解釈 that allows you to look at the 将来 where you will collect your rightly earned 奨励金. Guard against 阻喪 and don't be 忘れ勝ち of your past suffering because the Angel of 死亡 never refuses a 委託 and will ambush you even at your 自宅!

53A 蔵 LEAD

| ᵀ⁊ | | 蔵書 | 2B |
| 53A | | ぞうしょ | * |

My Entrails Harbour many Libraries

Originally concealing a wounded + incapacitated person with grass 蔵

臓	ゾウ	entrails, viscera	臓
内臓	ないぞう	entrails, viscera	53A
内	ナイ、ダイ、うち	inside	53A
蔵	ゾウ、くら	storehouse, harbor	蔵
蔵書	ぞうしょ	one's library	53A
書	ショ、か-く	write	53A

53B 支 LEAD

| ᵀ⁊ | | 支店 | 7 - 5 |

53B	しじ	*

The Skill of Drumming Up Support for Kabuki involves using the Limbs of the body as Forked Branches of a tree

Hand holding up branch, originally break off a branch 支

技	ギ、わざ	craft, skill	技
技巧	ぎこう	skill	53B
巧	コウ、たく-み	skill	53B
鼓	コ、つづみ	drum	鼓
鼓動	こどう	drumming	53B
動	ドウ、うご-く、うご-かす	move	53B
支	シ、ささ-える	branch, support	支
支店	しじ	branch office	53B
店	テン、みせ	store, premises	53B
伎	ギ、わざ	deed; skill	伎
歌舞伎	かぶき	Kabuki theatre	53B
歌	カ、うた、うた-う	song	53B
舞	ブ、ま-う、ま-い	dance, flit	53B
肢	シ	limb, part	肢
肢体	したい	the limbs	53B
体	タイ、テイ、からだ	body	53B
岐	キ	fork	岐
岐路	きろ	forked road	53B
路	ロ、じ	road, route	53B
枝	シ、えだ	branch	枝
枝角	えだずの	antlers	53B
角	カク、かど、つの	horn, angle	53B

53C 我 LEAD

ガ	我まま	2B8
53C	わがまま	*

Selfishness breeds Hungry Imps

Originally broad bladed halberd with tassels, notches for kill 我

我	ガ、われ、わ	I, self, my	我
我まま	わがまま	selfishness	53C
餓	ガ	starve	餓
餓鬼	がき	hungry imp, brat	53C
鬼	キ、おに	devil, demon, ghost	53C

53D 犬 LEAD

ガ	番犬	4A8
53D	ばんけん	*

It is a Condition not to kick a Prostrated Dog in the Jaws

Originally a pictograph of a dog on its hind legs barking 犬

状	ジョウ	condition, letter	状
状態	じょうたい	current status; condition; situation; circumstances; state	53D
態	タイ	appearance, intent	53D
伏	フク、ふ-せる、ふ-す	prostrated, bend down	伏
圧伏	あっぷく	overpower; subdue; keep down	53D
圧	アツ	pressure	53D
犬	ケン、いぬ	dog	犬
番犬	ばんけん	watchdog	53D

番	バン	turn, number, guard	53D
顎	ガク、あご、あぎと	jaw; chin; gill	顎
顎骨	あごぼね; がっこつ	jawbone	53D
骨	コツ、ほね	bone, frame	53D

53E 尊 LEAD

![glyph]		尊敬	3E11
53E		そんけい	*

Moreover, Respect the Law-Abiding Ones

Offer and pour wine for a superior 尊

猶	ユウ	moreover, still, hesitate, similar	猶
猶予	ゆうよ	postponement; deferment; extension	53E
予	ヨ	already, prior, I	53E
尊	ソン、たっと-い、とうと-い、たっと-ぶ、とうと-ぶ	value, esteem, your	尊
尊敬	そんけい	respect	53E
敬	ケイ、うやま-う	respect	53E
遵	ジュン	follow, obey	遵
遵法	じゅんぽう	law abiding	53E
法	ホウ、ハッ、ホッ	law	53E

53F 善 LEAD

![glyph]		親善	3 - 1
53F		しんぜん	*

Let us Repair to the Table for Virtuous Friendship

Originally sheep + argue, praiseworthy argument, fine debate 善

繕	ゼン、つくろ-う	repair, mend	繕
修繕	しゅうぜん	repairs	53F
修	シュウ、シュ、おさ-める、おさ-まる	practice, master	53F
膳	ゼン	small low table; tray	膳
配膳	はいぜん	set the table	53F
配	ハイ、くば-る	distribute	53F
善	ゼン、よ-い	good, virtuous	善
親善	しんぜん	friendship	53F
親	シン、おや、した-しい、した-しむ	intimate, parent	53F

53G 延 LEAD

| 延 | 延期 | 2 – 5 |
| 53G | えんき | * |

Deceive and Postpone

Lengthy protracted movement, foot + go and add mark 延

誕	タン	birth, deceive	誕
誕生日	たんじょうび	birthday	53G
生	セイ、ショウ、い-きる、い-かす、い-ける、う-まれる、う-む	life, birth, grow	53G
日	ニチ、ジツ、ひ、か	sun, day	53G
延	エン、の-びる、の-べる、の-ばす	extend, postpone	延
延期	えんき	postponement	53G

| 期 | キ、ゴ | period, expect | 53G |

Symphony of suffering souls. Offerings of 内臓 and 肢体 are to be sacrificed at the 岐路 where sheep go right and 我まま goats turn to the left. The dreaded 番犬 Cerberus 圧伏 any stragglers as no 猶予 will be granted but most are docile and 遵法. Rhadamanthus reposes himself in a chamber of 親善 and harmony as the 配膳 while beyond much wailing and gnashing of teeth is to be heard. A 誕生日 marking infinite suffering and indefinite 延期 of happiness.

54A 匿 MAGNESIA

| ℳ | | 匿名 | 3A1 |
| 54A | | とくめい | * |

The old boy Consented to having a Youthful Pseudonym

Originally old person tending to long pliant hair, weak, young 匿

諾	ダク	consent, agree	諾
承諾	しょうだく	consent	54A
承	ショウ、うけたまわ-る	acquiesce, hear, listen to	54A
若	ジャク、ニャク、わか-い、も-しくは	young, if	若
若年	じゃくねん	youth	54A
年	ネン、とし	year	54A
匿	トク	conceal	匿
匿名	とくめい	pseudonym	54A
名	メイ、ミョウ、な	name, fame	54A

54B 机 MAGNESIA

M	事務机	4 - 3
54B	じむつくえ	*

On the Office Desk a Skinny Joke Died From Hunger

Non general use character representing small table 机

机	キ、つくえ	desk, table	机
事務机	じむつくえ	office desk	54B
事	ジ、ズ、こと	thing, matter, act	54B
務	ム、つと-める	(perform) duty	54B
肌	はだ	skin, texture, grain	肌
素肌	すはだ	bare skin	54B
素	ソ、ス	element, base, bare	54B
冗	ジョウ	superfluous	冗
冗談	じょうだん	joke	54B
談	ダン	conversation, talk	54B
飢	キ、う-える	starve, hunger	飢
飢え死に	うえじ に	death from hunger	54B
死	シ、し-ぬ	death	54B

54C 栽 MAGNESIA

M	盆栽	3A
54C	ぼんさい	*

Publish the Bonsai Trial

Fancy halberd cutting/trimming 栽

載	サイ、の-せる、の-る	load, carry	載
掲載	けいさい	publication	54C

掲	ケイ、かか-げる	display, hoist, print	54C
栽	サイ	planting	栽
盆栽	ぼんさい	Bonsai	54C
盆	ボン	tray, Bon Festival	54C
裁	サイ、た-つ、さば-く	judge, decide, cut	裁
裁判	さいばん	trial	54C
判	ハン、バン	seal; stamp; judgment	54C

54D 座 MAGNESIA

ℳ	銀行口座	2B6
54D	ぎんこうこうざ	*

Keep your Frustration in a Bank Account

Two persons sitting on the ground under a roof, gathering 座

挫	ザ、サ、くじ.く、くじ.ける	crush; break; sprain; discourage	挫
挫折	ざせつ	frustration	54D
折	セツ、お-る、おり、お-れる	bend, break, occasion	54D
座	ザ、すわ-る	seat, sit, gather	座
銀行口座	ぎんこうこうざ	bank account	54D
銀	ギン	silver	54D
行	コウ、ギョウ、アン、い-く、ゆ-く、おこな-う	go, conduct, column	54D
口	コウ、ク、くち	mouth, opening	54D

54E 従 MAGNESIA

ℳ	従業員	2B4

54E	じゅうぎょういん	*

Employees must Comply with Vertical Lines

Originally two persons moving along a road 従

従	ジュウ、ショウ、ジュ、したが-う、したが-える	follow, comply	従
従業員	じゅうぎょういん	employee	54E
業	ギョウ、ゴウ、わざ	profession, deed, karma	54E
員	イン	member, official	54E
縦	ジュウ、たて	vertical, selfish	縦
縦線	じゅうせん	vertical line	54E
線	セン	line	54E

54F 株 MAGNESIA

ℳ	株式会社	4 - 6
54F	かぶしきかいしゃ	*

Especially Stocks in Vermilion Pearls have skyrocketed

Originally inside of a tree trunk, often red 朱

殊	シュ、こと	especially	殊
殊更	ことさら	especially	54F
更	コウ、さら、ふ-ける、ふ-かす	anew, change, again, grow late	54F
株	かぶ	stock, share, stump	株
株式会社	かぶしきかいしゃ	corporation, co., ltd.	54F
式	シキ	ceremony, form	54F
会	カイ、エ、あ-う	meet	54F

338

社	シャ、やしろ	company, Shinto shrine	54F
朱	シュ	vermilion, red	朱
朱肉	しゅにく	red ink pad	54F
肉	ニク	meat, flesh	54F
珠	シュ	jewel, pearl	珠
真珠	しんじゅ	pearl	54F
真	シン、ま	true, quintessence	54F

54G 脳 MAGNESIA

𝓜		頭脳	2 – 4
54G		ずのう	*

The fleshy Brain was heartily Distressed

Brain, hair, scoop, part of the head that is scooped out 脳

脳	ノウ	brain	脳
頭脳	ずのう	brain	54G
頭	トウ、ズ、ト、あたま、かしら	head, counter for large animals	54G
悩	ノウ、なや-む、なや-ます	worry, distress, tease	悩
苦悩	くのう	distress	54G
苦	ク、くる-しい、くる-しむ、くる-しめる、にが-い	painful, bitter	54G

Antique fossils and old fogies. The 承諾 of 若年 frequently is demanded by geriatrics behind 事務机 either through 冗談 or by threats. 裁判 by centenarians as old as gnarled 盆栽 who have plenty of 銀行口座 and lives riddled with 挫折. Consider the 縦線 on the grid where no youthful 従業員 will ever have a y-intercept, 殊更 in the Methuselah 株式会社 with its 969 stockholders! Sage

advice combined with 真珠 of wisdom and lots of 苦悩 running
around the 頭脳!

55A 斉 NIGHT

X	一斉	4A14
55A	いっせい	*

The Economists All Together Studied some sour Drugs

Similar heads of grain for religious offering 斉

済	サイ、す-む、す-ます	settle, finish	済
経済	けいざい	economy	55A
経	ケイ、キョウ、へ-る	pass, sutra, longitude	55A
斉	セイ	equal, similar	斉
一斉	いっせい	all together	55A
一	イチ、イツ、ひと、ひと-つ	one	55A
斎	サイ	purification, abstain, worship, a study	斎
書斎	しょさい	a study	55A
書	ショ、か-く	write	55A
剤	ザイ	medicine, drug	剤
薬剤	やくざい	drug	55A
薬	ヤク、くすり	medicine, drug	55A

55B 操 NIGHT

X	操縦 士	4 - 6
55B	そうじゅうし	*

Let's Transfer the Chaste Pilot from damp Seaweed to the Drying

Kiln

Chinese only birds chirping, three mouths in tree 操

繰	く-る	reel, turn	繰
繰り越す	くりこす	transfer	55B
越	エツ、こ-す、こ-える	cross, exceed, excel	55B
操	ソウ、みさお、あやつ-る	handle, chastity	操
操縦士	そうじゅうし	pilot	55B
縦	ジュウ、たて	vertical, selfish	55B
士	シ	warrior, scholar, man	55B
藻	ソウ、も	water weed, seaweed	藻
海藻	かいそう	seaweed	55B
海	カイ、うみ	sea	55B
燥	ソウ	dry, parch	燥
乾燥窯	かんそうがま	drying kiln	55B
乾	カン、かわ-く、かわ-かす	dry	55B
窯	ヨウ、かま	kiln, oven	55B

55C 虚 NIGHT

X	虚無 主義	8E25
55C	きょむしゅぎ	0|11

In the Theatre of Captive Nihilism Frolicking Tigger Underwear is Oppressed Without Reservation

Originally tiger, phonetic big, + large hill with a hollow crown 虚

劇	ゲキ	drama, intense	劇
劇場	げきじょう	theatre	55C

場	ジョウ、ば	place	55C
虜	リョ	captive, capture	虜
虜囚	りょしゅう	captive	55C
囚*	シュウ	captured, criminal, arrest	55C
虚	キョ、コ	empty, hollow, dip	虚
虚無主義	きょむしゅぎ	nihilism	55C
無	ム、ブ、な-い	not, non, cease to be	55C
主	シュ、ス、ぬし、おも	master, owner, main	55C
義	ギ	righteousness	55C
戯	ギ、たわむ-れる	play, frolic, joke	戯
戯画	ぎが	caricature	55C
画	ガ、カク	picture, stroke	55C
虎	コ、とら	tiger; drunkard	虎
虎穴	こけつ	tiger's den; dangerous place	55C
穴	ケツ、あな	hole	55C
膚	フ、はだ	skin	膚
膚着	はだぎ	underwear	55C
着	チャク、ジャク、き-る、き-せる、つ-く、つ-ける	arrive, wear	55C
虐	ギャク、しいた-げる	cruelty, oppress	虐
残虐	ざんぎゃく	cruelty	55C
残	ザン、のこ-る、のこ-す	leave, cruel, harm	55C
慮	リョ	thought, concern	慮
遠慮	えんりょ	reserve	55C
遠	エン、オン、とお-い	distant	55C

55D 恵 NIGHT

✗	仁恵	3C4
55D	じんけい	*

The Merciful Spear is my Specialty

Hand and round weighted device used in spinning 専

恵	ケイ、エ、めぐ-む	blessing, kindness	恵
仁恵	じんけい	mercy, graciousness, benevolence	55D
仁	ジン、ニ	virtue, benevolence, man	55D
穂	スイ、ほ	ear, spear (of grain)	穂
穂先	ほさき	spear	55D
先	セン、さき	previous, precede, tip	55D
専	セン、もっぱ-ら	exclusive, sole	専
専門	せんもん	specialty	55D
門	モン、かど	gate, door	55D

55E 郷 NIGHT

✗	望郷	2B1
55E	ぼうきょう	*

Echoes of Homesickness

Originally two persons meeting over dinner, feast, community 郷

響	キョウ、ひび-く	resound, echo, effect	響
響き渡る	ひびきわたる	resound	55E
渡	ト、わた-る、わた-す	cross, handover	55E
郷	キョウ、ゴウ	village, rural	郷
望郷	ぼうきょう	homesickness	55E

343

| 望 | ボウ、モウ、のぞ-む | wish, hope, gaze | 55E |

55F 革 NIGHT

| ✗ | 革命 | 3 - 4 |
| 55F | かくめい | * |

Ambition is the Boot of Revolution

Hornless creature with flaps of skin, hairless hide, change 革

覇	ハ	domination, rule	覇
覇気	はき	ambition	55F
気	キ、ケ	spirit	55F
靴	カ、くつ	shoe	靴
長靴	ながぐつ	boot	55F
長	チョウ、なが-い	long, senior	55F
革	カク、かわ	leather, reform	革
革命	かくめい	revolution	55F
命	メイ、ミョウ、いのち	life, order	55F

55G 没 NIGHT

| ✗ | 陥没 | 3A4 |
| 55G | かんぼつ | * |

Subsiding Cereals and Sea Shells were sinking

Originally hand holding a gong to strike large hanging bell 没

| 没 | ボツ | sink, disappear, die, lack, not | 没 |
| 陥没 | かんぼつ | cave-in, subsidence | 55G |

陥	カン、おちい-る、おとしい-れる	collapse	55G
穀	コク	grain, cereals	穀
穀物	こくもつ	cereals	55G
物	ブツ、モツ、もの	thing	55G
殻	カク、から	shell, husk, crust	殻
貝殻	かいがら	sea shell	55G
貝	かい	shell fish	55G

Microcosmic solidarity. Let us 一斉 conduct a 書斎 related to the effects on body and mind of 海藻 treated in a 乾燥窯. We should not be 虜囚 to some form of 虚無主義 as surely other philosophies that emphasise 仁恵 including a 専門 of social progress would 響き渡る more positively. Tomorrow's 革命 won't be coming but we should not give up the 覇気 to try to prevent a 陥没 of quality of life. When the mollusc loses it's 貝殻 it's like human beings losing their home.

56A 疑 OIL OF SATURN

疑	疑問	3 – 3
56A	ぎもん	*

If you Suspect Imitations, stare hard at the merchant

Originally old man in doubt where to turn 疑

疑	ギ、うたが-う	doubt, suspect	疑
疑問	ぎもん	doubt	56A
問	モン、と-う、と-い、とん	ask	56A
擬	ギ	imitate, model	擬
模擬	もぎ	imitation	56A
模	モ、ボ	copy, model, mould	56A

凝	ギョウ、こ-る、こ-らす	stiff, engrossed, elaborate	凝
凝視	ぎょうし	stare	56A
視	シ	see, look, regard	56A

56B 宣 OIL OF SATURN

| 🜔 | 宣伝 | 3E4 |
| 56B | せんでん | * |

Peeping Propaganda craves Constancy

Originally that which goes around a building, wall, fence 垣

垣	かき	fence, hedge	垣
垣間見る	かいまみる*	peep	56B
間	カン、ケン、あいだ、ま	space, gap	56B
見	ケン、み-る、み-える、み-せる	look, see, show	56B
宣	セン	promulgate, state	宣
宣伝	せんでん	propaganda	56B
伝	デン、つた-わる、つた-える、つた-う	convey, transmit	56B
恒	コウ	always, constant	恒
恒常	こうじょう	constancy	56B
常	ジョウ、つね、とこ	usual, always	56B

56C 処 OIL OF SATURN

| 🜔 | 処理 | 2 - 4 |
| 56C | しょり | * |

Basic Management has it all in hand

Visiting somewhere and stop sitting on a stool 処

拠	キョ	base, basis	拠
根拠	こんきょ	base, basis	56C
根	コン、ね	root, base	56C
処	ショ	deal with, place	処
処理	しょり	management	56C
理	リ	reason, principle	56C

56D 旦 OIL OF SATURN

![旦]	元旦	4A5
56D	がんたん	*

Abolishing Bravery is the Condition for Responsibility on New Year's Day

Simplification of carry, former ngu character dawn, sun over the horizon 旦

胆	タン	liver, gall, courage	胆
大胆	だいたん	bravery	56D
大	ダイ、タイ、おお、おお-きい、おお-いに	big	56D
但	ただ-し	but, however	但
但し付き	ただしずき	condition	56D
付	フ、つ-ける、つ-く	attach, apply	56D
担	タン、かつ-ぐ、にな-う	carry, bear	担
担当	たんとう	responsibility	56D
当	トウ、あ-たる、あ-てる	apply, hit, mark, appropriate, this	56D

旦	タン	daybreak; dawn; morning	旦
元旦	がんたん	New Year's Day	56D
元	ゲン、ガン、もと	originally, source	56D

56E 滑 OIL OF SATURN

| 𒀭 | 潤滑 | 3 – 5 |
| 56E | じゅんかつ | * |

Stop those Consenting Slippery Bones

Skull and vertebrae, bones + flesh of the body 骨

肯	コウ	consent, agree, vital	肯
肯定	こうてい	affirmation	56E
定	テイ、ジョウ、さだ-める、さだ-まる、さだ-か	fix, establish	56E
滑	カツ、すべ-る、なめ-らか	slide, slip, smooth	滑
潤滑	じゅんかつ	lubrication	56E
潤	ジュン、うるお-う、うるお-す、うる-む	moisten, enrich	56E
骨	コツ、ほね	bone, frame	骨
骨折	こっせつ	fracture	56E
折	セツ、お-る、おり、お-れる	bend, break, occasion	56E

56F 収 OIL OF SATURN

| 𒀭 | 収入 | 3B |

56F	しゅうにゅう		*	

An Examination of his Income made him Cry Out

Originally intertwined threads, assemble, gather 叫

糾	キュウ	entwine, examine	糾
糾明	きゅうめい	examination	56F
明	メイ、ミョウ、あ-かり、あか-るい、あか-るむ	clear, open, bright	56F
収	シュウ、おさ-める、おさ-まる	obtain, store, supply	収
収入	しゅうにゅう	income	56F
入	ニュウ、い-る、い-れる、はい-る	to get in, to go in, to come in	56F
叫	キョウ、さけ-ぶ	shout, yell	叫
叫び出す	さけびだす	cry out	56F
出	シュツ、スイ、で-る、だ-す	emerge, put out	56F

56G 為 OIL OF SATURN

🜩	行為	2B1
56G	こうい	*

Active Counterfeiters

Originally hand + prototype elephant, imitate form, image 為

為	イ	do, purpose	為
行為	こうい	action, act	56G
行	コウ、ギョウ、アン、い-く、ゆ-く、おこな-う	go, conduct, column	56G
偽	ギ、いつわ-る、にせ	false, lie	偽
偽札	にせさつ	counterfeit paper money	56G

| 札 | サツ、ふだ | paper money, note | 56G |

Pavane for a cyborg. To find out whether this creature is an 模擬 or the real thing, be sure to 凝視 intensely at the head and in order to remove any 疑問 just 垣間見る into its beady eyes. If there is too much 恒常 in its gaze, then this would be a 根拠 for assuming it to be non-human. Don't touch it but leave it to 処理 who will take 担当 if they have enough 大胆. Sustaining 骨折 could be 肯定 of its human origin but only a thorough 糾明 will bear this out -for 叫び出す loud! Let us perform a charitable 行為 instead and send this replicant on its way with a large plastic bag of 偽札.

Chapter 9 Sagittarius

57A 哀 PHILOSOPHICAL STONE

👑	悲哀	3 - 4
57A	ひあい	*

Survivors of the Ring felt Sadness

Mouth + clothing phonetic to express sound of wailing 哀

還	カン		return	還
生還者	せいかんしゃ		survivor	57A
生	セイ、ショウ、い-きる、い-かす、い-ける、う-まれる、う-む		life, birth, grow	57A
者	シャ、もの		person	57A
環	カン		ring, circle	環
環境	かんきょう		environment	57A
境	キョウ、ケイ、さかい		boundary, border	57A
哀	アイ、あわ-れ、あわ-れむ		sorrow, pity	哀
悲哀	ひあい		sadness	57A
悲	ヒ、かな-しい、かな-しむ		sad	57A

57B 補 PHILOSOPHICAL STONE

👑	補助	5E9
57B	ほじょ	*

We Support the Seizure of the Mammalian Bay Store

Jinmei character begin, use + hand holding tool, start to use,

351

phonetic patch 補

補	ホ、おぎな-う	make good, stop gap	補
補助	ほじょ	support	57B
助	ジョ、たす-ける、たす-かる、すけ	assist, help	57B
捕	ホ、と-らえる、と-らわれる、と-る、つか-まえる、つか-まる	seize, capture	捕
捕獲	ほかく	seizure	57B
獲	カク、え-る	obtain, gain, seize	57B
哺	ホ、はぐく.む、ふく.む	nurse; suckle	哺
哺乳動物	ほにゅうどうぶつ	mammal	57B
乳	ニュウ、ちち、ち	breasts, milk	57B
動	ドウ、うご-く、うご-かす	move	57B
物	ブツ、モツ、もの	thing	57B
浦	ホ、うら	coast, inlet, bay	浦
浦風	うらかぜ	bay breeze	57B
風	フウ、フ、かぜ、かざ	wind, style	57B
舗	ホ	shop, lay, pave	舗
店舗	てんぽ	shop, store	57B
店	テン、みせ	store, premises	57B

57C 享 PHILOSOPHICAL STONE

👑	享受者	4F9

| 57C | きょうじゅしゃ | | 1\|8 |

The Reception of Outlines from the Director of the Cram School was Mellow

Originally castle watchtower extending in two directions 享

享	キョウ	receive, have	享
享受者	きょうじゅしゃ	recipient	57C
受	ジュ、う-ける、う-かる	receive	57C
者	シャ、もの	person	57C
郭	カク	quarter, enclosure	郭
輪郭	りんかく	outlines	57C
輪	リン、わ	wheel, hoop	57C
塾	ジュク	juku (cram school)	塾
塾長	じゅくちょう	head of juku	57C
長	チョウ、なが-い	long, senior	57C
熟	ジュク、う-れる	ripe, mature, cooked	熟
老熟	ろうじゅく	mature skill, maturity, mellowness	57C
老*	ロウ、お-いる、ふ-ける	old, aged	57C

57D 凶 PHILOSOPHICAL STONE

👑	凶悪	2 - 3
57D	きょうあくな	*

Atrocious Chest Hair is a Disaster

Container/mouth + symbol for drawing attention, empty 凶

凶	キョウ	bad luck, disaster	凶

凶悪	きょうあくな	atrocious	57D
悪	アク、オ、わる-い	bad, hate	57D
胸	キョウ、むね、むな	chest, breast, heart	胸
胸毛	むなげ	chest hair	57D
毛	モウ、け	hair	57D

57E 乳 PHILOSOPHICAL STONE

| 👑 | | 乳房 | 4 - 9 |
| 57E | | にゅうぼう | * |

Confucius was Holed Up in the Fleeting World of Gay Breasts and Ovulations

Originally manually assist in removing a child from the vagina 乳

孔	コウ	hole, Confucius	孔
気孔	きこう	pore	57E
気	キ、ケ	spirit	57E
浮	フ、う-く、う-かれる、う-かぶ、う-かべる	float, fleeting, gay	浮
浮き世	うきよ	fleeting world	57E
世	セイ、セ、よ	world, society, age, generation	57E
乳	ニュウ、ちち、ち	breasts, milk	乳
乳房	にゅうぼう	breasts	57E
房	ボウ、ふさ	room, wife, tuft	57E
卵	ラン、たまご	egg, ovum, spawn	卵
排卵	はいらん	ovulation	57E
排	ハイ	reject, expel, push, anti-	57E

57F 敬 PHILOSOPHICAL STONE

👑	敬称	3 - 1
57F	けいしょう	*

Respect Approaching Miracles

Non general use character insignificance, person bending, speaking respectfully 敬

敬	ケイ、うやま-う	respect	敬
敬称	けいしょう	honorific title	57F
称	ショウ	name, praise	57F
警	ケイ	warn, approach	警
警告	けいこく	warning	57F
告	コク、つ-げる	proclaim, inform	57F
驚	キョウ、おどろ-く、おどろ-かす	surprise	驚
驚異	きょうい	miracle, wonder	57F
異	イ、こと	differ, strange	57F

57G 甲 PHILOSOPHICAL STONE

👑	甲虫	4A5
57G	こうちゅう	*

The First-Class Beetle pushed the Illustrated Barrow up the ABC Promontory

Hard-shelled seed with a split 甲

甲	コウ、カン	shell, armour, high, 1st, A	甲
甲虫	こうちゅう	beetle	57G
虫	チュウ、むし	insect, worm	57G
押	オウ、お-す、お-さえる	push	押

355

手押し車	ておしぐるま	barrow	57G
手	シュ、て、た	hand	57G
車	シャ、くるま	vehicle, chariot	57G
挿	ソウ、さ-す	insert	挿
挿絵	さしえ	(book) illustration	57G
絵	カイ、エ	picture	57G
岬	みさき	promontory, cape	岬
甲乙丙岬	"こう/おつ/へいみさき"	Cape ABC	57G
甲乙丙	こう/おつ/へい	ABC/123	57G
乙	オツ	odd, B, 2nd, stylish	57G
丙	ヘイ	C, 3rd	57G

Post human ruminations. Cockroaches have the upper hand as 生還者 in a devastated natural 環境 after the demise of the 哺乳動物. The 捕獲 of the world by Blattodea with their 老熟 social abilities will display the 輪郭 of a novel and perhaps less 凶悪 New Order. The decrease of human 胸毛 and 乳房 in this 浮き世 is as much a 警告 sign as it is heralding the 驚異 of the coming of the 甲虫 and Lucifuga who love feasting on Virgilian 挿絵 and picnicking on the 岬 of Lost Hope.

58A 鬼 QUICKSILVER

☻		鬼界	5B10
58A		きかい	1|8

Otherworldly Salesmanship Charmed some Ugly Gold Bullion

Person crouching wearing death mask, contact spirits dead 鬼

鬼	キ、おに	devil, demon, ghost	鬼
鬼界	きかい	nether world	58A
界	カイ	area, boundary	58A

魂	コン、たましい	soul, spirit	魂
商魂	しょうこん	salesmanship	58A
商*	ショウ、あきな-う	trade, deal, sell	58A
魅	ミ	bewitch, charm	魅
魅了	みりょう	charm, captivate, hold spellbound	58A
了	リョウ	complete, finish, understand	58A
醜	シュウ、みにく-い	ugly, shameful	醜
醜聞	しゅうぶん	scandal	58A
聞	ブン、モン、き-く、き-こえる	hear, ask, listen	58A
塊	カイ、かたまり	lump, clod, mass	塊
金塊	きんかい	gold bullion	58A
金	キン、コン、かね、かな	gold, money, metal	58A

58B 刺 QUICKSILVER

☥		名刺	2 – 4
58B		めいし	*

Whip and Stab the Imprudent Measures

Non general use character thorn, (tree/wood + tapering), phonetic beat 刺

刺	シ、さ-す、さ-さる	pierce, stab, thorn	刺
名刺	めいし	name card	58B
名	メイ、ミョウ、な	name, fame	58B
策	サク	policy, plan, whip	策
拙策	せっさく	poor policy, imprudent measures	58B
拙	セツ	clumsy, poor	58B

58C 暖 QUICKSILVER

☿	暖炉	4 – 3
58C	だん ろ	1|3

Talented Women Helped the Slackers get Stoved

Former ngu character at this point, originally draw up (hand down, up + rope) 暖

媛	エン、ひめ	beautiful woman; princess	媛
才媛	さいえん	talented woman	58C
才	サイ	talent, year of age	58C
援	エン	help	援
声援	せいえん	vocal support	58C
声*	セイ、ショウ、こえ、こわ	voice	58C
緩	カン、ゆる-い、ゆる-やか、ゆる-む、ゆる-める	loose, easy, slack	緩
緩緩	ゆるゆる	leisurely	58C
暖	ダン、あたた-か、あたた-かい、あたた-まる、あたた-める	warm	暖
暖炉	だんろ	fireplace, stove	58C
炉	ロ	furnace	58C

58D 岡 QUICKSILVER

☿	静岡	4 – 3
58D	しずおか	*

The Strength of his Fortitude resembled a Steel Cable in Shizuoka

Former ngu character hill, hill + net, draw in/up, formidable hill, phonetic strong 岡

剛	ゴウ	strength	剛
剛健	ごうけん	fortitude	58D
健	ケン、すこ-やか	healthy	58D
鋼	コウ、はがね	steel	鋼
鋼鉄	こうてつ	steel	58D
鉄	テツ	iron, steel	58D
綱	コウ、つな	cable, line, principle	綱
大綱	たいこう	main principles	58D
大	ダイ、タイ、おお、おお-きい、おお-いに	big	58D
岡	コウ、おか	hill; height; knoll; rising ground	岡
静岡	しずおか	Shizuoka (city)	58D
静	セイ、ジョウ、しず、しず-か、しず-まる、しず-める	quiet, calm	58D

58E 奉 QUICKSILVER

♀		棒紅	3A
58E		ぼうべに	*

The Incredible Lipstick cost an Annual Salary

Originally two hands offering thickly growing plant, offer 奉

奉	ホウ、ブ、たてまつ-る	offer, respectful	奉
信奉	しんぽう	faith, belief	58E
信	シン	trust, believe	58E

棒	ボウ		pole, bar, club	棒
棒紅	ぼうべに		lipstick	58E
紅	コウ、ク、べに、くれない		red, crimson, rouge	58E
俸	ホウ		salary, pay	俸
年俸	ねんぽう		annual, salary	58E
年	ネン、とし		year	58E

58F 誤 QUICKSILVER

☿		誤解	4 - 2
58F		ごかい	*

We Earnestly Fear Misunderstanding as it detracts from Pleasure

Originally mouth/say + man with head tilted, bragging 誤

呉	ゴ、くれ-る	give, Wu China	呉
呉呉も	くれぐれも	earnestly	58F
虞	ぐ、おそれ	fear, anxiety	虞
虞美人草	ぐびじんそう	poppy	58F
美	ビ、うつく-しい	beautiful, fine	58F
人	ジン、ニン、ひと	person	58F
草	ソウ、くさ	grass	58F
誤	ゴ、あやま-る	mistake, mis-	誤
誤解	ごかい	misunderstanding	58F
解	カイ、ゲ、と-く、と-かす、と-ける	unravel, explain, solve	58F
娯	ゴ	pleasure, amusement	娯
娯楽	ごらく	pleasure	58F
楽	ガク、ラク、たの-しい、たの-しむ	pleasure, music	58F

58G 丘 QUICKSILVER

☿	丘陵	3 – 2
58G	きゅうりょう	5|2

Mounds and Hillocks want to become big Mountains

Originally two hills 丘

阜	フ、おか	hill; mound; left village radical	阜
岐阜県	ぎふけん	Gifu Prefecture	58G
岐	キ	fork	58G
県	ケン	prefecture	58G
丘	キュウ、おか	hill	丘
丘陵	きゅうりょう	hill, hillock	58G

361

陵*	リョウ、みささぎ	imperial tomb, mound	58G
岳	ガク、たけ	peak, imposing	岳
山岳	さんがく	mountains	58G
山	サン、やま	mountain	58G

No time to go wobbly. Notes on a 醜聞 followed the delirious 魅了 of 拙策 by incompetent CEOs. This is the 名刺 of a 才媛 who can clean up the Augean stables flowing over with many years of 緩緩 sloth, sleaze and indolence. The organisation's 大綱 having been violated for so long, there is a need for 剛健 and a determination of 鋼鉄. ”棒紅 maketh the woman”, she said with an unshakable 信奉 in the power of a decent 年俸. This lady is no 虞美人草, lest there be 誤解 of my intentions. The 娯楽 is all mine and I will banish you to some isolated 丘陵 in 岐阜県 if you stand in my way!

59A 既 QUINTESSENCE

| ㊅ | | 慨嘆 | 3A12 |
| 59A | | がいたん | * |

Outlines of Ready-Made Lamentations

Chinese only not without, person kneeling with head turned, unable 既

概	ガイ		roughly, in general	概
概略	がいりゃく		outline	59A
略	リャク		abbreviate, outline	59A
既	キ、すで-に		already, finished	既
既製	きせい		ready-made	59A
製	セイ		manufacture	59A
慨	ガイ		lament, deplore	慨
慨嘆	がいたん		lamentation	59A

| 嘆 | タン、なげ-く、なげ-かわしい | lament, admire | 59A |

59B 尉 QUINTESSENCE

ŒŒ		小尉	2 − 2
59B		しょい	*

The difference between Condolences and a Military Rank is in the heart

Press down with something hot, ironing, put into shape 尉

慰	イ、なぐさめ-る、なぐさ-む	comfort, console, amusement	慰
慰問	いもん	condolence	59B
問	モン、と-う、と-い、とん	ask	59B
尉	イ	military rank	尉
小尉	しょい	ensign	59B
小	ショウ、ちい-さい、こ、お	small	59B

59C 茂 QUINTESSENCE

ŒŒ		繁茂	3A5
59C		はんも	*

Show Superiority and Luxuriant Contempt

Pictograph of halberd/battle as 茂

越	エツ、こ-す、こ-える	cross, exceed, excel	越
優越	ゆうえつ	superiority	59C
優	ユウ、やさ-しい、すぐ-れる	superior, gentle, actor	59C

茂	モ、しげ-る	grow thickly	茂
繁茂	はんも	luxuriant/dense growth	59C
繁	ハン	profuse, rich, complex	59C
蔑	ベツ、ないがしろ、なみ.する、くらい、さげす.む	ignore; despise; neglect; ridicule	蔑
侮蔑	ぶべつ	scorn; disdain; contempt; slight	59C
侮	ブ、あなど-る	scorn, despise	59C

59D 隠 QUINTESSENCE

⊕	雲隠れ	3 - 2
59D	くもがくれ	*

Moderation Suddenly Disappeared behind the Clouds

Chinese only compassion, care 隠

穏	オン、おだ-やか	peace, moderation	穏
穏和	おんわ	moderation	59D
和	ワ、オ、やわ-らぐ、やわ-らげる、なご-む、なご-やか	Japan, peace, soft	59D
急	キュウ、いそ-ぐ	hurry, emergency, sudden	急
緩急	かんきゅう	in case of emergency	59D
緩	カン、ゆる-い、ゆる-やか、ゆる-む、ゆる-める	loose, easy, slack	59D
隠	イン、かく-す、かく-れる	hide	隠
雲隠れ	くもがくれ	be hidden behind clouds, disappear	59D

| 雲 | ウン、くも | cloud | 59D |

59E 激 QUINTESSENCE

🜚		憤激	2 – 13
59E		ふんげき	*

Pride & Fury

Water, release (literally strike a person) and white, phonetic to beat, water striking 傲

傲	ゴウ、おご.る、あなど.る	be proud	傲
傲然	ごうぜん	haughty	59E
然	ゼン、ネン	duly, thus, so, but	59E
激	ゲキ、はげ-しい	violent, fierce, strong, intense	激
憤激	ふんげき	fury	59E
憤	フン、いきどお-る	indignant, angry	59E

59F 唐 QUINTESSENCE

🜚		唐本	2 – 2
59F		とうほん	*

Chinese Sugar & spice

Originally mouth + hands holding pestle, phonetic brag/boast 唐

唐	トウ、から	(T'ang) China	唐
唐本	とうほん	Chinese book	59F
本	ホン、もと	root, true, book, this	59F
糖	トウ	sugar	糖
砂糖	さとう	sugar	59F

砂	サ、シャ、すな	sand, gravel, grain	59F

59G 甘 QUINTESSENCE

⊕	甘え	7B18
59G	あまえ	0|2

The Sweet Dark Blue Perfume of Four Animals Accounted for her Immense Patience

Originally something held in the mouth, savoured, sweet 甘

甘	カン、あま-い、あま-える、-あま-やかす	sweet, presume upon	甘
甘え	あまえ	presumption	59G
紺	コン	dark blue, dye	紺
紺色	こんいろ	dark blue	59G
色	ショク、シキ、いろ	colour, sensuality	59G
香	コウ、キョウ、か、かお-り、かお-る	fragrance, incense	香
香水	こうすい	perfume	59G
水	スイ、みず	water	59G
匹	ヒツ、ひき	match, common, cloth, animal counter	匹
四匹	よんひき	four animals	59G
四*	シ、よ、よ-つ、よっ-つ、よん	four	59G
勘	カン	endure, consider, investigate, sense	勘
勘定	かんじょう	bill, account	59G
定	テイ、ジョウ、さだ-める、さだ-まる、さだ-か	fix, establish	59G

甚	ジン、はなは-だ、はなは-だしい	great(ly), extreme	甚
甚大	じんだい な	immense	59G
大	ダイ、タイ、おお、おお-きい、おお-いに	big	59G
堪	カン、た-える	endure, withstand	堪
堪忍	かんにん	patience	59G
忍	ニン、しの-ぶ、しの-ばせる	endure, stealth	59G

Matters of the cloth. The end of sartorial splendour is a cause for grief and 慨嘆 now that the march of 既製 fashion is virtually unstoppable. It is time for 慰問 and to mourn the passing of the 優越 of bespoke tailoring. There can be nothing but 侮蔑 for those mass-produced horrors of depressing 穏和, the 雲隠れ of which can only be a blessing. Beware of the 憤激 of the few remaining 傲然 fashionistas who are not prepared to 砂糖 coat this unfortunate state of affairs. They have lost 堪忍 a long time ago and their 甚大 frustration with cheap fabrics is reaching boiling point. And as far as their views on 紺色 cottons are concerned: don't go there darling!

60A 患 RECTIFICATION

| ✉ | 患者 家族 | 2 |
| 60A | かんじゃかぞく | * |

Patiently Skewering sweethearts and Relatives

Pierced heart, afflicted 患

患	カン、わずら-う	disease, afflicted	患
患者家族	かんじゃかぞく	patient and relatives	60A
者	シャ、もの	person	60A
家	カ、ケ、いえ、や	house, specialist	60A
族	ゾク	clan, family	60A

串	カン、セン、くし	shish kebab; spit; skewer	串
串刺し	くしざし	skewer	60A
刺	シ、さ-す、さ-さる	pierce, stab, thorn	60A

60B 喝 RECTIFICATION

	喝さい	7C13
60B	かっさい	*

He had an Audience with a Smelly & Thirsty Ruler but he was Scolded for displaying Complicated Coarse Brown Cloth

Chinese only range of interrogatives, say, encircle, surround and person: ask and/or threaten 喝

謁	エツ	audience (with ruler)	謁
拝謁	はいえつ	audience	60B
拝	ハイ、おが-む	worship, respectful	60B
匂	にお-う	fragrant; stink; glow; insinuate	匂
匂い袋	においぶくろ	sachet	60B
袋	タイ、ふくろ	bag, pouch	60B
渇	カツ、かわ-く	thirst, parched	渇
渇き	かわき	thirst	60B
喝	カツ	shout, scold	喝
喝さい	かっさい	applause	60B
掲	ケイ、かか-げる	display, hoist, print	掲
掲示板	けいじばん	noticeboard	60B
示	ジ、シ、しめ-す	show	60B
板	ハン、バン、いた	board, plate	60B
葛	カツ、くず、つづら	arrowroot; kudzu	葛
葛藤	かっとう	conflict; complication; troubles; discord	60B

368

藤	トウ、ふじ	wisteria	60B
褐	カツ	brown, coarse cloth	褐
褐色	かっしょく	brown	60B
色	ショク、シキ、いろ	colour, sensuality	60B

60C 壊 RECTIFICATION

⬜		壊滅	2B
60C		かいめつ	*

Destroy yearning for Idleness

Wrap Chinese only conceal/carry in the sleeve, eye, variant of multitude 懐

壊	カイ、こわ-す、こわ-れる	break, destroy, ruin	壊
壊滅	かいめつ	destruction	60C
滅	メツ、ほろ-びる、ほろ-ぼす	destroy	60C
懐	カイ、ふところ、なつ-かしい、なつ-かしむ、なつ-く、なつ-ける	bosom, yearn, fond	懐
懐手	ふところで	idleness	60C
手	シュ、て、た	hand	60C

60D 卸 RECTIFICATION

⬜		卸売	2 - 2
60D		おろしうり	*

Wholesale Drivers

Originally drive a cart 卸

卸	おろ-す、おろし	wholesale, grate	卸
卸売	おろしうり	wholesale	60D
売	バイ、う-る、う-れる	sell	60D
御	ギョ、ゴ、おん	handle, drive, honourable, your	御
御者	ぎょしゃ	driver	60D
者	シャ、もの	person	60D

60E 喚 RECTIFICATION

▱		叫喚	2 - 5
60E		きょうかん	*

A Scream in Exchange for Ventilation

Chinese only lively, women's genitals + spread thighs with hands, sex 喚

喚	カン	shout, yell	喚
叫喚	きょうかん	cry, scream	60E
叫	キョウ、さけ-ぶ	shout, yell	60E
換	カン、か-える、か-わる	exchange	換
換気	かんき	ventilation	60E
気	キ、ケ	spirit	60E

60F 融 RECTIFICATION

▱		金融	2 - 3
60F		きんゆう	*

Spacing bankruptcies will improve Finance

Large pot on stand 隔

隔	カク、へだ-てる、ひだ-たる	separate, interpose	隔
間隔	かんかく	spacing	60F
間	カン、ケン、あいだ、ま	space, gap	60F
融	ユウ	dissolve, melt	融
金融	きんゆう	finance	60F
金	キン、コン、かね、かな	gold, money, metal	60F

60G 兼 RECTIFICATION

	兼用	5A5
60G	けんよう	1|1

In the Kamakura Period fear and Loathing Combined with Cheap Humility

Originally hand holding two rice plants, doing two things at once
兼

鎌	レン、かま	sickle; scythe; trick	鎌
鎌倉時代	かまくらじだい	Kamakura Period	60G
倉	ソウ、くら	warehouse, sudden	60G
時	ジ、とき	time	60G
代	ダイ、タイ、か-わる、か-える、よ、しろ	replace, world, generation, fee	60G
嫌	ケン、ゲン、きら-う、いや	dislike(d)	嫌
嫌悪	けんお	loathing	60G
悪	アク、オ、わる-い	bad, hate	60G
兼	ケン、か-ねる	combine, unable	兼
兼用	けんよう	dual purpose	60G
用	ヨウ、もち-いる	use	60G
廉	レン	honest, cheap, angle	廉

371

廉価	れんか	low price	60G
価*	カ、あたい	price, value, worth	60G
謙	ケン	humble, modest	謙
謙譲	けんじょう	humility	60G
譲	ジョウ、ゆず-る	hand over, yield	60G

I wouldn't drink that if I were you. Turning the 串刺し of specially treated meat, making intoxicating 匂い袋 or preparing 褐色 poisonous potions are some of the methods to wreak the 壊滅 of unwanted companions. Indeed, 懐手 is the devil's workshop so let's tell the 御者 to make haste and to procure those herbs at 卸売 prices. Of course, tampering with 換気 also works well as long as 叫喚 are prevented. It is prudent to have some 間隔 between the lethal drops otherwise securing 金融 will be jeopardised. Sometimes that intense feeling of 嫌悪 becomes just too much so that offering a goblet of fragrant wine will serve the 兼用 of providing temporary contentment for one and permanent relief for the other: a 廉価 to pay to be sure!

61A 挟 SAL-AMMONIAC

✖		板挟み	4C10
61A		いたばさみ	*

The dire Straits of Cramped Dilemma's raise no Smile

Non general use character insert, big person squeezed between two others 挟

峡	キョウ	ravine, gorge	峡
海峡	かいきょう	straits	61A
海	カイ、うみ	sea	61A
狭	キョウ、せま-い、せば-める、せば-まる	narrow, small	狭

狭苦しい	せまくるしい	cramped	61A
苦	ク、くる-しい、くる-しむ、くる-しめる、にが-い	painful, bitter	61A
挟	キョウ、はさ-む、はさ-まる	insert, pinch, squeeze between	挟
板挟み	いたばさみ	dilemma	61A
板	ハン、バン、いた	board, plate	61A
頬	キョウ、ほお	cheek	頬
頬笑み	ほおえみ	smile	61A
笑	ショウ、わら-う、え-む	laugh, smile	61A

61B 巨 SAL-AMMONIAC

✳	巨人	3A5
61B	きょじん	*

The Denial of the Giant created a huge Distance

Carpenter's square characterised by its large size 巨

拒	キョ、こば-む	refuse, resist	拒
拒否	きょひ	denial	61B
否	ヒ、いな	no, decline, deny	61B
巨	キョ	huge, giant	巨
巨人	きょじん	giant	61B
人	ジン、ニン、ひと	person	61B
距	キョ	distance, cockspur	距
距離	きょり	distance	61B
離	リ、はな-れる、はな-す	separate, leave	61B

61C 乙 SAL-AMMONIAC

✖	乙 に	3A3
61C	おつ に	*

Oddly, the Dry Battery Begged to be wet

Double bladed sword, unusual 乙

乙	オツ	odd, B, 2nd, stylish	乙
乙 に	おつ に	strangely	61C
乾	カン、かわ-く、かわ-かす	dry	乾
乾電池	かんでんち	dry battery	61C
電	デン	electricity	61C
池	チ、いけ	pond, lake	61C
乞	コツ、キツ、キ、キケ、コチ、こ.う	beg; invite; ask	乞
乞食	こじき	beggar	61C
食	ショク、ジキ、く-う、く-らう、た-べる	food, eat	61C

61D 仰 SAL-AMMONIAC

✖	信仰	3
61D	しんこう	*

Welcome to all Suppressed Creeds

Chinese only raise, bending person looking up respectfully 仰

迎	ゲイ、むか-える	greet, welcome, meet	迎
歓迎会	かんげいかい	reception	61D
歓	カン	rejoice, merry	61D

会	カイ、エ、あ-う	meet	61D
抑	ヨク、お-さえる	restrain, press down	抑
抑圧	よくあつ	suppression	61D
圧	アツ	pressure	61D
仰	ギョウ、コウ、あお-ぐ、おお-せ	lookup, state, respect	仰
信仰	しんこう	faith, creed	61D
信	シン	trust, believe	61D

61E 屈 SAL-AMMONIAC

✖		窮屈		4 - 2
61E		きゅうくつ		0|1

Dig a Narrow Ditch in the Slums

Originally tail/genitals, testes, put out/remove balls, castrate 屈

掘	クツ、ほ-る	dig	掘
掘り出す	ほりだす	unearth	61E
出	シュツ、スイ、で-る、だ-す	emerge, put out	61E
屈	クツ	submit, crouch	屈
窮屈	きゅうくつ	narrow, cramped	61E
窮*	キュウ、きわ-める、きわ-まる	distress, extreme	61E
堀	ほり	moat, ditch, canal	堀
堀川	ほりかわ	canal	61E
川	セン、かわ	river	61E
窟	クツ、あな、いわや	cavern	窟
貧民窟	ひんみんくつ	slums	61E

貧	ヒン、ビン、まず-しい	poor, meagre	61E
民	ミン、たみ	people, populace	61E

61F 缶 SAL-AMMONIAC

🜹	缶切り	3A7
61F	かんきり	*

Opening a Can of Depressing Ceramic Wares

Secure vessel for pouring liquid into 缶

缶	カン	can, boiler	缶
缶切り	かんきり	can opener	61F
切	セツ、サイ、き-る、き-れる	cut	61F
鬱	ウツ、うっ.する、ふさ.ぐ、しげ.る	gloom; depression; melancholy	鬱
憂鬱	ゆううつ	depression	61F
憂	ユウ、うれ-える、うれ-い、う-い	grief, sorrow	61F
陶	トウ	ceramic, happy, educate	陶
陶器	とうき	ceramic ware	61F
器	キ、うつわ	vessel, utensil, skill	61F

61G 孤 SAL-AMMONIAC

🜹	孤立	2A6
61G	こりつ	*

Bow in Isolation

Non general use character melon, phonetic alone 孤

弧	コ	arc, arch, bow	弧
弧形	こけい	arc	61G
形	ケイ、ギョウ、かた、かたち	shape, pattern	61G
孤	コ	orphan, lonely	孤
孤立	こりつ	isolation	61G
立	リツ、リュウ、た-つ、た-てる	stand, rise, leave	61G

It was more fun in hell. Shady characters from the Hunger 海峡 flashed cruel and unusual 頬笑み when the warden 拒否 them to go beyond the 距離 across Bedlam Point: a place where no 乾電池 would work and that even 乞食 would avoid. The inmates there experienced such terrible 抑圧 that many would lose their 信仰. Do not start 掘り出す there because you won't like what you will find and never venture close to that dismal 堀川. The 窮屈 cells were filled with patients suffering from 憂鬱 and the dangerous ones were for safety reasons even denied the use of a 缶切り. Lives spent in 孤立 under the grim 弧形 of the most sombre melancholy.

62A 偶 SILVER

| | 偶然 | 4A4 |
| 62A | ぐうぜん | * |

In the Corner I met a Fool By Chance

Chinese only begin, not clear/open, scorpion with twisting tail 偶

隅	グウ、すみ	corner, nook	隅
隅石	すみいし	corner stone	62A
石	セキ、シャク、コク、いし	stone, rock	62A
遇	グウ	meet, receive, treat	遇
待遇	たいぐう	reception	62A

待	タイ、ま-つ	wait	62A
愚	グ、おろ-か	foolish	愚
愚人	ぐじん	fool	62A
人	ジン、ニン、ひと	person	62A
偶	グウ	by chance, spouse, doll	偶
偶然	ぐうぜん	by chance	62A
然	ゼン、ネン	duly, thus, so, but	62A

62B 堅 SILVER

🏛		堅固	3 - 3
62B		けんご	*

A Tight and Solid Pretence of Wisdom

Chinese only hard and wise, hand presses the eye? 堅

緊	キン	tight, compact	緊
緊張	きんちょう	tension	62B
張	チョウ、は-る	stretch	62B
堅	ケン、かた-い	firm, solid, hard	堅
堅固	けんご	firm, steady	62B
固	コ、かた-める、かた-まる、かた-い	hard, firm, solid	62B
賢	ケン、かしこ-い	wise	賢
賢立つ	かしこだて	pretence of wisdom	62B
立	リツ、リュウ、た-つ、た-てる	stand, rise, leave	62B

62C 傑 SILVER

		豪傑	5D7
62C		ごうけつ	1|1

Last Year Flash the Hero Behaved in a Neighbourly manner

Chinese only bird's roost, heroic 傑

年	ネン、とし	year	年
去年	きょねん	last year	62C
去	キョ、コ、さ-る	go, leave, past	62C
瞬	シュン、またた-く	flash, twinkle, blink	瞬
瞬く間	またたくまに	in the twinkling of an eye	62C
間	カン、ケン、あいだ、ま	space, gap	62C
傑	ケツ	outstanding	傑
豪傑	ごうけつ	hero, great man	62C
豪*	ゴウ	strength, splendour, Australia	62C
舞	ブ、ま-う、ま-い	dance, flit	舞
振舞い	ふるまい	behaviour	62C
振	シン、ふ-る、ふ-るう	wave, swing, air, manner, after	62C
隣	リン、とな-る、となり	neighbour, adjoin	隣
隣接	りんせつ	adjacency	62C
接	セツ、つ-ぐ	contact, join	62C

62D 傘 SILVER

		相合傘	4A5
62D 並		あいあいがさ	*

Shady Mel & Shifty Barry Share an Umbrella

Pictograph of a parasol 傘
Originally billowing vapours, later used to speak + rain 雲

曇	ドン、くも-る	to cloud, dim, mar	曇
曇天	どんてん	dull (cloudy) weather	62D
天	テン、あめ、あま	heaven, sky	62D
桑	ソウ、くわ	mulberry	桑
桑原	くわばら	mulberry field	62D
原	ゲン、はら	plain, origin	62D
雲	ウン、くも	cloud	雲
浮雲	うきぐも	drifting or floating cloud; instability	62D
浮	フ、う-く、う-かれる、う-かぶ、う-かべる	float, fleeting, gay	62D
傘	サン、かさ	umbrella, parasol	傘
相合傘	あいあいがさ	sharing an umbrella; under one umbrella	62D
相	ソウ、ショウ、あい	mutual, minister, aspect	62D
合	ゴウ、ガッ、カッ、あ-う、あ-わす、あ-わせる	meet, join, fit	62D

62E 慶 SILVER

| ⛩ | 慶弔 | 5 - 11 |
| 62E | けいちょう | 2\|03 |

Beauty's Foolish Recommendations give Joy at the Base of the Mountain

Deer, love and goodness 慶

| 麗 | レイ、うるわ-しい | beautiful | 麗 |

華麗	かれい	splendid, magnificent	62E
華*	カ、ケ、はな	flower, showy, China	62E
鹿	ロク、か、しか、しし	deer	鹿
馬鹿	ばか	simpleton; dimwit; sluggard	62E
馬	バ、うま、ま	horse	62E
薦	セン、すす-める	recommend, mat	薦
推薦	すいせん	recommendation	62E
推	スイ、お-す	infer, push ahead	62E
慶	ケイ	joy	慶
慶弔	けいちょう	congratulations and condolences	62E
弔	チョウ、とむら-う	mourn, funeral	62E
麓	ロク、ふもと	foot of a mountain	麓
山麓	さんろく	foot or base of a mountain	62E
山	サン、やま	mountain	62E

62F 需 SILVER

	需要	4C15
62F	じゅよう	3‖05

Tango Endurance Demands Confucianism

Non general use character however, originally beard, beard soaked by the rain 需

端	タン、はし、は、はた	extremity, edge, bit, upright	端
端午	たんご	Boys' Day (May 5)	62F
午*	ゴ	noon	62F
耐	タイ、た-える	endure, bear	耐
耐久	たいきゅう	endurance	62F

久*	キュウ、ク、ひさ-しい	long time	62F
需	ジュ	need, demand	需
需要	じゅよう	demand	62F
要	ヨウ、い-る	need, vital, pivot	62F
儒	ジュ	Confucianism	儒
儒教	じゅきょう	Confucianism	62F
教	キョウ、おし-える、おそ-わる	teach	62F

62G 雇 SILVER

| | 回顧 | 2 |
| 62G | かいこ | * |

In the Employment of Retrospection

Bird + door, ungainly flapping of a quail 雇

雇	コ、やと-う	employ, hire	雇
雇い人	やといにん	employee	62G
人	ジン、ニン、ひと	person	62G
顧	コ、かえり-みる	look back	顧
回顧	かいこ	retrospection	62G
回	カイ、エ、まわ-る、まわ-す	turn, rotate	62G

Only fools and horses. 愚人 rely on things to happen 偶然 and resort to a 賢立つ to explain away the lack of 堅固 results. On the other hand, the 振舞い of our valiant 豪傑 is certainly not that of 浮雲 during a spell of 曇天. A shared vision is like 相合傘 gathering 華麗 ideas but repulsing 馬鹿 and inappropriate 推薦. It goes without saying that the 需要 for 耐久 is paramount. And a follower of 儒教 would argue that rueful 20/20 回顧 is a poor substitute for hiring 雇い人 that can get the job done.

63A 頃 TIN

𝄢	日頃	2 - 3
63A	ひごろ	*

Keiko Recently became Trendy

Character indicates slumped head, person fallen to one side 頃

傾	ケイ、かたむ-く、かたむ-ける	incline, dedicate	傾
傾向	けいこう	tendency; trend; inclination;	63A
向	コウ、む-く、む-ける、む-かう、む-こう	face towards, beyond	63A
頃	ケイ、ころ	time; about; toward	頃
日頃	ひごろ	recently	63A
日	ニチ、ジツ、ひ、か	sun, day	63A

63B 執 TIN

𝄢	執着	2 - 3
63B	しゅうちゃく	*

Earnest had a Serious Attachment

Old form shows shackles + kneeling person, shackle a prisoner, seize 執

摯	シ、いた.る	gift; seriousness	摯
真摯	しんし	earnest	63B
真	シン、ま	true, quintessence	63B
執	シツ、シュウ、と-る	take, grasp, execute	執

| 執着 | しゅうちゃく | attachment; adhesion; tenacity | 63B |
| 着 | チャク、ジャク、き-る、き-せる、つ-く、つ-ける | arrive, wear | 63B |

63C 舟 TIN

| ⛵ | 渡し舟 | 6A14 |
| 63C | わたしぶね | * |

The Red Conveyor Belt Ferried a Bowling General Metaphorically

Boat 舟

丹	タン	red, sincere	丹
丹念	たんねん	assiduity; diligence; application	63C
念	ネン	thought, concern	33C
搬	ハン	carry, transport	搬
搬送帯	はんそうたい	conveyor belt	63C
送	ソウ、おく-る	send	63C
帯	タイ、お-びる、おび	wear, zone	63C
舟	シュウ、ふね、ふな	boat	舟
渡し舟	わたしぶね	ferry boat	63C
渡	ト、わた-る、わた-す	cross, handover	63C
盤	バン	tray, board, bowl, plate	盤
水盤	すいばん	bowl	63C
水	スイ、みず	water	63C
般	ハン	general, time, carry	般
一般	いっぱん	general	63C
一	イチ、イツ、ひと、ひと-つ	one	63C

喩	ユ、たと.える、さと.す	metaphor	喩
比喩	ひゆ	metaphor	63C
比	ヒ、くら-べる	compare, ratio	63C

63D 薫 TIN

🔧		薫香	2B4
63D		くんこう	*

A Medal with Incense

Pleasant smelling smoke 薫

勲	クン		merit	勲
勲章	くんしょう		medal	63D
章	ショウ		badge, chapter	63D
薫	クン、かお-る		aroma, fragrance, aura	薫
薫香	くんこう		incense	63D
香	コウ、キョウ、か、かお-り、かお-る		fragrance, incense	63D

63E 渓 TIN

🔧		渓谷	2A4
63E		けいこく	*

Cocky Gorge and Hen-Picked Valley

Originally valley + Chinese only 'doubt' twisting threads 渓

鶏	ケイ、にわとり	chicken, hen, cock	鶏
鶏卵	けいらん	hen's egg	63E
卵	ラン、たまご	egg, ovum, spawn	63E

渓	ケイ	valley, gorge	渓
渓谷	けいこく	valley, gorge	63E
谷	コク、たに	valley, gorge	63E

63F 譲 TIN

	互譲	4E7
63F	ごじょう	0|3

Hand Over your Daughter and you shall have my Brewing Soil

Originally people accusing each other 譲

譲	ジョウ、ゆず-る	hand over, yield	譲
互譲	ごじょう	concession, compromise, conciliation	63F
互*	ゴ、たが-い	mutual, reciprocal, together	63F
嬢	ジョウ	young lady, daughter	嬢
お嬢さん	おじょうさん	young lady, daughter	63F
醸	ジョウ、かも-す	brew, cause	醸
醸造	じょうぞう	brewing	63F
造	ゾウ、つく-る	make, build	63F
壌	ジョウ	earth, soil	壌
土壌	どじょう	earth, soil	63F
土	ド、ト、つち	earth	63F

63G 企 TIN

	企て	2A
63G	くわだて	*

Scheming for Happiness

Person + foot, phonetic precarious, standing on tiptoe 企

企	キ、くわだ-てる	plan, undertake	企
企て	くわだて	plot, scheme	63G
祉	シ	well-being, happiness	祉
福祉国家	ふくしこっか	welfare state	63G
福	フク	good fortune	63G
国	コク、くに	country, region	63G
家	カ、ケ、いえ、や	house, specialist	63G

Erst kommt das Fressen, dann die Moral. The regrettable 傾向 towards mindless escapism 日頃 can be seen in the 執着 of many viewers to fatuous cooking programs hosted by sometimes 真摯 but always jovial presenters. The proliferation of those media personalities who, like a 搬送帯 or a quaint little 渡し舟, bring you on a 水盤 fresh produce and reassuring bonhomie has become de rigueur. There might not be any 勲章 of merit but who could dismiss those fabulous 鶏卵 sourced in that scenic 渓谷 where the 土壌 has such special qualities? The お嬢さん intoned that she will make no 互譲 to substandard organic sprouts (to be used in home 醸造) and that any 企て to improve the diet of obese citizens of the 福祉国家 would be warmly welcomed!

Chapter 10 Capricorn

64A 荒 VITRIOL

⌖	荒れ 狂う	2 - 3
64A	あれくるう	*

The Blunderer goes Berserk

Chinese only vast watery waste, (river + death) 荒

慌	コウ、あわ-てる、あわ-ただしい	be flustered	慌
慌て者	あわたもの	blunderer	64A
者	シャ、もの	person	64A
荒	コウ、あら-い、あ-れる、あ-らす	rough, wild, waste	荒
荒れ狂う	あれくるう	rage, run amok	64A
狂	キョウ、くる-う、くる-おしい	lunatic, mad	64A

64B 膝 VITRIOL

⌖	諸膝	2
64B	もろひざ	*

On Both Black Knees Lapping it up

Tree + drops of moisture, resin, sap of the lacquer-tree 漆

漆	シツ、うるし	lacquer, varnish	漆
漆黒	しっこく	jet black	64B

黒	コク、くろ、くろ-い	black	64B
膝	シツ、ひざ	knee; lap	膝
諸膝	もろひざ	both knees	64B
諸	ショ、もろ	various, many	64B

64C 竜 VITRIOL

		竜巻	4C9
64C		たつまき	*

When under Siege, Wind Whirls and Water Falls as the Dragon Attacks

Dragon, fearsome, flying 竜

籠	ロウ、ル、かご、こ.める、こも.る、こ.む	basket; devote oneself; seclude oneself; cage	籠
籠城	ろうじょう	under siege	64C
城	ジョウ、しろ	castle	64C
竜	リュウ、たつ	dragon	竜
竜巻	たつまき	whirlwind	64C
巻	カン、ま-く、ま-き	roll, reel, volume	64C
滝	たき	cascade, waterfall	滝
清滝	きよたき	clear waterfall	64C
清	セイ、ショウ、きよ-い、きよ-まる、きよ-める	pure, clean	64C
襲	シュウ、おそ-う	attack, inherit	襲
襲来	しゅうらい	invasion	64C
来	ライ、く-る、きた-る、きた-す	come	64C

64D 顕 VITRIOL

(key)		顕微 鏡	2B1
64D		けんびきょう	*

Microscopic Humidity

Chinese only motes, small particles of dust, sunlight + double thread 顕

顕	ケン	manifest, visible	顕
顕微鏡	けんびきょう	microscope	64D
微	ビ	tiny, obscure, faint, secretive	64D
鏡	キョウ、がかみ	mirror	64D
湿	シツ、しめ-る、しめ-す	damp, moist, humid	湿
湿度	しつど	humidity	64D
度	ド、ト、タク、たび	degree, times	64D

64E 秀 VITRIOL

(key)		誘惑	3 - 7
64E		ゆうわく	*

She was Seduced by the Transparency of His Excellency

Rice plant + bending person, rice plant bent (heavy head), excellent 秀

誘	ユウ、さそ-う	invite, tempt, lead	誘
誘惑	ゆうわく	seduction	64E
惑	ワク、まど-う	be confused	64E

透	トウ、す-く、す-かす、す-ける	clear, transparent	透
透明	とうめい	transparent	64E
明	メイ、ミョウ、あ-かり、あか-るい、あか-るむ	clear, open, bright	64E
秀	シュウ、ひい-でる	excel, excellent	秀
秀逸	しゅういつ	excellence	64E
逸	イツ	escape, go astray, fast, excel	64E

64F 珍 VITRIOL

⌨		珍奇	5 - 9
64F 並		ちんき	*

I Truly would like to Examine EC's Strange Braziers

Jewel and person + hair, phonetic pure/unblemished: rare 珍
Originally pictograph of the roots of a tree, essence/origin 本

本	ホン、もと	root, true, book, this	本
本格	ほんかく	original method, orthodox, genuine	64F
格	カク、コウ	standard, status	64F
診	シン、み-る	diagnose, examine	診
健診	けんしん	physical examination	64F
健	ケン、すこ-やか	healthy	64F
体	タイ、テイ、からだ	body	体

欧州共同体	おうしゅうきょうどうたい	European Community, EC	64F
欧	オウ	Europe, eu-	64F
州	シュウ、す	state, province	64F
共	キョウ、とも	together	64F
同	ドウ、おな-じ	same	64F
珍	チン、めずら-しい	rare, curious	珍
珍奇	ちんき	strange, rare, curious	64F
奇	キ	strange, odd	64F
鉢	ハチ、ハツ	bowl, pot, skull	鉢
火鉢	ひばち	brazier	64F
火	カ、ひ、ほ	fire	64F

64G 升 VITRIOL

⌐━	升目	3 - 2
64G	ますめ	*

Erratic Flies like to Top Up on Liquid Measures

Ladle 升

飛	ヒ、と-ぶ、と-ばす	fly	飛
突飛	とっぴ	erratic; wild; extraordinary	64G
突	トツ、つ-く	thrust, lunge, protrude	64G
昇	ショウ、のぼ-る	rise, ascend	昇
上昇	じょうしょう	rise, ascend, climb	64G
上	ジョウ、ショウ、うえ、うわ、かみ、あ-げる、あ-がる、のぼ-る	up, top, over, go up	64G

升	ショウ、ます	liquid measure	升
升目	ますめ	measure	64G
目	モク、ボク、め、ま	eye, ordinal, suffix	64G

Dark sporting matter. After too many drinks a well-known player started to 荒れ狂う and ended up falling down on 諸膝 outside in the street. As the sports bar seemed 籠城 whilst an 襲来 from a rival club was a distinct possibility, it was time to brace oneself for the 湿度 of fervent battle. The 秀逸 of the side was never in doubt although there were accusations regarding lack of 透明. Management would always claim that there was no need for a 健診 of the victims and that it was best to ignore 珍奇 bodily symptoms. It was argued that one should make allowances for the 突飛 behaviour of athletes because their 上昇 to the top is more important than the unfortunate experiences of a few supporters...

65A 寿 WATER

▽	寿命	2D11
65A	じゅみょう	*

Cast your Life Span in lead

Originally old man who has lived a long time 寿

鋳	チュウ、い-る	cast, found, mint	鋳
鋳鉄	ちゅうてつ	cast iron	65A
鉄	テツ	iron, steel	65A
寿	ジュ、ことぶき	long life, congratulation	寿
寿命	じゅみょう	life span	65A
命	メイ、ミョウ、いのち	life, order	65A

65B 叔 WATER

▽		叔父	5 – 5
65B		おじ	*

Chastity was Supervised by her Relatively Quiet Uncle

Originally hand pulling up a potato 叔

淑	シュク		pure, graceful	淑
貞淑	ていしゅく		chastity	65B
貞	テイ		chastity, virtue	65B
督	トク		supervise, urge	督
監督	かんとく		supervision	65B
監	カン		supervise, watch	65B
戚	セキ、いた-む、うれ-える		grieve	戚
親戚	しんせき		relatives	65B
親	シン、おや、した-しい、した-しむ		intimate, parent	65B
寂	ジャク、セキ、さび、さび-しい、さび-れる		quiet, lonely	寂
閑寂	かんじゃく		quiet, tranquillity	65B
閑	カン		leisure, quiet	65B
叔	シュク		uncle, young brother	叔
叔父	おじ*		uncle	65B
父	フ、ちち		father	65B

65C 盾 WATER

▽		後盾	2B1
65C		うしろだて	0|1

Backing the Vicious Circle

Eye + shield and possibly piercing/intently 盾

盾	ジュン、たて	shield, pretext	盾
後盾	うしろだて	backing	65C
後*	ゴ、コウ、のち、うし-ろ、あと、おく-れる	behind, after, delay	65C
循	ジュン	follow	循
悪循環	あくじゅんかん	vicious circle	65C
悪	アク、オ、わる-い	bad, hate	65C
環	カン	ring, circle	65C

65D 雌 WATER

▽		雌牛	2D8
65D		めうし	*

The Ultraviolet Rays Transformed him into a Purple Cow

Non general use character this/here, foot/stop + sitting person 雌

紫	シ、むらさき	purple, violet	紫
紫外線	しがいせん	ultraviolet rays	65D
外	ガイ、ゲ、そと、ほか、はず-す、はず-れる	outside, other, undo	65D
線	セン	line	65D
雌	シ、め、めす	female	雌
雌牛	めうし	cow, heifer	65D
牛	ギュウ、うし	cow	65D

65E 崩 WATER

▽	山崩れ	2B4
65E	やまくずれ	*

A Landslide of mountaineering books dropped off the Bookshelf

String of matching jewels, matching join 崩

崩	ホウ、くず-れる、くず-す	crumble, collapse	崩
山崩れ	やまくずれ	landslide	65E
山	サン、やま	mountain	65E
棚	たな	shelf, trellis	棚
本棚	ほんだな	bookshelf	65E
本	ホン、もと	root, true, book, this	65E

65F 瀬 WATER

▽	瀬戸	2C6
65F	せと	*

Channel your Request through shallow waters

Originally bundle, money, slash/cut, profit financially 頼

瀬	せ	shallows, rapids	瀬
瀬戸	せと	strait, channel	65F
戸	コ、と	door	65F
頼	ライ、たの-む、たの-もしい、たよ-る	request, rely	頼
依頼	いらい	request	65F
依	イ、エ	depend, as is	65F

65G 隻 WATER

▽	三隻	2 - 5
65G	さんせき	0|1

Both Sides of Three Ships

Bird and hand, one of a pair, as opposed to a pair 隻

双	ソウ、ふた	pair, both	双
双方	そうほう	both sides	65G
方	ホウ、かた	side, way, square, direction, person	65G
隻	セキ	one of a pair, ship counter	隻
三隻	さんせき	three ships/boats	65G
三*	サン、み、み- つ、みっ-つ	three	65G

Visions of virtue. The average 寿命 of virtue was sometimes prolonged by using 鋳鉄 to secure the 貞淑 of female 親戚. In addition, strict 監督 and vigorous 後盾 by male relatives was deemed necessary to avoid a 悪循環 of sensual cause and sexual effect. It is prudent to prevent 雌牛 from wondering off into the 紫外線 part of the spectrum just as it is imperative to divert water in order to avoid triggering a 山崩れ. Ensure that you safely navigate the 瀬戸 of wickedness and attempt to steer your fragile 三隻 of Faith, Hope and Charity without fail to the other end.

66A 帝 WHITE LEAD

⌇	帝国	3A5
66A	ていこく	0|1

Meet the Clear Vision of the Imperial Deadline

Two-tier table + cross-struts and item, variant of altar 帝

諦	テイ、あきら-める	abandon; give up	諦
諦観	ていかん	clear vision; resignation (as in reconciling oneself)	66A
観	カン	watch, observe	66A
帝	テイ	emperor	帝
帝国	ていこく	empire	66A
国	コク、くに	country, region	66A
締	テイ、し-まる、し-める	bind, tighten, close	締
締め切り	しめきり	deadline	66A
切	セツ、サイ、き-る、き-れる	cut	66A

66B 卓 WHITE LEAD

⩘		食卓	4 − 12
66B 並		しょくたく	*

Top of the Mourning for a Fast Gr(e)as(s)y Table Snack

Core meaning high/excellent 卓
Sun and one line cutting another representing cutting/opening, sun breaking through 早

悼	トウ、いた-む	grieve, mourn	悼
哀悼	あいとう	mourning	66B
哀	アイ、あわ-れ、あわ-れむ	sorrow, pity	66B
早	ソウ、サッ、はや-い、はや-まる、はや-める	early, fast, prompt	早
素早い	すばやい	fast, quick, nimble, agile	66B

素	ソ、ス	element, base, bare	66B
草	ソウ、くさ	grass	草
青草	あおくさ	green grass	66B
青	セイ、ショウ、あお、あお-い	blue, green, young	66B
卓	タク	table, excel, high	卓
食卓	しょくたく	dining table	66B
食	ショク、ジキ、く-う、く-らう、た-べる	food, eat	66B

66C 逮 WHITE LEAD

⊆		逮捕	2B9
66C		たいほ	*

Slavery is an Arresting system

Originally seizing an animal by the tail 逮

隷	レイ	slave, prisoner	隷
奴隷制	どれいせい	slavery	66C
奴	ド	slave, servant, guy	66C
制	セイ	system, control	66C
逮	タイ	chase, seize	逮
逮捕	たいほ	arrest	66C
捕	ホ、と-らえる、と-らわれる、と-る、つか-まえる、つか-まる	seize, capture	66C

66D 庶 WHITE LEAD

☒	庶民	2A4
66D	しょみん	*

Intercept that Plebeian Circuit-Breaker

Originally put things on a fire, many things 庶

遮	シャ、さえぎ-る	obstruct, interrupt	遮
遮断器	しゃだんき	circuit-breaker	66D
断	ダン、た-つ、ことわ-る	cut, decline, warn, judge, be decisive	66D
器	キ、うつわ	vessel, utensil, skill	66D
庶	ショ	multitude, various, illegitimate	庶
庶民	しょみん	hoi polloi	66D
民	ミン、たみ	people, populace	66D

66E 尼 WHITE LEAD

☒	尼寺	6A5
66E	あまでら	*

Nuns with Muddy Feet avoid Golden Showers, Leaky Congress and general Promiscuity

Two slumped figures, phonetically 'ni' of 'bikuni', Sanskrit nun 尼

尼	ニ、あま	nun, priestess	尼
尼寺	あまでら	convent (bikuni)	66E
寺	ジ、てら	temple	66E
泥	デイ、どろ	mud, adhere to	泥
泥足	どろあし	muddy feet	66E

400

足	ソク、あし、た-りる、た-る、た-す	leg, foot, sufficient	66E
尿	ニョウ	urine	尿
尿意	にょうい	nature's call	66E
意	イ	mind, thought, will	66E
漏	ロウ、も-る、も-れる、も-らす	leak	漏
粗漏	そろう	carelessness	66E
粗	ソ、あら-い	coarse, rough	66E
尾	ビ、お	tail	尾
交尾	こうび	copulation	66E
交	コウ、まじ-わる、まじ-える、ま-じる、ま-ざる、ま-ぜる	mix, exchange	66E
尻	コウ、しり	buttocks; hips; butt; rear	尻
尻癖	しりくせ	incontinence; promiscuity	66E
癖	ヘキ、くせ	habit, kink	66E

66F 替 WHITE LEAD

⚏		両替え	2 - 2
66F		りょうがえ	1|2

Money -2,000,001 yen- Exchanged hands in that sweaty Dive

Two persons speaking, having an 'exchange' 替

替	タイ、か-える、か-わる	exchange, swap	替
両替え	りょうがえ	money changing	66F
両	リョウ	both, pair, coin	66F
弐拾万壱円	2,000,001 yen	2,000,001 yen	66F

401

弐	ニ	two	66F
拾	シュウ、ジュウ、ひろ-う	pickup, gather, ten	66F
万	マン、バン	ten thousand, myriad	66F
壱	イチ	one	66F
円*	エン、まる-い	round, yen	66F
潜	セン、ひそ-む、もぐ-る	dive, lurk, hide	潜
潜水	せんすい	diving	66F
水	スイ、みず	water	66F

66G 捜 WHITE LEAD

⚎	捜索隊	2B6
66G	そうさくたい	*

The Search Party was looking for a Lean Figure

Originally searching for something by torchlight in a building 捜

捜	ソウ、さが-す	investigate	捜
捜索隊	そうさくたい	search party	66G
索	サク	rope, search	66G
隊	タイ	corps, unit	66G
痩	ソウ、や-せる	get thin	痩
痩身	そうしん	a lean figure	66G
身	シン、み	body	66G

The devil is in the detail. After aiming for paradise, a 諦観 with regard to the limits of this earthly 帝国 of passion, pain and 哀悼 could be salutary. The 青草 yonder is always greener just as the other 食卓 is so much better prepared than the one in front of you. Perception is a form of 奴隷制 that easily can lead to the 逮捕 of

402

critical faculties and it is doubtful if the "healthy" sentiment of the 庶民 could act as a 遮断器. The supernatural goings on in the 尼寺 of Loudun for example referred to 尻癖 and other acts of 粗漏 behaviour. Also, 両替 and the seemingly innocent activity of 潜水 were investigated by the authorities. In due course even a 捜索隊 was dispatched with instructions to find all those with suspiciously 痩身!

67A 縄 WINE

	縄目	3B18
67A	なわめ	*

Turtles & Snakes get Cracking and tie the Knot

Thread and pictograph of a tadpole 縄

亀	キ、かめ	turtle	亀
亀裂	きれつ	crack; crevice; fissure; chap	67A
裂	レツ、さ-く、さ-ける	split, rend, rip	67A
蛇	ジャ、ダ、へび	snake, serpent	蛇
蛇革	へびがわ	snakeskin	67A
革	カク、かわ	leather, reform	67A
縄	ジョウ、なわ	rope, cord	縄
縄目	なわめ	knot	67A
目	モク、ボク、め、ま	eye, ordinal suffix	67A

67B 棟 WINE

	病棟	3
67B	びょうとう	*

Petition the Freezing Ward

403

Originally raised earthen path around a field, raised, exposed 棟

陳	チン	state, show, old	陳
陳情	ちんじょう	petition	67B
情	ジョウ、セイ、なさ-け	feeling, pity, fact	67B
凍	トウ、こお-る、こご-える	freeze	凍
凍結	とうけつ	freezing	67B
結	ケツ、むす-ぶ、ゆ-う、ゆ-わえる	bind, join, end	67B
棟	トウ、むね、むな	ridge pole, building	棟
病棟	びょうとう	ward	67B
病	ビョウ、ヘイ、や-む、やまい	illness	67B

67C 伐 WINE

⩔		征伐	2A5
67C		せいばつ	*

The Punishment of Cutty Z

Halberd cutting down 伐

伐	バツ	attack, cut down	伐
征伐	せいばつ	punishment	67C
征	セイ	subjugate, travel	67C
閥	バツ	faction, clan, lineage	閥
財閥	ざいばつ	Zaibatsu (conglomerates)	67C
財	ザイ、サイ	wealth, assets	67C

67D 焦 WINE

𝖁	黒焦げ	2A2
67D	くろこげ	*

Scorch the Hidden Reef

Bird roasting over a fire, scorching, charring, fretting 焦

焦	ショウ、こ-げる、こ-がす、こ-がれる、あせ-る	scorch, fret	焦
黒焦げ	くろこげ	charring	67D
黒	コク、くろ、くろ-い	black	67D
礁	ショウ	(hidden) reef	礁
岩礁	がんしょう	reef	67D
岩	ガン、いわ	rock, crag	67D

67E 苗 WINE

𝖁	苗字	3 - 1
67E	みょうじ	*

The Family Name is a Depiction of our Pet Cat

Plants still in the field, not ready yet for cropping 苗

苗	ビョウ、なえ、なわ	seedling, offspring	苗
苗字	みょうじ	family name	67E
字	ジ、あざ	letter, symbol	67E
描	ビョウ、えが-く	depict, draw, write	描
描写	びょうしゃ	depiction	67E
写	シャ、うつ-す、うつ-る	copy, transcribe	67E
猫	ビョウ、ねこ	cat	猫

愛猫	あいびょう	pet cat	67E
愛	アイ	love	67E

67F 徴 WINE

Ⅴ		特徴	3C3
67F		とくちょう	*

This is Characteristic of Smiling Punishment

Core meaning small, secretive 徴

徴	チョウ、しるし	sign, summon, levy	徴
特徴	とくちょう	characteristic	67F
特	トク	special	67F
微	ビ	tiny, obscure, faint, secretive	微
微笑	びしょう	smile	67F
笑	ショウ、わら-う、え-む	laugh, smile	67F
懲	チョウ、こ-りる、こ-らす、こ-らしめる	chastise, learn	懲
懲罰	ちょうばつ	punishment	67F
罰	バツ、バチ	penalty, punishment	67F

67G 沈 WINE

Ⅴ		消沈	2A4
67G		しょうちん	*

Downcast Spirits were hanging around my Bedside

Originally hanging down in water, to sink 沈

沈	チン、しず-む、しず-める	sink	沈
消沈	しょうちん	depression; low spirits; dejection	67G
消	ショウ、き-える、け-す	extinguish, vanish, consume	67G
枕	チン、まくら	pillow	枕
枕元	まくらもと	near one's pillow; at one's bedside	67G
元	ゲン、ガン、もと	originally, source	67G

Cat's paw and monkey's fist. The redoubtable boa 縄目 fashioned from 蛇革 was extensively used in the 病棟 under 凍結 conditions and could be employed for 征伐 or, depending on the resources of the 財閥, turned into a 岩礁 knot. The latter could also effectively be applied to restrain the 愛猫 although that again would be an unfortunate 描写 of cruel and unusual 懲罰. Let's settle for a beautiful 微笑 instead because having an unfettered furry friend 枕元 is by far the best remedy against 消沈.

68A 幣 YEAR

⌒⌐	弊害	3A5
68A	へいがい	*

The Evil Coin Cover-Up

Cutting up by hand of small bits of cloth, offerings to gods 幣

弊	ヘイ	my (humble), evil, exhaustion	弊
弊害	へいがい	evil, abuse	68A
害	ガイ	harm, damage	68A
幣	ヘイ	offering, money	幣
貨幣	かへい	coin, money	68A

407

貨	カ	goods, money	68A
蔽	ヘイ、おお-う	cover; shade; mantle; capsize; be ruined	蔽
隠蔽	いんぺい	concealment; suppression; hiding; cover-up	68A
隠	イン、かく-す、かく-れる	hide	68A

68B 凡 YEAR

～	平凡	3 - 2
68B	へいぼん	*

Mediocre Philanthropy Sets Sail

Wind cloth, sail 凡

凡	ボン、ハン	mediocre, common, toughly, in general	凡
平凡	へいぼん	mediocrity	68B
平	ヘイ、ビョウ、たい-ら、ひら	flat, even, calm	68B
汎	ハン、う-かぶ、ひろ-い	pan-	汎
汎愛	はんあい	philanthropy	68B
愛	アイ	love	68B
帆	ハン、ほ	sail	帆
帆掛け船	ほかけぶね	sail boat	68B
掛	か-ける、か-かる、かかり	be connected, apply, hang, depend, cost	68B
船	セン、ふね、ふな	boat, ship	68B

68C 峰 YEAR

∿	主峰	3D3
68C	しゅほう	*

Bumblebees can really Stitch Up those Main Peaks

Chinese only butt, gore, in Chinese only compounds sharp 峰

蜂	ホウ、はち	bee; wasp; hornet	蜂
花蜂	はなばち	bumblebee	68C
花	カ、はな	flower, blossom	68C
縫	ホウ、ぬ-う	sew, titch	縫
縫針	ぬいばり	sewing needle	68C
針	シン、はり	needle	68C
峰	ホウ、みね	peak, top	峰
主峰	しゅほう	main peak	68C
主	シュ、ス、ぬし、おも	master, owner, main	68C

68D 曹 YEAR

∿	軍曹	3A1
68D	ぐんそう	*

The Sergeant issued an SOS from the Water Tank

Originally two well matched people, (doubling of east/sack) 曹

曹	ソウ	official, companion	曹
軍曹	ぐんそう	sergeant	68D
軍	グン	military, army	68D
遭	ソウ、あ-う	encounter, meet	遭
遭難信号	そうなんしんごう	SOS	68D

難	ナン、かた-い、むずか-しい	difficult, trouble	68D
信	シン	trust, believe	68D
号	ゴウ	number, call, sign	68D
槽	ソウ	tank, tub, vat	槽
水槽	すいそう	water tank	68D
水	スイ、みず	water	68D

68E 某 YEAR

〜	媒介	3A1
68E	ばいかい	*

Mediation in a Certain Place smacks of a Plot

Sweet produce of certain trees 某

媒	バイ	intermediary	媒
媒介	ばいかい	mediation	68E
介	カイ	mediate, shell	68E
某	ボウ	a certain-, some-	某
某所	ぼうしょ	a certain place	68E
所	ショ、ところ	place, situation	68E
謀	ボウ、ム、はか-る	plot, stratagem	謀
陰謀	いんぼう	plot, intrigue	68E
陰	イン、かげ、かげ-る	shadow, secret, negative (yin)	68E

68F 卑 YEAR

〜	卑劣	2B10
68F	ひれつ	*

The grimy Tombstone of Baseness

Originally hand holding a wine-pressing basket, the last drops 卑

碑	ヒ	tombstone, monument	碑
石碑	せきひ	tombstone	68F
石	セキ、シャク、コク、いし	stone, rock	68F
卑	ヒ、いや-しい、いや-しむ、いや-しめる	lowly, mean, despise	卑
卑劣	ひれつ	baseness	68F
劣	レツ、おと-る	be inferior	68F

68G 徹 YEAR

∿		徹夜	2 - 1
68G		てつや	*

Clear the All-Night Removal

Originally remove pot from a stand, remove clear 徹

徹	テツ	go through, clear, remove	徹
徹夜	てつや	all night	68G
夜	ヤ、よ、よる	night	68G
撤	テツ	remove, withdraw	撤
撤収	てっしゅう	removal	68G
収	シュウ、おさ-める、おさ-まる	obtain, store, supply	68G

Patent leather and concrete shoes. As widely practised in the worlds of politics and finance, it is prudent to have effective 隠蔽 in place when some 弊害 needs to be covered up. The red sails of the corporate 帆掛け船 are not dyed with the blood of competitors and the flag of obvious 汎愛 flutters merrily. The 縫針 that were used have nothing to do with the bones of deceased rival directors whilst that 主峰 is quite distinct from the other Twin Peaks from which no 遭難信号 has ever been transmitted. Whatever happened in a sealed 水槽 will stay there: it is no use spreading rumours about a 陰謀 in a 某所 and a certain time. We categorically deny all 卑劣 whilst laying a wreath at the 石碑 of our slain opponents and confirm that there will be no 徹夜 soul searching after the 撤収 of their regional headquarters!

69A 僕 YELLOW AMBER

ꙩ	公僕	3 - 4
69A	こうぼく	*

Strike the Public Servant Professionally

Originally slave carrying chamber-pot and turds, rough 僕

撲	ボク	strike, beat	撲
打撲	だぼく	strike, blow	69A
打	ダ、う-つ	hit, strike	69A
僕	ボク	man servant, I	僕
公僕	こうぼく	public servant	69A
公	コウ、おおやけ	public, fair, lord	69A
業	ギョウ、ゴウ、わざ	profession, deed, karma	業
偉業	いぎょう	great enterprise; exploits	69A
偉	イ、えら-い	great, grand	69A

69B 揺 YELLOW AMBER

ꙩ	揺り いす	2E4
69B	ゆりいす	*

Rocking Chair meaty Folk song

Unclear swaying meat vessel 揺

揺	ヨウ、ゆ-れる、ゆ-る、ゆ-らぐ、ゆ-るぐ、ゆ-する	shake, swing	揺
揺りいす	ゆりいす	rocking chair	69B
謡	ヨウ、うたい、うた-う	Noh chant, song	謡
民謡	みんよう	folk song	69B
民	ミン、たみ	people, populace	69B

69C 冒 YELLOW AMBER

ざ		冒険	2 - 4
69C		ぼうけん	*

Mad Hat had a dumb Adventure

Protective helmet worn over the eyes, fighting man 冒

帽	ボウ	cap, headgear	帽
帽子	ぼうし	hat	69C
子	シ、ス、こ	child	69C
冒	ボウ、おか-す	defy, risk, attack	冒
冒険	ぼうけん	adventure	69C
険	ケン、けわ-しい	steep, severe, perilous	69C

413

69D 慢 YELLOW AMBER

ㆡ	腕自慢	4C15
69D 並	うでじまん	*

An Account of Proud Manga Skill is to be found in this Cartoon

Non general use character full/expansive 慢
Old form shows pot for steaming rice and lid, come together 会

会	カイ、エ、あ-う	meet	会
会計	かいけい	account, reckoning, bill	69D
計	ケイ、はか-る、はか-らう	measure	69D
慢	マン	lazy, rude, boastful	慢
腕自慢	うでじまん	proud of one's skill	69D
腕	ワン、うで	arm, skill	69D
自	ジ、シ、みずか-ら	self	69D
漫	マン	random, diffuse, involuntary	漫
漫画	まんが	manga	69D
画	ガ、カク	picture, stroke	69D
絵	カイ、エ	picture	絵
下絵	したえ	rough sketch, cartoon, design	69D
下	カ、ゲ、した、しも、もと、さ-げる、さ-がる、くだ-る、くだ-す	base, under, lower	69D

69E 避 YELLOW AMBER

ざ	避妊	4 - 16
69E	ひにん	*

Her Accomplished Habit of Avoiding Pregnancies encouraged Wallflowers

Buttocks, opening, needle, anal penetration 避

璧	ヘキ、たま	sphere; ball	璧
完璧	かんぺき	perfect; complete; flawless;	69E
完	カン	complete	69E
癖	ヘキ、くせ	habit, kink	癖
習癖	しゅうへき	habit	69E
習	シュウ、なら-う	learn, train	69E
避	ヒ、さ-ける	avoid	避
避妊	ひにん	contraception	69E
妊	ニン	pregnant woman	69E
壁	ヘキ、かべ	wall	壁
壁紙	かべがみ	wallpaper	69E
紙	シ、かみ	paper	69E

69F 噴 YELLOW AMBER

ざ	噴水	3 - 2
69F	ふんすい	*

A Tumultuous Fountain of Indignation

Make a 'pon' sound with the mouth 噴

墳	フン	(burial-) mound	墳
古墳	こふん	tumulus	69F
古	コ、ふる-い、ふる-す	old	69F
噴	フン、ふ-く	emit, spout, gush	噴
噴水	ふんすい	fountain	69F
憤	フン、いきどお-る	indignant, angry	憤
憤慨	ふんがい	indignation	69F
慨	ガイ	lament, deplore	69F

69G 抜 YELLOW AMBER

ᡒ		手抜かり	2B7
69G		てぬうかり	1|2

That Haircut is a painful Omission

Obscure element dog, phonetic extract 抜

髪	ハツ、かみ	hair	髪
散髪	さんぱつ	haircut	69G
散*	サン、ち-る、ち-らす、ち-らかす、ち-らかる	scatter	69G
抜	バツ、ぬ-く、ぬ-ける、ぬ-かす、ぬ-かる	pluck, extract, miss	抜
手抜かり	てぬうかり	omission	69G
手	シュ、て、た	hand	69G

There and back again. It does not happen often that 偉業 are conducted without a fair deal of 打撲 followed by the inevitable 民謡 relating the grand 冒険 and heroic 帽子 tricks. Alternatively, these magnificent feats can be represented through 下絵 or 漫画. No fraudulent 会計 will be permitted of course and if there will be

416

representations on 壁紙, only the most 完璧 rendition will do. The stuff of legends with a 古墳 located near a mysterious 噴水 where, after drinking from the restorative waters, 散髪 will be reversed and 手抜かり shall be rectified.

70A 寮 ZINC

⼑	寮生	4B6
70A	りょうせい	*

There is no Clear Remedy for Boarding Students and Colleagues

Chinese only fuel used in sacrifices 寮

瞭	リョウ、あき-らか	clear	瞭
明瞭	めいりょう	clarity; clearness;	70A
明	メイ、ミョウ、あ-かり、あか-るい、あか-るむ	clear, open, bright	70A
療	リョウ	cure, heal	療
療法	りょうほう	remedy	70A
法	ホウ、ハッ、ホッ	law	70A
寮	リョウ	hostel, dormitory	寮
寮生	りょうせい	boarding student	70A
生	セイ、ショウ、い-きる、い-かす、い-ける、う-まれる、う-む	life, birth, grow	70A
僚	リョウ	colleague, official	僚
同僚	どうりょう	colleague	70A
同	ドウ、おな-じ	same	70A

70B 累 ZINC

乄	累計	2B8
70B	るいけい	*

The Sum Total of a Base Umpire

Originally three fields suggesting build up, accumulation 累

累	ルイ	accumulate, involve	累
累計	るいけい	sum total	70B
計	ケイ、はか-る、はか-らう	measure	70B
塁	ルイ	fort, baseball, base	塁
塁審	るいしん	base umpire	70B
審	シン	judge, investigate	70B

70C 腕 ZINC

乄	手腕家	3C5
70C	しゅわんか	*

I Grudgingly admired Shuwanka's Ability to find the Address

Originally straighten a bent body, display of strength 腕

怨	エン、オン、ウン、うら.む、うらみ、うら.めしい	grudge; show resentment; be jealous	怨
怨恨	えんこん	grudge	70C
恨	コン、うら-む、うら-めしい	resent, regret	70C
腕	ワン、うで	arm, skill	腕
手腕家	しゅわんか	able individual; man of ability	70C
手	シュ、て、た	hand	70C

家	カ、ケ、いえ、や	house, specialist	70C
宛	エン、あて、ずつ	address	宛
宛先	あてさき	address	70C
先	セン、さき	previous, precede, tip	70C

70D 励 ZINC

⿻	策励	2 - 8
70D	さくれい	*

Whipping it up in Tochigi Prefecture

Formerly showing a scorpion, phonetically expressing to strive 励

励	レイ、はげ-む、はげ-ます	encourage, strive	励
策励	さくれい	urging; whipping (up)	70D
策	サク	policy, plan, whip	70D
栃	レイ、とち	horse chestnut	栃
栃木県	とちぎけん	Tochigi Prefecture	70D
木	ボク、モク、き、こ	tree, wood	70D
県	ケン	prefecture	70D

70E 併 ZINC

⿻	併用	5 - 11
70E	へいよう	*

The Collapse of the Earthen Wall Jointly staked a Flower Vase and Roasted Rice Cake

Non general character put together, two persons and matching stakes 併

瓦	ガ、グラム、かわら	tile	瓦
瓦解	がかい	collapse; downfall	70E
解	カイ、ゲ、と-く、と-かす、と-ける	unravel, explain, solve	70E
塀	ヘイ	fence, wall	塀
土塀	どべい	earthen wall	70E
土	ド、ト、つち	earth	70E
併	ヘイ、あわ-せる	unite, join	併
併用	へいよう	joint use	70E
用	ヨウ、もち-いる	use	70E
瓶	ビン	bottle, jug, jar	瓶
花瓶	かびん	flower vase	70E
花	カ、はな	flower, blossom	70E
餅	ヘイ、もち	mochi rice cake	餅
焼餅	やきもち	(1) jealousy; (2) roasted rice cake	70E
焼	ショウ、や-く、や-ける	burn, roast	70E

70F 麻 ZINC

𠂆		麻薬		4A7
70F		まやく		*

Narcotic Devils were ready to Scrape and Grind the sinners

Originally cloth plant, hemp, flax 麻

麻	マ、あさ	hemp, flax, numb	麻
麻薬	まやく	narcotic	70F
薬	ヤク、くすり	medicine, drug	70F
魔	マ	demon, devil	魔

悪魔	あくま	devil (mara)	70F
悪	アク、オ、わる-い	bad, hate	70F
摩	マ	rub, graze, scrape	摩
摩擦	まさつ	friction	70F
擦	サツ、す-る、す-れる	rub, chafe, brush	70F
磨	マ、みが-く	polish, scour, rub	磨
研磨	けんま	grinding	70F
研	ケン、と-ぐ	hone, refine	70F

70G 涙 ZINC

		空涙	2A3
70G		そらなみだ	*

No more Returns of the Crocodile Tears

Originally crouching dog and door, semantically unclear 戻

戻	レイ、もど-す、もど-る	return, bring back, rebel, bend, vomit	戻
返戻	へんれい	return	70G
返	ヘン、かえ-す、かえ-る	return	70G
涙	ルイ、なみだ	tear	涙
空涙	そらなみだ	crocodile tears	70G
空	クウ、そら、あ-く、あ-ける、から	sky, empty	70G

Let not the dragon be my guide. 明瞭 of purpose and a strong resolve will provide a 療法 for the 累計 of 怨恨 that seem to have accumulated at this 宛先. There is a need for 手腕家 who could engage in 策励 positive energies in 栃木県 to effectively banish 焼餅 and to prevent a 瓦解 of the protective 土塀. If the latter falls

421

the path will be clear for 悪魔 to wreak havoc and an era of everlasting 摩擦 will commence: a 返戻 to times of wailing accompanied by copious 空涙!

Index & Definitions of Alchemical Symbols

	1	AIR	Equals breath, breeze, spirit, wind, weather
	2	ALEMBIC	Or capitellum (helmet) is a vessel set over the retort to receive and collect vapours
	3	ALUM	Grows as hair on fire-resistant salamanders; asbestos
	4	AMALGAM	A composition of gold or silver and quick silver
	5	ANTIMONY	Also mineral or chemical wolf. Could be used as universal medicine making all other medicine redundant
	6	ARMENIAN BOLE	Red clay, cure against the bite of poisonous snakes
	7	ATHANOR	An oven that is adapted for composing the stone of the philosophers
	8	BALM	A preserver of all bodies from destruction and putrefaction
	9	BATH OF VAPOURS	A furnace in which the distillatory vase is suspended only over the steam of water in such a manner that the waters do not touch the body
	10	BISMUTH	Weissmuth or white substance, bright metal of white colour
	11	BLACK BRIMSTONE	Also horse brimstone, used externally by veterinary surgeons

⊏	12 BLOOD STONE	Synonym for gold
⚛	13 BORAX	Also atincar or rock borax, mineral salt used in foldering, brazing and calling gold
▥	14 BRICK	The plural (Latin lateres) refers to iron tiles
Ⓡ	15 CALCINATION	Calcination of bodies is combustion which takes place in a strong heat
ЖO	16 CAMPHOR	Can be used for medicinal or culinary purposes
Tm	17 CAPUT MORTUUM	Residue in the retort from which the phlegmatic part has been extracted
☿	18 CINNABAR	Used by Venetian painters because of its blood-colour, also used as an antidote in medicine
♀	19 COPPER, VENUS	A metallic body of bluish colour with a dark ruddy tinge, igneous and fusible
⚡	20 CORAL	A substance that originated from the head of the Medusa
Ʊ	21 CRUCIBLE	A melting vessel made of some earth which can absolutely withstand fire
✦	22 DAY	To be distinguished from Nychthemeron which is night & day: 24 hours
╫B	23 DECOCTION	Thick juice made by boiling grain or animal/vegetables
⊒	24 DIGEST	To slowly draw out effective ingredients from drugs by using solvents whilst subjected to stable temperatures

	25 DISSOLUTION	The vaporising of matter and the capture of the condensed moisture thereof in another vessel
	26 DISTILLATION	A process in which the essence is extracted in the form of a liquid
	27 DRAGON'S BLOOD	Synonym for cinnabar, also used as medicine against scratches and the French disease
	28 DRAM	A weight of 3,373 grams
	29 EARTH	Red earth from Lemnos was famous for protecting against poison and plague
	30 EBULLITION	The act, process, or state of boiling or bubbling up
	31 EFFERVESCENCE	To escape from a liquid as bubbles; bubble up
	32 ELEMENT	The elements are the matrices of substances: fire, air, water, and earth are the four universal matrices
	33 EQUAL PARTS	From all parts the same quantity
	34 ESSENCE	Essence is a simple extract which contains the whole nature and perfection of the substances from which it is derived
	35 EXTRACTION	Extraction is the separation of the essential part from the body
	36 FERMENTATION	The incorporation of a fermenting substance with a substance which is to be fermented

𝄪	37	FILTRATION	Subduction by filtration in a colander; but this process in the chymical filter may also be called straining, or percolation
△	38	FIRE	Fire for the stone of the philosophers
♓	39	FIRST MATTER	Soul and heaven of the elements
♀	40	FIXATION	To make firm, to solidify
♄	41	FLOWERS OF SATURN	Lead oxide, the red form is known as litharge and the yellow form as massicot
⊡	42	FURNACE	A furnace or oven
♇	43	GLASS	Glass, sieve, riddle for distillation, grave, churchyard, because the stone lies hidden therein, and is driven up and down
♋	44	GLUE OF THE WISE	Special sticky substances used for sealing off the apparatus for distillation
⚶	45	GOLD, SUN	Called sol by the chemists, and dedicated to the sun, is the most tempered of all the metals
♆	46	GRADE OF FIRE	There are four different grades of fire ranging from tepid to the highest possible level of heat
⚷	47	GRANATE	It is a transparent, ruby-coloured gem, like the blossom of the pomegranate, and is more dusky than the carbuncle
♑	48	GUM	A transforming substance on account of its adhesive quality. The "glue of the world" is the medium between mind and body

♉	49	GYPSUM	Its use is chiefly in external application, on account of its extremely drying and destroying nature
⧖	50	HOUR	Time measured by an hourglass
♁	51	IRON, MARS	This metal is attributed to mars by the chemist, and is so called, because of its many uses in war
♋	52	JUNIPER	Juniper berries are a spice used in a wide variety of culinary dishes and best known for the primary flavouring in gin
♄	53	LEAD, SATURN	Lead with a heavy metallic body, very little whiteness and much of earthy nature
ℳ	54	MAGNESIA	Magnesia is produced when silver and quicksilver are united so as to form a heavy fluid metal. It is also the matter of the philosopher's stone
✕	55	NIGHT	Calling the one day and the other night for darkness to obscure and day for shining bright.
♄	56	OIL OF SATURN	Also liquor saturni, lead acetate
♔	57	PHILOSOPHICAL STONE	Universal medicine by which age is renewed in youth, metals are transmuted, and all diseases are cured
☿	58	QUICKSILVER, MERCURY	Primary matter of metals, incorporates volatility
⚗	59	QUINTESSENCE	A concoction that contains all the powers and qualities of substances in the purest form
⌐	60	RECTIFICATION	Concentration of a fluid through distillation

✳	61 SAL-AMMONIAC	Salmiac, corrosive and desiccating, best from a camel's discharge
⚛	62 SILVER, MOON	The luna of chemists, the metal ranked next after gold
⚓	63 TIN, JUPITER	Tin, white metallic substance, not pure, livid
⚭	64 VITRIOL	Also roman vitriol, green atrament, a mixture of salt and sulphates
▽	65 WATER	A dry mineral first substance, a catholic water which dissolves all metals
⩘	66 WHITE LEAD	Synonym for tin
⩔	67 WINE	Medicinal drugs used to be mixed with wine
∿	68 YEAR	The annus chymicus or annus philosophicus lasts for 30 days and 30 nights
♄	69 YELLOW AMBER	Once thought to have derived from the seed of wales and worn around the neck as an amulet
⚴	70 ZINC	Element: term first used by Paracelsus (c. 1526) due to the form of the crystals after smelting

Index Signature Characters

亜 ア	next, sub-, Asia	20A
愛 アイ	love	39E
哀 アイ、あわ-れ、あわ-れむ	sorrow, pity	57A
委 イ	committee; entrust to; leave to; devote; discard	26G
医 イ	doctor; medicine	28C
以 イ	starting point, means, use, through, because	38B
胃 イ	stomach	42G
為 イ	do, purpose	56G
尉 イ	military rank	59B
偉 イ、えら-い	great, grand	48C
異 イ、こと	differ, strange	51A
域 イキ	area, limits	51C
員 イン	member, official	25B
隠 イン、かく-す、かく-れる	hide	59D
因 イン、よ-る	cause, be based on, depend on	48A
宇 ウ	eaves, roof, heaven	51D
羽 ウ、は、はね	wing, feather, bird counter	11G
永 エイ、なが-い	long, lasting	30E
易 エキ、イ、やさ-しい	easy, change, divination	43D

園	エン、その	garden, park	6C
鉛	エン、なまり	lead	13F
延	エン、の-びる、の-べる、の-ばす	extend, postpone	53G
炎	エン、ほのお	inflammation, flame, blaze	24D
王	オウ	king	6B
央	オウ	centre	32A
桜	オウ、さくら	cherry	9A
乙	オツ	odd, b, 2nd, stylish	61C
卸	おろ-す、おろし	wholesale, grate	60D
音	オン、イン、おと、ね	sound	3G
可	カ	approve, can, should	16E
佳	カ	beautiful, good	42E
渦	カ、うず	whirlpool, eddy	46E
加	カ、くわ-える、くわ-わる	add, join	42F
家	カ、ケ、いえ、や	house, specialist	9D
化	カ、ケ、ば-ける、ば-かす	change, bewitch	2A
果	カ、は-たす、は-てる、は-て	fruit, result, carryout	42B
貝	かい	shellfish	3F
介	カイ	mediate, shell	18C
拐	カイ	deceive, kidnap, bend	40A
戒	カイ、いまし-める	command, admonish	36C
快	カイ、こころよ-い	pleasant, cheerful	24E
壊	カイ、こわ-す、こわ-れる	break, destroy, ruin	60C
灰	カイ、はい	ashes	27C

各	カク、おのおの	each	28D
角	カク、かど、つの	horn, angle	18G
革	カク、かわ	leather, reform	55F
且	か-つ	furthermore, besides	18A
喝	カツ	shout, scold	60B
滑	カツ、すべ-る、なめ-らか	slide, slip, smooth	56E
感	カン	feeling	17C
官	カン	government, official	30D
漢	カン	Han China, man	34F
観	カン	watch, observe	36G
監	カン	supervise, watch	51G
敢	カン	daring, tragic	52C
喚	カン	shout, yell	60E
缶	カン	can, boiler	61F
甘	カン、あま-い、あま-える、-あま-やかす	sweet, presume upon	59G
寒	カン、さむ-い	cold, midwinter	33A
貫	カン、つらぬ-く	pierce	45F
干	カン、ほ-す、ひ-る	dry, defence	23C
巻	カン、ま-く、ま-き	roll, reel, volume	50G
患	カン、わずら-う	disease, afflicted	60A
牙	ガ、ゲ、きば	tusk; fang	41A
我	ガ、われわ、わが	I, self, my	53C
害	ガイ	harm, damage	34A
慨	ガイ	lament, deplore	59A
楽	ガク、ラク、たの-しい、たの-しむ	pleasure, music	12B

431

眼	ガン、ゲン、まなこ	eye	22D
幾	キ、いく	how many, how much	34C
鬼	キ、おに	devil, demon, ghost	58A
企	キ、くわだ-てる	plan, undertake	63G
貴	キ、たっと-い、とうと-い、たっと-ぶ、とうと-ぶ	precious, revered	51F
机	キ、つくえ	desk, table	54B
基	キ、もと、もとい	base	30A
旧	キュウ	old, past	39F
丘	キュウ、おか	hill	58G
及	キュウ、およ-ぶ、およ-び、およ-ぼす	reach, extend, and	31G
九	キュウ、ク、ここの、ここの-つ	nine	4E
球	キュウ、たま	sphere, ball	23F
弓	キュウ、ゆみ	bow	40F
巨	キョ	huge, giant	61B
居	キョ、い-る	be, reside	43A
虚	キョ、コ	empty, hollow, dip	55C
去	キョ、コ、さ-る	go, leave, past	28A
協	キョウ	cooperate	44C
享	キョウ	receive, have	57C
凶	キョウ	bad luck, disaster	57D
鏡	キョウ、がかみ	mirror	36D
京	キョウ、ケイ	capital	16B
郷	キョウ、ゴウ	village, rural	55E
挟	キョウ、はさ-む、はさ-まる	insert, pinch, squeeze between	61A

橋	キョウ、はし	bridge	24C
斤	キン	axe, weight	15C
禁	キン	ban, forbid	47A
義	ギ	righteousness	37C
疑	ギ、うたが-う	doubt, suspect	56A
暁	ギョウ、あかつき	dawn, light, event	35E
仰	ギョウ、コウ、あお-ぐ、おお-せ	look up, state, respect	61D
玉	ギョク、たま	ball, sphere, coin	1F
吟	ギン	recite	5F
区	ク	ward, section	31F
句	ク	phrase, clause	48F
空	クウ、そら、あ-く、あ-ける、から	sky, empty	4B
屈	クツ	submit, crouch	61E
薫	クン、かお-る	aroma, fragrance, aura	63D
君	クン、きみ	lord, you Mr	32B
具	グ	equip, means	31B
偶	グウ	by chance, spouse, doll	62A
軍	グン	military, army	21C
慶	ケイ	joy	62E
系	ケイ	lineage, connection	6G
径	ケイ	path, direct	26E
渓	ケイ	valley, gorge	63E
敬	ケイ、うやま-う	respect	57F
恵	ケイ、エ、めぐ-む	blessing, kindness	55D
形	ケイ、ギョウ、かた、かたち	shape, pattern	15E

頃	ケイ、ころ	time; about; toward	63A
契	ケイ、ちぎ-る	pledge, join	49B
傑	ケツ	outstanding	62C
穴	ケツ、あな	hole	27A
欠	ケツ、か-ける、か-く	lack	29D
結	ケツ、むす-ぶ、ゆ-う、ゆ-わえる	bind, join, end	40D
県	ケン	prefecture	31A
倹	ケン	thrifty, frugal	41F
顕	ケン	manifest, visible	64D
犬	ケン、いぬ	dog	53D
兼	ケン、か-ねる	combine, unable	60G
堅	ケン、かた-い	firm, solid, hard	62B
拳	ケン、こぶし	fist	49C
建	ケン、コン、た-てる、た-つ	build, erect	33B
見	ケン、み-る、み-える、み-せる	look, see, show	4D
激	ゲキ、はげ-しい	violent, fierce, strong, intense	59E
玄	ゲン	occult, black	50A
元	ゲン、ガン、もと	originally, source	18B
言	ゲン、ゴン、い-う、こと	word, say, speak	19F
原	ゲン、はら	plain, origin	9E
孤	コ	orphan, lonely	61G
顧	コ、かえり-みる	look back	62G
己	コ、キ、おのれ	I, me, you, self	7E
戸	コ、と	door	9G
古	コ、ふる-い、ふる-す	old	15A
孝	コウ	filial piety	13A
洪	コウ	flood, vast	25E

康	コウ	peace, health	34E
航	コウ	sail, voyage	38G
侯	コウ	marquis, lord	41C
講	コウ	lecture	49F
荒	コウ、あら-い、あ-れる、あ-らす	rough, wild, waste	64A
岡	コウ、おか	hill; height; knoll; rising ground	58D
黄	コウ、オウ、き、こ	yellow	9C
考	コウ、かんが-える	consider	19A
甲	コウ、カン	shell, armour, high, 1st, a	57G
行	コウ、ギョウ、アン、い-く、ゆ-く、おこな-う	go, conduct, column	11F
工	コウ、ク	work	7B
幸	コウ、さいわ-い、さち、しあわ-せ	happiness, luck	25D
更	コウ、さら、ふ-ける、ふ-かす	anew, change, again, grow late	32C
高	コウ、たか-い、たか、たか-まる、たか-める	tall, high, sum	16C
耕	コウ、たがや-す	till, plough	48B
広	コウ、ひろ-い、ひろ-まる、ひろ-める、ひろ-がる、ひろ-げる	wide, spacious	8B
交	コウ、まじ-わる、まじ-える、ま-じる、ま-ざる、ま-ぜる	mix, exchange	4F
刻	コク、きざ-む	chop, mince, engrave	50D
黒	コク、くろ、くろ-い	black	13D
谷	コク、たに	valley, gorge	15G

告	コク、つ-げる	proclaim, inform	37E
護	ゴ	defend, protect	50F
誤	ゴ、あやま-る	mistake, mis-	58F
号	ゴウ	number, call, sign	29F
合	ゴウ、ガッ、カッ、あ-う、あ-わす、あ-わせる	meet, join, fit	7F
左	サ、ひだり	left	3B
才	サイ	talent, year of age	11B
債	サイ	debt, loan	44F
栽	サイ	planting	54C
砕	サイ、くだ-く、くだ-ける	break, smash	38C
妻	サイ、つま	wife	14E
采	サイ、と-る	dice; form; appearance; take; colouring; general's baton	39G
最	サイ、もっと-も	most, -est	40C
作	サク、サ、つく-る	make	10B
察	サツ	judge, surmise, realise	29A
皿	さら	dish, bowl, plate	22F
傘	サン、かさ	umbrella, parasol	62D
参	サン、まい-る	attend, go, be in love, be at a loss, 3	40E
山	サン、やま	mountain	1A
座	ザ、すわ-る	seat, sit, gather	54D
司	シ	administer, official	41E
至	シ、いた-る	go, reach, peak	11C
市	シ、いち	city, market	15D

氏 シ、うじ	clan, family, Mr	13B
志 シ、こころざ-す、こころざし	will, intent	42D
刺 シ、さ-す、さ-さる	pierce, stab, thorn	58B
支 シ、ささ-える	branch, support	53B
死 シ、し-ぬ	death	21A
子 シ、ス、こ	child	1G
止 シ、と-まる、と-める	stop	11D
旨 シ、むね	tasty, good, gist	22E
紫 シ、むらさき	purple, violet	65D
式 シキ	ceremony, form	23B
識 シキ	knowledge	47F
七 シチ、なな、なな-つ、なの	seven	4A
膝 シツ、ひざ	knee; lap	64B
失 シツ、うしな-う	lose	37F
執 シツ、シュウ、と-る	take, grasp, execute	63B
舎 シャ	house, quarters	47E
車 シャ、くるま	vehicle, chariot	2C
者 シャ、もの	person	23D
尺 シャク	measure, foot	52D
朱 シュ	vermilion, red	54F
首 シュ、くび	head, neck, chief	8E
主 シュ、ス、ぬし、おも	master, owner, main	20B
秋 シュウ、あき	autumn	20D
収 シュウ、おさ-める、おさ-まる	obtain, store, supply	56F
宗 シュウ、ソウ	religion, main	46A
舟 シュウ、ふね、ふな	boat	63C

437

周	シュウ、まわ-り	circumference, around	12D
叔	シュク	uncle, young brother	65B
宿	シュク、やど、やど-る、やど-す	lodge, shelter, house	32E
出	シュツ、スイ、で-る、だ-す	emerge, put out	23G
俊	シュン	excellence, genius	44G
処	ショ	deal with, place	56C
庶	ショ	multitude, various, illegitimate	66D
章	ショウ	badge, chapter	26B
尚	ショウ	furthermore, esteem	43F
将	ショウ	command, about to	52E
焦	ショウ、こ-げる、こ-がす、こ-がれる、あせ-る	scorch, fret	67D
象	ショウ、ゾウ	elephant, image	31C
升	ショウ、ます	liquid measure	64G
詔	ショウ、みことのり	imperial edict	33F
宵	ショウ、よい	evening	25G
色	ショク、シキ、いろ	colour, sensuality	7E
娠	シン	pregnancy	28G
辛	シン、から-い	sharp, bitter	14A
心	シン、こころ	heart, feelings	11E
臣	シン、ジン	retainer, subject	43B
進	シン、すす-む、すす-める	advance	22G
真	シン、ま	true, quintessence	22A

身	シン、み	body	20C
申	シン、もう-す	say, expound	10A
字	ジ、あざ	letter, symbol	2F
侍	ジ、さむらい	attend (upon)	10E
自	ジ、シ、みずか-ら	self	17G
事	ジ、ズ、こと	thing, matter, act	15F
耳	ジ、みみ	ear	4C
弱	ジャク、よわ-い、よわ-る、よわ-まる、よわ-める	weak	10C
需	ジュ	need, demand	62F
受	ジュ、う-ける、う-かる	receive	21E
寿	ジュ、ことぶき	long life, congratulation	65A
充	ジュウ、あ-てる	full, fill, provide	23E
従	ジュウ、ショウ、ジュ、したが-う、したが-える	follow, comply	54E
十	ジュウ、ジッ、とお、と	ten	3C
重	ジュウ、チョウ、え、おも-い、かさ-ねる、かさ-なる	heavy, pile, -fold	25A
述	ジュツ、の-べる	state, relate	41D
盾	ジュン、たて	shield, pretext	65C
縄	ジョウ、なわ	rope, cord	67A
乗	ジョウ、の-る、の-せる	ride, mount, load	21B
譲	ジョウ、ゆず-る	hand over, yield	63F
須	ス、あごひげ、すべか-らく …べ-し	ought; by all means; necessarily	12G
垂	スイ、た-れる、た-らす	suspend, hang down	50E
寸	スン	measure, inch	7D

439

瀬	せ	shallows, rapids	65F
制	セイ	system, control	47B
斉	セイ	equal, similar	55A
勢	セイ、いきお-い	power, force	35B
西	セイ、サイ、にし	west	14F
青	セイ、ショウ、あお、あお-い	blue, green, young	3E
井	セイ、ショウ、い	well	33G
正	セイ、ショウ、ただ-しい、ただ-す、まさ	correct	5B
星	セイ、ショウ、ほし	star	26F
成	セイ、ジョウ、な-る、な-す	become, make, consist	30C
隻	セキ	one of a pair, ship counter	65G
赤	セキ、シャク、あか、あか-い、あか-らむ、あか-らめる	red	5D
石	セキ、シャク、コク、いし	stone, rock	2E
昔	セキ、シャク、むかし	olden times, past	32D
夕	セキ、ゆう	evening	4G
折	セツ、お-る、おり、お-れる	bend, break, occasion	41B
説	セツ、ゼイ、と-く	preach, explain	16F
宣	セン	promulgate, state	56B
泉	セン、いずみ	spring	17E
先	セン、さき	previous, precede, tip	3A
外	セン、し-める、うらな-う	divine, occupy	12A
銭	セン、ぜに	sen, coin, money	35C
是	ゼ	proper, this	30G

舌	ゼツ、した	tongue	12C
然	ゼン、ネン	duly, thus, so, but	29C
前	ゼン、まえ	before, front	14B
全	ゼン、まった-く	whole, completely	32F
善	ゼン、よ-い	good, virtuous	53F
遡	ソ、さかのぼ-る	go upstream; retrace the past	48G
壮	ソウ	manly, strong, grand, fertile	33E
創	ソウ	start, wound	41G
僧	ソウ	priest	48D
曹	ソウ	official, companion	68D
争	ソウ、あらそ-う	conflict, vie	38A
送	ソウ、おく-る	send	24B
捜	ソウ、さが-す	investigate	66G
相	ソウ、ショウ、あい	mutual, minister, aspect	21G
走	ソウ、はし-る	run	19G
窓	ソウ、まど	window	43G
操	ソウ、みさお、あやつ-る	handle, chastity	55B
即	ソク	immediate, namely, accession	35D
則	ソク	rule, model, standard	39B
足	ソク、あし、た-りる、た-る、た-す	leg, foot, sufficient	3D
息	ソク、いき	breath, rest, child	27E
束	ソク、たば	bundle, manage	31D

尊	ソン、たっと-い、とうと-い、たっと-ぶ、とうと-ぶ	value, esteem, your	53E
蔵	ゾウ、くら	storehouse, harbour	53A
族	ゾク	clan, family	26C
属	ゾク	belong, genus	44D
逮	タイ	chase, seize	66C
帯	タイ、お-びる、おび	wear, zone	33D
替	タイ、か-える、か-わる	exchange, swap	66F
択	タク	choose, select	27B
宅	タク	house, home	52G
卓	タク	table, excel, high	66B
単	タン	simple, single, unit	33C
旦	タン	daybreak; dawn; morning	56D
探	タン、さぐ-る、さが-す	search, probe	26A
台	ダイ、タイ	platform, stand	14C
大	ダイ、タイ、おお、おお-きい、おお-いに	big	1B
代	ダイ、タイ、か-わる、か-える、よ、しろ	replace, world, generation, fee	28F
暖	ダン、あたた-か、あたた-かい、あたた-まる、あたた-める	warm	58C
池	チ、いけ	pond, lake	8G
知	チ、しる	know	17F
築	チク、きず-く	build	46B
中	チュウ、なか	middle, inside, China	1C
虫	チュウ、むし	insect, worm	5G

朝	チョウ、あさ	court, morning	16D
兆	チョウ、きざ-す、きざ-し	sign, omen, trillion	36A
調	チョウ、しら-べる、ととの-う、ととの-える	adjust, investigate, tone, tune	10F
徴	チョウ、しるし	sign, summon, levy	67F
丁	チョウ、テイ	block, exact	2B
鳥	チョウ、とり	bird	46D
長	チョウ、なが-い	long, senior	16A
直	チョク、ジキ、ただ-ちに、なお-す、なお-る	direct, upright, fix	16G
沈	チン、しず-む、しず-める	sink	67G
珍	チン、めずら-しい	rare, curious	64F
追	ツイ、お-う	chase, pursue	28E
通	ツウ、ツ、とお-る、とお-す、かよ-う	pass, way, commute	13E
廷	テイ	court, government office	30B
亭	テイ	pavilion, inn	44B
帝	テイ	emperor	66A
弟	テイ、ダイ、デ、おとうと	younger brother	14D
適	テキ	suitable, fit, go	52B
的	テキ、まと	target, like, adjectival suffix	35G
徹	テツ	go through, clear, remove	68G
田	デン、た	rice field	7A
斗	ト	dipper, measure	9F

刀	トウ、かたな	sword	13C
唐	トウ、から	(T'ang) China	59F
豆	トウ、ズ、まめ	beans, miniature	19D
棟	トウ、むね、むな	ridgepole, building	67B
匿	トク	conceal	54A
屯	トン	barracks, camp, post	47G
豚	トン、ぶた	pig, pork	40G
奴	ド	slave, servant, guy	38E
度	ド、ト、タク、たび	degree, times	22B
土	ド、ト、つち	earth	6A
銅	ドウ	copper	6F
童	ドウ、わらべ	child	24G
那	ナ	what?	45C
内	ナイ、ダイ、うち	inside	8A
南	ナン、ナ、みなみ	south	18E
尼	ニ、あま	nun, priestess	66E
日	ニチ、ジツ、ひ、か	sun, day	1D
乳	ニュウ、ちち、ち	breasts, milk	57E
妊	ニン	pregnant, swollen	45G
忍	ニン、しの-ぶ、しの-ばせる	endure, stealth	50C
能	ノウ	ability, can, Noh	46G
脳	ノウ	brain	54G
派	ハ	faction, send	35F
波	ハ、なみ	wave	27F
博	ハク、バク	extensive, spread, gain, gamble	38D
白	ハク、ビャク、しろ、しら、しろ-い	white	6D

発	ハツ、ホツ	discharge, start, leave	19C
犯	ハン、おか-す	crime, violate, commit, assault	45A
半	ハン、なか-ば	half, middle	19B
反	ハン、ホン、タン、そ-る、そ-らす	oppose, anti, reverse	21F
煩	ハン、ボン、わずら-う、わずら-わす	trouble, pain, torment	51E
馬	バ、うま、ま	horse	8C
倍	バイ	double, -fold	29B
媒	バイ	intermediary	68E
売	バイ、う-る、う-れる	sell	8F
爆	バク	burst, explode	45D
伐	バツ	attack, cut down	67C
抜	バツ、ぬ-く、ぬ-ける、ぬ-かす、ぬ-かる	pluck, extract, miss	69G
番	バン	turn, number, guard	15B
非	ヒ	not, un-, fault	27G
卑	ヒ、いや-しい、いや-しむ、いや-しめる	lowly, mean, despise	68F
比	ヒ、くら-べる	compare, ratio	29E
避	ヒ、さ-ける	avoid	69E
必	ヒツ、かなら-ず	necessarily	42C
筆	ヒツ、ふで	writing brush	12F
票	ヒョウ	vote, label, sign	39D
表	ヒョウ、おもて、あらわ-す、あらわ-れる	show, surface, list	20E
苗	ビョウ、なえ、なわ	seedling, offspring	67E

父	フ、ちち	father	17B
付	フ、つ-ける、つ-く	attach, apply	34D
布	フ、ぬの	cloth, spread	37D
夫	フ、フウ、おっと	husband, man	39A
不	フ、ブ	not, un-, dis-	32G
風	フウ、フ、かぜ、かざ	wind, style	17D
副	フク	deputy, vice-, sub-	24A
復	フク	again, repeat	42A
噴	フン、ふ-く	emit, spout, gush	69F
武	ブ、ム	military, warrior	47C
仏	ブツ、ほとけ	Buddha, France	11A
生	セイ、ショウ、い-きる、い-かす、い-ける、う-まれる、う-む	life, birth, grow	1E
分	ブン、フン、ブ、わ-ける、わ-かれる、わ-かる、わ-かつ	divide, minute, understand	5C
丙	ヘイ	c, 3rd	23A
弊	ヘイ	my (humble), evil, exhaustion	68A
併	ヘイ、あわ-せる	unite, join	70E
並	ヘイ、なみ、なら-べる、なら-ぶ、なら-びに	row, line, rank with, ordinary	49G
兵	ヘイ、ヒョウ	soldier	39C
平	ヘイ、ビョウ、たい-ら、ひら	flat, even, calm	19E
編	ヘン、あ-む	edit, knit, book	51B
変	ヘン、か-わる、か-える	change, strange	37G
片	ヘン、かた	one side, piece	45B
米	ベイ、マイ、こめ	rice, America	20F
補	ホ、おぎな-う	make good, stopgap	57B

保	ホ、たも-つ	preserve, maintain	44E
歩	ホ、ブ、フ、ある-く、あゆ-む	walk	18D
方	ホウ、かた	side, way, square, direction, person	10G
崩	ホウ、くず-れる、くず-す	crumble, collapse	65E
包	ホウ、つつ-む	wrap, envelop	36E
峰	ホウ、みね	peak, top	68C
豊	ホウ、ゆたか	abundant, rich	49E
北	ホク、きた	north, flee	7G
墓	ボ、はか	grave	44A
棒	ボウ	pole, bar, club	58E
冒	ボウ、おか-す	defy, risk, attack	69C
僕	ボク	manservant, I	69A
没	ボツ	sink, disappear, die, lack, not	55G
凡	ボン、ハン	mediocre, common, toughly, in general	68B
麻	マ、あさ	hemp, flax, numb	70F
毎	マイ	each, every	12E
妹	マイ、いもうと	younger sister	5E
末	マツ、バツ、すえ	end, tip	34B
慢	マン	lazy, rude, boastful	69D
妙	ミョウ	exquisite, strange, mystery	14G
民	ミン、たみ	people, populace	35A
矛	ム、ほこ	halberd, lance, spear	46C

明	メイ、ミョウ、あ-かり、あか-るい、あか-るむ	clear, open, bright	7C
面	メン、おも、おもて、つら	face, aspect, mask	27D
免	メン、まぬか-れる	escape, avoid	31E
綿	メン、わた	cotton, cotton wool	48E
茂	モ、しげ-る	grow thickly	59C
盲	モウ	blind	52F
目	モク、ボク、め、ま	eye, ordinal, suffix	2G
門	モン、かど	gate, door	17A
夜	ヤ、よ、よる	night	13G
厄	ヤク	misfortune, disaster	49A
役	ヤク、エキ	role, service, duty	25C
輸	ユ	transport, send	46F
由	ユ、ユウ、ユイ、よし	reason, means, way	30F
悠	ユウ	compose, distant, long time, ample	45E
融	ユウ	dissolve, melt	60F
勇	ユウ、いさ-む	courage; cheer up; be in high spirits; bravery; heroism	43C
憂	ユウ、うれ-える、うれ-い、う-い	grief, sorrow	52A
有	ユウ、ウ、ある	have, exist	29G
雄	ユウ、お、おす	male, powerful	49D
誘	ユウ、さそ-う	invite, tempt, lead	64E
予	ヨ	already, prior, I	18F

与	ヨ、あた-える	give, convey, impart, involvement	21D
余	ヨ、あま-る、あま-す	excess, ample, I	47D
陽	ヨウ	sunny, male, positive (yang)	8D
曜	ヨウ	day of the week	10D
妖	ヨウ、あや-しい、なまめ-く	attractive	43E
要	ヨウ、い-る	need, vital, pivot	34G
羊	ヨウ、ひつじ	sheep	26D
揺	ヨウ、ゆ-れる、ゆ-る、ゆ-らぐ、ゆ-るぐ、ゆ-する、ゆ-さぶる、ゆ-すぶる	shake, swing, rock	69B
利	リ、き-く	profit, gain, effect	36F
里	リ、さと	village, league	9B
陸	リク	land	36B
立	リツ、リュウ、た-つ、た-てる	stand, rise, leave	2D
竜	リュウ、たつ	dragon	64C
留	リュウ、ル、と-める、と-まる	stop, fasten	50B
呂	リョ、ロ	spine; backbone	20G
寮	リョウ	hostel, dormitory	70A
量	リョウ、はか-る	measure, quantity	37A
良	リョウ、よ-い	good	38F
倫	リン	principles, ethics	37B
林	リン、はやし	woods, forest	40B
累	ルイ	accumulate, involve	70B
涙	ルイ、なみだ	tear	70G
令	レイ	order, rule	28B

励	レイ、はげ-む、はげ-ます	encourage, strive	70D
列	レツ	row, line	22C
錬	レン	refine, train, drill	25F
録	ロク	record, inscribe	24F
六	ロク、む、む-つ、むっ-つ、むい	six	5A
腕	ワン、うで	arm, skill	70C

Bibliography & Online Resources

Coulmas, Florian (1981), Ueber Schrift, Suhrkamp Taschenbuch Wissenschaft

DeFrancis, John (1984), Chinese Language: Fact and Fantasy, University of Hawaii Press

Henshall, Kenneth G. (1995), A Guide to Remembering Japanese Characters, Tuttle

Jim Breen's WWWJDIC [Online] Available http://www.csse.monash.edu.au/ (2014)

Nozaki Kanji Frequency List: [Online] Available http://web.archive.org/web/20080320143000/http://nozaki-lab.ics.aichi-edu.ac.jp/nozaki/asahi/kanji.html (2014)

Ostler, Nicolas (2006), Empires of the Word, Harper Perennial

Rick Harbaugh's Zhongwen Chinese Character Genealogy: [Online] Available http://zhongwen.com/ (2014)

Seeley, Christopher (2000), A History of Writing in Japan, Ateneo de Manilla University Press

Shirakawa, Shizuka (2003), 常用漢字解, Heibonsha

Shirakawa, Shizuka (2006), 人名字解, Heibonsha

Toyoda, Etsuko: 'Enhancing Autonomous L2 Vocabulary Learning Focusing on the Development of Word-Level Processing Skills' 2007 [Online] Available www.readingmatrix.com/articles/etsuko_toyoda/article.pdf (2014)

Alchemy and Astrology

Bobrick, Benson (2006), The Fated Sky: Astrology in History, Simon & Schuster

Eliade, Mircea (1979), The Forge and the Crucible: The Origins and Structure of Alchemy, The University of Chicago Press http://www.levity.com/alchemy/

De Sphaera Mundi [Online] Available 1230

Gettings, Fred (1981), Dictionary of Occult, Hermetic and

Alchemical Sigils, Routledge & Kegan Paul Ltd

Klibansky, Raymond, Panofsky, Erwin, Saxl, Fritz (1992), Saturn und Melancholie: Studien zur Geschichte der Naturphilosophie und Medizin, der Religion und der Kunst, Suhrkamp Taschenbuch Wissenschaft

Maier, Michael: 'Atalanta Fugiens' 1617 [Online] Available

Poisson, Albert: 'Theories et Symboles des Alchimistes Le Grand Oeuvre' 1891 [Online] Available http://chrysopee.url.ph/_ouvrages/377.pdf (2014)

Rulandus, Martin: 'A Lexicon of Alchemy or Alchemical Dictionary'1612 [Online] Available http://www.rexresearch.com/rulandus/rulxa.htm (2014)

Splendor Solis 1532 [Online] Available

Mnemonics

Carruthers, Mary (2008), The Book of Memory: A Study of Memory in Medieval Culture, Cambridge Studies in Medieval Literature

Higbee, Kenneth L. (2001), Your Memory: How It Works and How to Improve It, Da Capo Press

Rossi, Paolo (2000), Logic and the Art of Memory: The Quest for a Universal Language, University of Chicago Press

Yates, Frances (2014), The Art of Memory, Random House UK

Made in the USA
Middletown, DE
25 February 2020